STUDY GUIDE

BUSINESS

STUDY GUIDE

John S. Bowdidge ▼ *George Swales*
Southwest Missouri State   *Southwest Missouri State*

THIRD EDITION

BUSINESS
▼

Ricky W. Griffin ▼ *Ronald J. Ebert*
Texas A&M University   *University of Missouri-Columbia*

Prentice Hall, Englewood Cliffs, New Jersey 07632

Production Editor: *John A. Nestor*
Acquisitions Editor: *Don Hull*
Supplements Acquisitions Editor: *Lisamarie Brassini*
Prepress Buyer: *Trudy Pisciotti*
Manufacturing Buyer: *Patrice Fraccio*

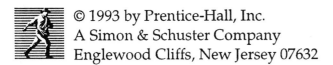

Printed in the United States of America

10   9   8   7   6   5   4   3   2   1

ISBN 0-13-094459-9

Prentice-Hall International (UK) Limited, *London*
Prentice-Hall of Australia Pty. Limited, *Sydney*
Prentice-Hall Canada Inc., *Toronto*
Prentice-Hall Hispanoamericana, S.A., *Mexico*
Prentice-Hall of India Private Limited, *New Delhi*
Prentice-Hall of Japan, Inc., *Tokyo*
Simon & Schuster Asia Pte. Ltd., *Singapore*
Editora Prentice-Hall do Brasil, Ltda., *Rio de Janeiro*

CONTENTS

PREFACE

TO THE STUDENT

We hope you will find this Study Guide to accompany the third edition of Griffin and Ebert's BUSINESS not only a helpful, but also an enjoyable aid in studying this subject. So that you may get the most benefit from this Study Guide, we would like to detail the different components within it.

Chapter Overview - Reading this overview will allow you to absorb the main points of a chapter in just a matter of seconds. Although this quick summary is never a substitute for reading the entire chapter in the text, it can help you review major ideas after you have already read the text chapter.

Learning Objectives - Often a student asks, "What does the professor want us to out of this chapter. The list of objectives, which are also found also in your textbook, answers that question.

Discussion of the Opening Case - Cases in the textbook are quick accounts of often quite complicated situations. This section provides a little more explanation and insight of the case. The questions will make you consider the case in even more depth. This section will boost your analytical thinking and better prepare you for in-class discussions of the case.

Annotated Key Terms - At the end of each chapter in the textbook you will find a list of Key Terms used in that chapter. Here, we have provided those terms and their definitions all in one convenient spot. This section of the Study Guide is perfect for you to use to preview the terms before reading the chapter and review them for exams.

True-False Questions - To quickly test your knowledge of a textbook chapter, take this ten-question quiz. The answers and a textbook page reference for each answer are provided at the end of each Study Guide chapter.

Multiple Choice Questions - To further warm up for a test, try these multiple-choice questions. Again their answers and textbook page references can be found at the end of the Study Guide chapter.

Writing To Learn - This section is a perfect opportunity to help you develop your writing skills while reinforcing the main concepts of the chapter. We hope you discover that writing can be fun.

Discussion of the Closing Case - As with the Opening Case, this discussion may present other thoughts and concepts that will illuminate and enliven the issue . Hopefully, this section will help you to generate your own ideas and opinions in a class discussion.

An Additional Case - Your Study Guide authors once aspired to be new Ernest Hemingways, but the closest we have come to realizing those dreams is to write these Additional Cases. We hope you think of them as great fiction. We also hope you notice that each one relates to the subject matter of the chapter. This creative section, therefore, should serve as further reinforcement of the chapter concepts.

Answers to True-False and Multiple Choice Questions - Not only does the end of each Study Guide chapter contain answers to a total of thirty questions, but for each answer there is also a page reference that allows you to read about the relevant material in the textbook to better understand why you got a question right or wrong.

TO THE PROFESSOR

Although we are a bit biased, we feel that this Study Guide is indeed a strong supplement to the third edition of Griffin and Ebert's BUSINESS. The thirty questions provided will put students in a testing frame of mind and some professors may even want to draw actual test questions from these. Discussions of cases can open up vistas of thought and will serve as a catalyst to the student's own thinking. The Writing to Learn exercises can help you pick worthwhile topics for student exposition and can serve as in-class exercises or out-of-class homework assignments. The Learning Objectives and Annotated Key Terms provide convenience. And finally, the colorful Additional Case ties the chapter concept up in one neat and enjoyable case.

John S. Bowdidge
George S. Swales, Jr.

STUDY GUIDE

BUSINESS

CHAPTER ONE

UNDERSTANDING THE AMERICAN BUSINESS SYSTEM

CHAPTER OVERVIEW

A business is an organization that seeks to earn profits by providing goods or services. Profits are the difference between a business's revenues and its expenses. An economic system is a nation's system for allocating its resources among its citizens, and these resources are often called factors of production-- natural resources, labor, capital, and entrepreneurs. The two most basic forms of planned economies are communism (in which the government owns and operates all industry) and socialism (in which the government owns and operates only selected major industries). Market economies rely on markets, not the government, to decide what, when, and for whom to produce. Demand is the willingness and ability of buyers to purchase a product or service. Supply is the willingness and ability of producers to offer a good or service for sale. Buyers will demand more as the price drops; producers will offer more as the price rises. Pure competition involves many small firms selling a greatly-similar product. In monopolistic competition, there are many firms selling purposely-differentiated products. In an oligopoly, there are only a handful of sellers (or firms). A monopoly exists when there is only one seller. Stability is the condition in which the balance between the money available and the goods produced remains about the same. Productivity describes how much is produced relative to the resources used to produce it.

LEARNING OBJECTIVES

1.   Define the nature of U.S. business and its goals.

2.   Differentiate between types of economic systems based on the way each one controls and uses the factors of production.

3.   Describe how demand and supply affect resource distribution in the United States.

4.   Identify the elements of private enterprise and the various degrees of competition in the U.S. economic system.

5.   Explain the criteria used to assess how well an economy meets its goals and how the U.S. government attempts to manage the economy.

DISCUSSION OF THE OPENING CASE

There are many things to be learned and quite a few intriguing business principles to be encountered by reading about the resurgence of Harley-Davidson. In this section, we shall comment on only two aspects, but your teacher can easily touch on others. First of all, we notice that when it came to sharpening up production techniques and procedures at the Harley-Davidson plant, the executives consulted extensively with the actual workers who would be putting those very techniques and procedures into operation and who had worked in similar operations in the past. This certainly seems logical, seeking the advice of people who are closest to the action. Now, we are not saying that people on the assembly line will dictate what models we shall make and how many. No, someone at a higher level, with a better understanding of company goals and targets, should make that kind of determination. A person at the higher level is much better qualified for such judgments. But the executives high on the firm's organization chart do not understand assembly-line production problems the way assembly-line workers do. Logical as seeking their advice may seem, too many organizations issue edicts that will affect lowest-echelon personnel without ever seeking to see what will make sense with those lowest-echelon personnel. Second, a basic business problem that jumps out at us off the page is that of obtaining significant financing when there are no guaranteed prospects that the loans involved can be paid back. Although later in the life of a firm, operations may produce considerable profits that can support further operations, in the beginning there is a gaping absence of funds. To fill the void, we must find some lender with faith in the organization. We saw that Citibank was willing to stick by Harley-Davidson a little longer. Then along came Bob Koe of Heller Financial Services. Heller Financial was taking a heavy risk; it was possible that Harley might not be successful and that loans to the firm might not be fully repaid. But in the lending business, there will always be risks, just as there will always be sick people in the field of medicine. In this case, the loans to Harley-Davidson were a good investment.

1. If you were an executive with Heller Financial Services, what are some of the questions you would want to ask of Harley-Davidson executives before you made a loan to them.

2. If Harley-Davidson had been in business for so long, why did they need such a great magnitude of fresh funds during the period that the case covers?

3. What are some disadvantages that would have followed from Harley-Davidson executives implementing changes on the assembly-line without consulting the assembly-line workers?

4. What are some ways in which William G. Davidson rescued the firm?

ANNOTATED KEY TERMS

<u>Business</u> - An organization that seeks to earn profits by providing goods or services.

<u>Profit</u> - The positive difference between a business's revenues and its expenses.

Economic System - A nation's system for allocating its resources among its citizens.

Factors of Production - The resources used in the production of goods and services: natural resources, labor, capital, and entrepreneurs.

Natural Resources - Materials supplied by nature--for example, land, water, mineral deposits, and trees.

Labor - The mental and physical capabilities of people. Also called human resources.

Capital - The funds needed to operate a business enterprise.

Entrepreneur - A person who accepts the opportunities and risks involved in creating and operating a business.

Planned Economy - An economy that relies on a centralized government to control all or most factors of production and to make all or most production decisions.

Market Economy - An economy in which individuals control production factors and decisions.

Communism - A planned economic system in which the government owns and operates all industry.

Socialism - A planned economic system in which the government owns and operates only selected major industries. Smaller businesses may be privately owned.

Market - A mechanism for exchange between buyers and sellers of a particular good or service.

Capitalism - A market economy that provides for the private ownership of the factors of production and encourages entrepreneurship by offering profits as an incentive.

Mixed Economy - An economy that has characteristics of both planned and market economies.

Privatization - The process of converting government enterprises into privately owned companies.

Demand - The willingness and ability of producers to offer a good or service for sale.

Supply - The willingness and ability of producers to offer a good or service for sale.

Law of Demand - The principle that buyers will purchase (demand) more of a product as its price drops and will purchase (demand) less of a product as its price increases.

Law of Supply - The principle that producers will offer more for sale as the price of a product rises, but will offer less for sale as the price drops.

Demand Curve - A graph that shows how many products will be demanded (bought) at different prices.

Supply Curve - A graph that shows how many products will be supplied (offered for sale) at different prices.

Equilibrium Price - The price at which the quantity of goods demanded and the quantity of goods supplied are equal; the profit-maximizing price of a good. This is commonly referred to as the market price.

Surplus - A situation in which quantity supplied exceeds quantity demanded.

Shortage - A situation in which quantity demanded exceeds quantity supplied.

Private Enterprise - A system that allows individuals within a society to pursue their own interests without governmental regulation or restriction.

Private Property - The right to buy, own, use, and sell almost any item.

Freedom of Choice - The right to choose what to buy or sell, including one's labor.

Competition - The vying among businesses for the same resources or customers.

Pure Competition - A market or industry characterized by a very large number of small firms, producing an identical product. In pure competition, no single firm is powerful enough to influence the price of its product in the marketplace.

Monopolistic Competition - A market or industry characterized by (1) a large number of buyers and (2) a large number of sellers, trying to differentiate their products from those of their competitors. It is relatively easy for a firm to enter or leave a monopolistically competitive market.

Oligopoly - A market or industry characterized by a handful of (generally very large) sellers that have the power to influence the price of their products.

Monopoly - A market or industry in which there is only one producer and that producer has the power to set the price of its product.

Natural Monopoly - An industry in which one company can most efficiently supply all the product or service that is needed.

Stability - In economic terms, the condition in which the balance between the money available in an economy and the goods produced in that economy remains about the same.

Inflation - A period of widespread price increases throughout an economic system.

Recession - A period characterized by a decrease in employment, income, and production. Recessions may occur on a local, statewide, or national level.

Depression - A particularly severe and long-lasting recession.

Unemployment - The level of joblessness among people actively seeking work.

Growth - An increase in the amount of goods and services produced by a nation's resources.

Gross National Product (GNP) - The total value of all the goods and services produced by an economic system in a one-year period.

Real Gross National Product - Gross national product adjusted for inflation and changes in the value of a country's currency.

Productivity - A measure of economic growth that compares how much is produced to the resources used to produce it.

Balance of Trade - The difference between a country's exports to other nations and its imports from other countries.

Budget Deficit - A situation in which the federal government spends more money in one year than it takes in.

National Debt - The total amount the United States owes to its creditors.

Monetary Policies - Government policies for managing the economy that focus on controlling the size of the nation's money supply.

Fiscal Policies - Government policies for managing the economy that revolve around the ways the government collects and spends its revenues.

TRUE-FALSE QUESTIONS

1. A major determinant of how organizations operate are the kinds of economic systems that characterize the countries in which they do business.

2. Land and mineral deposits are examples of capital.

3. Planned economies rely on individuals to control production factors and choices.

4. The market price is the price at which the quantity of goods demanded and the quantity of goods supplied are equal.

5. Market economies are based on private enterprise.

6. All industries are equally competitive.

7. Since substantial price competition would reduce every seller's profits, perfectly competitive firms use product differentiation to attract customers.

8. Like most utilities, your local electric company is a natural monopoly.

9. The biggest threat to economic stability is inflation.

10. The United States has the third highest real GNP of any industrial nation in the world.

MULTIPLE CHOICE QUESTIONS

1. The positive difference between a business' revenues and its expenses are

   a. factors of production.
   b. supplied resources.
   c. liabilities.
   d. profits.

2. Natural resources, labor, capital, and entrepreneurs are called

   a. human contributions.
   b. economic systems.
   c. factors of production.
   d. market economies.

3. The funds needed to operate an enterprise are called

   a. natural resources.
   b. capital.
   c. labor.
   d. entrepreneurs.

4. Communism is an example of a

   a. planned economy.
   b. market economy.
   c. mixed economy.
   d. capitalistic theory.

5.   A mechanism for exchange between buyers and sellers of a particular good or service is called a

a.   planned economy.
b.   socialistic state.
c.   monopoly.
d.   market.

6.   Producers will offer more for sale as the price of a product rises, but will offer less for sale as the price drops according to the

a.   communist view of the economy.
b.   government.
c.   law of supply.
d.   law of demand.

7.   The Wealth of Nations was written by

a.   Karl Marx.
b.   Adam Smith.
c.   Chet Huntley.
d.   Milton Friedman.

8.   Which of the following is not an element of private enterprise?

a.   public property rights
b.   profits
c.   competition
d.   freedom of choice

9.   When two or more businesses vie for the same resources, it is called

a.   freedom of choice.
b.   private property.
c.   profits.
d.   competition.

10.   Agriculture is a good example of

a.   monopoly in the United States.
b.   oligopoly in the United States.
c.   pure competition in the United States.
d.   monopolistic competition in the United States.

11. When an industry has only a handful of very large sellers, it is referred to as

    a. perfect competition.
    b. an oligopoly.
    c. a monopoly.
    d. monopolistic competition.

12. As an economic goal, the condition in which the balance between the money available and the goods produced remains about the same is called

    a. stability.
    b. inflation.
    c. recession.
    d. employment.

13. When people are unemployed because they lack the skills needed to perform available jobs, it is called

    a. frictional unemployment.
    b. seasonal unemployment.
    c. cyclical unemployment.
    d. structural unemployment.

14. As an economic goal, an increase in the amount of goods and services produced by a nation's resources is called

    a. employment.
    b. inflation.
    c. growth.
    d. stability.

15. The total value of all goods and services produced by an economic system in a one-year period is called the country's

    a. contribution margin.
    b. gross national product.
    c. inflation rate.
    d. real GNP.

16. An economic measure of growth that describes how much is produced relative to the resources used to produce it is

    a. productivity.
    b. balance of trade.
    c. national debt.
    d. unemployment.

17. The difference between a country's exports to other countries and its imports from other countries is called the

    a. national debt.
    b. measure of productivity.
    c. employment index.
    d. balance of trade.

18. When the U.S. Government spends more money than it takes in, it is referred to as

    a. the balance of trade.
    b. monetary politics.
    c. a budget deficit.
    d. productive endeavor.

19. Federal tax increases and budget cuts are examples of

    a. monetary policies.
    b. fiscal policies.
    c. balance of trade policies.
    d. stability policies.

20. An organization that seeks to earn profits by providing goods or services is a

    a. business.
    b. government agency.
    c. school.
    d. foreign country.

WRITING TO LEARN

1. Describe the four factors of production. How do these factors impact our economic growth?

2. What are the major types of economic systems? How do these systems manage the factors of production?

3. How is an equilibrium price attained in a market economy?
   What are the differences between supply and demand and the law of demand and law of supply?

4. Private enterprise requires the presence of what four elements? Discuss each of the four elements and their importance in a market economy that is based on private enterprise.

5.   Discuss and give examples of the four basic degrees of competition within a private enterprise system.

DISCUSSION OF THE CLOSING CASE

Just about every student in this course has heard something about the earliest days of Colonel Sanders' Kentucky Fried Chicken--an absorbing tale of how to get a successful business started. But we are currently in an era in which knowing how to internationalize could possibly be the necessary step for continued survival. It would seem that the Kentucky Fried Chicken organization has learned some important lessons in how to successfully start up operations overseas. The key lesson upon which we shall dwell seems to be to quickly as possible put the foreign operation in the hands of residents of that foreign land. The case points out that the KFC chief for China is Mr. Wang, a native Chinese. There are several reasons why such a move is wise. A native of that foreign land has a better sense of how to market a product to his or her countrymen than any American could ever have. Often, however, this "better sense" is violated by stubborn American executives. For example, were you aware that American car makers still ship automobiles to Japan that have the steering wheel on the wrong side? Your response is probably: "Surely you jest!" No, it's true. Certainly, at some point, a Japanese must have said to an American auto firm: "Don't you Americans know that our roads are like those of the British? We want steering wheels on the right side of the auto. You must make them that way!" But Detroit hasn't been listening. In addition, sending American executives abroad is far more expensive than hiring "nationals"--residents of the foreign land. During the summer of 1991, a Parisian branch of an American firm was in the process of sending home as many Americans as possible and turning the operation over to French employees. The main reason given at the time was expenses. An American executive usually receives a bonus for overseas assignments, along with housing allowances, travel expenses, and numerous provisions for the entire family of the executive--cash outlays that are not involved when hiring a national. Beyond the expenses, the American executive is usually not fluent in the language of the nation where he or she is sent, and this can sometimes constitute a barrier to good business. So KFC has largely decided to let "nationals" take care of its chicken in China.

1.   How important is it for an American executive stationed in Paris, for example, to be able to speak French fluently? What effect could this have on the firm's business?

2.   If you were CEO of Kentucky Fried Chicken, how much advice would you accept from Mr. Wang concerning slight alterations in the KFC menu for Chinese consumption?

3.   If you could be instantly transported to the KFC store in Beijing, do you think that you would feel at home there? Why or why not?

4.   If you were giving directions to Mr. Wang, which of the following ideas would be top priority in your instructions? (a) Teach the Chinese the wonders of Colonel Sanders' great-tasting chicken, or (b) Do whatever you must do to make KFC a sales success.

AN ADDITIONAL CASE

The hauling away of trash is an important business in Palmetto Heights, a growing and prestigious suburb of a huge Atlantic- coast city. There is lively competition among the four trash haulers. Now, it would seem a logical question to ask how there can be "competition" when a resident usually books a trash hauler almost for life. Thus, contracts, if you will, are set and there is little room for four trash haulers to be jockeying for customers. Yes, that is a logical question that could be asked in a logical context. But Palmetto Heights is hardly a logical context! Here's what we mean.

The large Atlantic-coast city adjacent to Palmetto Heights is what is called a "branch office town." That means this major metropolis houses large regional offices for many, many of America's largest corporations. As a result, energetic and fast- rising executives are continuously moving in and out of these branch offices as they climb their way to the top tier of the executive world.

What does all of this have to do with Palmetto Heights? Well, it means that choice properties in this attractive suburb are being constantly bought and sold by these executive families who are regularly arriving and departing. Now, this doesn't mean that real estate price tags are especially high or especially low. It does mean that numerous sales commissions are being earned by agents working the Palmetto Heights market. In fact, several national real estate journals have referred to Palmetto Heights as the "real estate turnover capital of the world." Do you have a figure on how long the average American home owner stays in a particular house? Well, that average figure for Palmetto Heights is 1.794 years. This figure greatly impacts the trash hauling industry.

The figure tells us that in Palmetto Heights there is no such thing as a resident who "books a trash hauler almost for life." With such rapid turnover of real property, the four trash haulers of Palmetto Heights are always faced with a fresh supply of potential new customers. In addition to that, in an effort to keep the town always beautiful, the City Council passed an ordinance that requires each homeowner to engage in a contract with a trash hauler. As you might guess, the haulers crammed this through the council. But the pro-hauler legislation has a snag in it that the haulers don't appreciate; contracts come up for renewal each year! This means that every resident in town (while thinking of where to sign a new contract) becomes each year a potential new customer. So, yes, there is competition aplenty for the hauling of trash in Palmetto Heights.

A new arrival in Palmetto Heights would assume that because of this highly-competitive environment, prices for trash service would be low. Think again. That's not the case in Palmetto Heights. Each of the four trash services (Shakespeare Sanitation, Pursely Pickups, HAUL Incorporated, and Tidy Tim) charge just about the same monthly fee. When one service alters its fee, the other three follow suit immediately. Actually, "follow suit" is an inaccurate expression. There is no leader who is "followed." Price rises by the four are simultaneous. And here's how that works--if we can believe Sally Fisher, who works in the pro shop at Royal Palm Golf and Country Club in nearby Coral Estates. We can't use Sally's real name because what she has told us is possible grounds for Federal prosecution, and she fears retaliation from the haulers. We have also disguised the name of the golf course. Nevertheless, Sally says that every once in awhile the CEOs of the four haulers-- Shakespeare, Pursely, HAUL, and Tidy Tim--meet at Royal Palm Golf and Country Club for a round of golf. A caddy has reported to Sally that all during such a game, the four CEOs discuss how much to raise trash-hauling fees for Palmetto Heights. By the end of 18 holes, an increase would be determined. Within weeks, Sally (who is a resident of Palmetto Heights) would get a notice that her trash service would experience an increased fee. The increase was always the figure that the caddy had relayed to Sally.

Although the four haulers may have been very cooperative in setting fees, they still compete fiercely with one another, mostly through gimmicks. Shakespeare's pickup crews deliver a poinsettia to the door of each patron at Christmastime. Tidy Tim gives out free trash sacks. HAUL Incorporated sprinkles free grass seed on the lawns of customers. Pursely encloses free movie passes with its monthly bills. At least that is what the four haulers did up until recently when one of their group tried a new tack. Shakespeare Sanitation now sponsors five softball teams strictly for kids of their customers. They've even arranged with the Recreation Board for the five teams to make up their own league, called, of course, the Shakespeare League. The other three services are scrambling and stumbling over one another in an effort to start a public relations gimmick that will be equally successful. For the Shakespeare League, the cost involved has been modest but the public relations dividends have been tremendous.

As a counterattack, Pursely is thinking of underwriting a portion of the costs of the Palmetto Heights Junior Ballet--maybe even having a "Pursely Night." Tidy Tim's executives were toying with the idea of a gigantic Christmas Party for the underprivileged children of Palmetto Heights. However, a quick check of demographics of the suburb indicated that--you guessed it--there are no underprivileged children of Palmetto Heights! HAUL is planning to pick up the expenses of the annual Fourth of July fireworks extravaganza at Independence Park. The finale, of course, will consist of the letters H-A-U-L being spelled out in fireworks!

Although the general public isn't supposed to know about it, Sally Fisher and her caddy friend tell us that the four trash CEOs have already thought about how to react to a new trash hauler trying to enter the Palmetto Heights market. Granted, it would be difficult for any new firm to duplicate all the special services that the four trash haulers now provide the suburb. But suppose a lone individual with a small pickup truck offered to haul away your trash at half the going rate? Would you be interested? If so, then the new kid on the block could be a threat; and that threat must be dealt with.

1.   Surely, you've spotted the "degree of competition" existing in Palmetto Heights' trash service industry. Name it. Then go on to indicate the characteristics that gave you clues.

2.   If the four CEOs can agree on service charges, can they also agree when it is time to stop escalating all their special gimmicks?

3.   Really, what chance would a new trash service have to break into this market? Explain. What are some techniques that such a new service might employ to break through?

4.   If a new trash service came in to offer the same basic service at half the going rate, what

might the four CEOs do to combat this lone attractive feature of the new service?

ANSWERS TO TRUE-FALSE QUESTIONS

1.	T	(p. 5)	6.	F	(p. 13)
2.	F	(p. 5)	7.	F	(p. 15)
3.	F	(p. 6-7)	8.	T	(p. 15)
4.	T	(p. 8)	9.	T	(p. 16)
5.	T	(p. 10)	10.	F	(p. 19)

ANSWERS TO MULTIPLE-CHOICE QUESTIONS

1.	D	(p. 5)	11.	B	(p. 15)
2.	C	(p. 5)	12.	A	(p. 16)
3.	B	(p. 6)	13.	D	(p. 17)
4.	A	(p. 7)	14.	C	(p. 18)
5.	D	(p. 7)	15.	B	(p. 18)
6.	C	(p. 8)	16.	A	(p. 19)
7.	B	(p. 10)	17.	D	(p. 20)
8.	A	(p. 10)	18.	C	(p. 20)
9.	D	(p. 11)	19.	B	(p. 20)
10.	C	(p. 13)	20.	A	(p. 5)

CHAPTER TWO

SETTING UP BUSINESS IN THE UNITED STATES

CHAPTER OVERVIEW

All business owners must decide which form of legal organization best suits their business: sole proprietorship, partnership, or corporation. Ease of forming is an advantage of the sole proprietorship and partnership, but a major disadvantage is unlimited liability. A corporation offers limited liability but has the drawback of double taxation. Chief Justice John Marshall defined a corporation in 1819 as "an artificial being, invisible, intangible, and existing only in contemplation of the law." In a cooperative, a group of sole proprietorships or partnerships agrees to work together for their common benefit. S-corporations enjoy the advantages of limited liability and easy transfer of ownership without the disadvantages of the regular corporate form. The corporation, in the process of formation, develops articles of incorporation and corporate bylaws, and then sells shares of stock--common and/or preferred--in the business. The governing body of the corporation is the board of directors which communicates with the rest of the stockholders through the annual report. A subsidiary corporation is one that is owned by another corporation (called the parent). A history of American business stretches through the Colonial Period, the Factory System and the Industrial Revolution, the Entrepreneurial Era, the Production Era, the Marketing Era, and the Glo-bal Era.

LEARNING OBJECTIVES

1.   Identify the major forms of business ownership.

2.   Discuss sole proprietorships and partnerships and identify their advantages and disadvantages.

3.   Describe cooperative and regular corporations and identify their advantages and disadvantages.

4.   Describe the basic issues involved in creating and managing a corporation.

5.   Identify recent trends and issues in corporate ownership.

6.   Trace the history of business in the United States.

DISCUSSION OF THE OPENING CASE

The chapter in your textbook has pointed out that, at least in theory, stockholders of a corporation elect a board of directors and that the board controls the executives of the firm. In theory, the board and the corporate executives always act with the idea that they are always representing the mass of stockholders of the firm. In one sense of the word, the executives are "agents" for the owners, or stockholders. In the field of finance, there is a concept called the "agency problem." This term refers to the fact that company executives will often tend to act with their own selfish best interests in mind rather than in the interests of the stockholders. As a rule, with a very large corporation, it is difficult for stockholders to do much about this. When a stockholders meeting is coming up, stockholders are asked--by mail--to sign a proxy which gives the executives or key board members the authority to vote for the stockholders who cannot be present for the meeting. Most stockholders willingly comply. This allows the "inside group" to make all the decisions on behalf of stockholders. The latter group normally has no idea what is being voted on anyway-- although the fate of their investment in the company is being greatly affected. When a board of directors is made up largely of company executives, how can these executives be "agents" for the board when they are indeed most of the board? The "agency problem" is seen most vividly when there is an attempt at a hostile takeover. When Firm A indicates it wants to buy up large numbers of shares of stock in Firm B and at a premium price, Firm A begins to fight back. But wait? WHO is "fighting back" in the name of Firm A? It isn't necessarily the stockholders, because they may be delighted to sell their shares at the premium price. No, fighting back in the clothing of "Firm A" is the management of the firm. And they are fighting back to avoid a takeover, not with the goal of looking out for the stockholders, but obsessed with repulsing a move that could cost them their jobs! The court decision referred to in the Time-Warner case--allowing corporate managers to act without resort to a stockholder vote-- was a blow to the rights of stockholders. But the Time-Warner stockholders were an exceptional group. They did what few such bodies dare to do: they challenged the managers through the Securities and Exchange Commission and gained a measure of satisfaction.

1.   Despite the court ruling early in the Time-Warner case, do you feel that the stockholders were victorious in their battle with the corporate executives? Why or why not?

2.   Do stockholders with minds of their own tend to impede the progress of a firm's executives toward corporate goals? Explain.

3.   Keeping the Time-Warner case in mind, explain just who is the corporation?

4.   Evaluate the ruling of the court that corporate managers of Time-Warner can make key decisions without subjecting these decisions to a stockholder vote.

ANNOTATED KEY TERMS

Sole Proprietorship - A business owned (and usually operated) by one person, who is responsible for all of the firm's debts.

Unlimited Liability - A major disadvantage to sole proprietorships and partnerships: business owners are responsible for paying off all the debts of the business.

General Partnership - A business with two or more owners, who share in the operation of the firm and in financial responsibility for the firm's debts.

Limited Partnership - A type of partnership that allows for two types of partners: limited partners and active partners.

Limited Partners - Partners who invest their money in a business without being liable for the debts incurred by active partners.

Active Partners - Partners who take an active role in running a business and bear the responsibility for its survival and growth.

Master Limited Partnership - An arrangement in which an organization sells shares of the business to investors and pays all profits back to these investors.

Cooperative - A form of business ownership in which a group of sole proprietorships or partnerships agree to work together for their common benefit.

Corporation - A business considered by law to be a legal entity separate from its owners and with many of the legal rights and privileges of a person; a form of business organization in which owners' liability is limited to their investment in the firm.

Public Corporation - A corporation whose stock is widely held and available for sale to the general public.

Private Corporation - A corporation whose stock is held by only a few people and is not available for sale to the general public.

Limited Liability - One of the major advantages of corporations: investors' liability is limited to their personal investments in the company.

S-Corporation - A small business whose owners enjoy the limited liability benefits of corporate ownership, but the taxation advantages of a partnership. Limited Liability Company (LLC) - A company that has the same advantages of an S-corporation, but with fewer rules and regulations.

18

Articles of Incorporation - The document required by the state in which a corporation receives its charter. The articles include such information as the corporation's name, its purpose, how much stock it intends to issue, and the corporation's address.

Corporate Bylaws - The document in which the rules and regulations of a corporation are set out. The bylaws detail how directors will be elected, how they will serve, their basic responsibilities, and how new stock will be issued.

Stock - A share of ownership in a corporation.

Stockholder/Shareholder - One who owns shares of stock in a corporation.

Dividends - The business profits distributed to shareholders, paid on a per share basis.

Preferred Stock - Stock that guarantees its owners a fixed dividend and priority over assets, but no voting rights in the corporation.

Common Stock - Stock that guarantees its owners voting rights in a company, but last claim to a company's assets.

Proxy - Authorization granted by shareholders for someone else to vote their shares.

Board of Directors - The governing body of a corporation, charged with overseeing the day-to-day operations of the business.

Chief Executive Officer (CEO) - The top manager hired by the board of directors to run a corporation.

Inside Directors - Members of a corporation's board of directors, who are employees of the company and who have primary responsibility for the corporation.

Outside Directors - Members of a corporation's board of directors, who are not employees of the corporation in the normal course of business.

Corporate Merger - The union of two corporations to form a new corporation.

Acquisition - The purchase of one company by another company.

Subsidiary Corporation - A corporation owned by another corporation.

Parent Corporation - A corporation that owns another subsidiary corporation.

Multinational Corporation - A corporation that conducts operations and marketing activities on an international level.

Joint Venture - A collaboration between two or more organizations on a new enterprise.

Employee Stock Ownership Plan (ESOP) - An arrangement in which a corporation buys its own stock with loaned funds and holds it in trust for its employees. Employees "earn" the stock, based on some condition such as seniority. Employees control the stock's voting rights immediately, even though they may not take physical possession of the stock until specified conditions are met.

Institutional Investors - Large investors, such as mutual funds and pension funds, that purchase large blocks of a corporation's stock.

Industrial Revolution - A major change in goods production that began in England in the mid-eighteenth century and was characterized by a shift to the factory system, mass production, and the specialization of labor.

Factory System - A process in which all the materials and workers required to produce items are brought together in one place.

Mass Production - The manufacture of a good of uniform quality in large numbers.

Specialization - The breaking down of complex operations into individual tasks to permit concentration in performing each task.

Production Era - The period during the early twentieth century in which U.S. business focused almost exclusively on improving productivity and manufacturing methods.

Sales Era - The period during the 1930s in which U.S. business focused on developing sales forces, advertising, and keeping products readily available.

Marketing Concept - The philosophy that all businesses start with the customer: business must identify and satisfy consumer wants to be profitable.

TRUE-FALSE QUESTIONS

1.   Sole proprietorships account for about six percent of total business revenues in the United States.

2.   There is a legal limit of twelve partners that may form a general partnership.

3.   Partnerships are among the least popular legal forms of organization.

4.   Limited liability is the biggest disadvantage of regular corporations.

5.   The greatest potential drawback of the corporate form of organization is double taxation.

6. Bondholders are the owners of a corporate business.

7. Common stock must be issued by every corporation, big or small.

8. A summary of the company's financial health issued by the board of directors is called a proxy.

9. A collaboration between two or more organizations on a new enterprise is called a joint venture.

10. An ESOP is essentially a trust established on behalf of the employees of a corporation.

MULTIPLE CHOICE QUESTIONS

1. The very first legal form of business organization, dating back to ancient times is the

   a. limited partnership.
   b. general partnership.
   c. corporation.
   d. sole proprietorship.

2. Which of the following is not an advantage of the sole proprietorship form of business?

   a. simple to form
   b. freedom
   c. unlimited liability
   d. low start-up costs

3. The greatest drawback of general partnerships is their

   a. ability to borrow funds.
   b. unlimited liability.
   c. ease of organization.
   d. legal standing for tax purposes.

4. The Boston Celtics basketball team is structured as a

   a. master limited partnership.
   b. corporation.
   c. sole proprietorship.
   d. Subchapter-S corporation.

5.	A form of business ownership in which a group of sole proprietorships or partnerships agree to work together for their common benefit is the

	a. sole proprietorship.
	b. master limited partnership.
	c. Subchapter-S corporation.
	d. cooperative.

6.	Ocean Spray, Riceland, and Blue Diamond Growers are examples of

	a. sole proprietorships.
	b. corporations.
	c. cooperatives.
	d. general partnerships.

7.	Chief Justice John Marshall's definition of a business form that is "an artificial being, invisible, intangible, and existing only in contemplation of the law" describes a

	a. partnership.
	b. corporation.
	c. cooperative.
	d. sole proprietorship.

8.	Gallo Wine, Levi Strauss, and UPS are examples of

	a. private corporations.
	b. sole proprietorships.
	c. general partnerships.
	d. cooperatives.

9.	The biggest advantage of a regular corporation is

	a. ease of transferring ownership.
	b. costs of formation.
	c. lack of regulation.
	d. limited liability.

10.	Which of the following specialized forms of corporate organization enjoys the advantages of limited liability and easy transfer of ownership without many of the disadvantages of the regular corporate form?

	a. a limited liability company
	b. a limited partnership
	c. a Subchapter-S corporation
	d. a cooperative

11. Which of the following forms of ownership has the same advantages of a S-corporation, but with fewer rules and regulations?

a. master limited partnerships
b. limited liability companies
c. general partnerships
d. Section-409 corporations

12. Which of the following specify the corporation's name, its purpose, how much stock it intends to issue, the corporation's address, and other information that the state requires?

a. articles of incorporation
b. corporate bylaws
c. mechanics liens
d. partnership agreement

13. Business profits are distributed among stockholders in the form of

a. preferred stock.
b. bonds.
c. assets.
d. dividends.

14. Which of the following guarantees those who own it a fixed dividend, much like the interest payment earned on a savings account?

a. common stock
b. bonds
c. preferred stock
d. treasury stock

15. By law, the governing body of a corporation is its

a. chief executive officer.
b. board of directors.
c. chief operating officer.
d. employees.

16. Directors of a board composed of employees of the company such as the president and executive vice president are called

a. inside directors
b. outside directors.
c. a board of aldermen.
d. an oversight committee.

17. When one corporation buys another outright, the move is called a(n)

    a. merger.
    b. conglomerate.
    c. diversification.
    d. acquisition.

18. A corporation that is owned by another corporation is a

    a. parent corporation.
    b. Subchapter-S corporation.
    c. subsidiary corporation.
    d. multinational corporation.

19. A collaboration between two or more organizations on a new enterprise is called a

    a. multinational corporation.
    b. joint venture.
    c. ESOP.
    d. merger.

20. Which of the following concepts suggests that all businesses start with the customer?

    a. the marketing concept
    b. the production concept
    c. the sales concept
    d. the manufacturing concept

WRITING TO LEARN

1. Describe the types of business organizations. What are the advantages and disadvantages of each?

2. What are the advantages of a Subchapter-S corporation? What is an LLC? How does an LLC differ from a Subchapter-S corporation?

3. What steps are involved in creating a corporation? Why do corporations sell stock and bonds? What are the advantages of a corporation having an outside board of directors?

4. Discuss some recent trends in corporate ownership. Why would two or more organizations want to form a joint venture? What is an ESOP?

5. Discuss the production, marketing and global eras. How do they differ? What is meant by the marketing concept?

DISCUSSION OF THE CLOSING CASE

The Hard Rock Cafes have been fabulously successful. Unfortunately, their story is not necessarily the fate of every new business venture. The text has pointed out that a problem with the sole proprietorship, and the partnership as well, is difficulty in lining up sufficient financial resources. This is still very definitely a problem for small businesses getting started--even a cafe in London! Most businesses need this large starting capital to carry the firm through the opening lean months when sales revenues are not sufficient to support the operations of the company. In the worst case scenario, sales revenues never reach expected levels, and the company exists largely on borrowed capital. When the firm is unable to repay the borrowed funds, bankruptcy-- of whatever chapter--follows. But this "worst case scenario" that is all too familiar <u>never occurred for Hard Rock Cafes</u>. Apparently, revenues were healthy right from the start and so were net profits. A successful eating establishment has a break in this way over some other businesses in that it can draw revenues on the first day of operation. The minute a cafe opens for its very first day of business at 6:00 A.M., a quickly prepared breakfast at a cost to the firm of $.85 can sell for $2.99--instantly ringing up a profit of $2.14! A new auto manufacturer, on the other hand, may go on for <u>many months</u> spending money (in designing, developing, building and shipping autos) before the very first car is sold. For Hard Rock Cafes, these quick and freely-flowing profits meant that for expansion there would be retained earnings from profitable operation to buttress any borrowed funds. And plenty of expansion was on the way. When we stop to consider the enormous outlay of funds necessary for the Hard Rock Cafes to reach across the world, we appreciate how sales success not only added dollars for expansion but also--and perhaps more important--convinced bankers and other interested investors that here was a good place to lend money!

1. Suppose the first Hard Rock Cafe had taken a year or two to "catch on" with the British public. What would this have done to change their story?

2. Do you feel that the Hard Rock Cafes have run their course? If so, what changes ought they to make? If not, then why not?

3. How successful will the Hard Rock Cafe Hotel and Casino be in Las Vegas? Is branching out from the original format a good idea? Why or why not?

4. Think of a small locally-owned restaurant in your town. What is to prevent that restaurant from enjoying the successful fate of the Hard Rock Cafes?

AN ADDITIONAL CASE

Bixit Corporation is a large manufacturer of greeting cards and accessories located in Oak Grove, Utah. At some time or other, you have sent a Bixit to a friend on a special occasion. But, if you live in the United States, you haven't done it very often, because well over 90 percent of Bixit's cards are manufactured for the European market. Bixit has 20,000,000 shares of common stock outstanding; price per share at last quotation from New York was $14. [When most of those shares were sold originally, they brought around $3 a share.] There are around 20,000 shareholders of Bixit. Industry analysts have wrtten about Bixit for numerous national and international publications. Although these critics perceive the firm in varying ways, most analysts agree that Bixit operates as if it were not aware of what is going on in the greeting-card industry.

First of all, these industry analysts say almost unanimously that the greeting-card market right now is about as receptive as it will ever be. But Bixit has done nothing in the first half of the 1990s to exploit this favorable atmosphere. Although sales seem to be holding their own, Bixit's market share has dropped-- and no one at the Oak Grove headquarters seems concerned. Bixit's approach to social responsibility has been admirable; but can you carry such an attitude too far? Several institutions in Oak Grove owe their very existence to Bixit. Here's the list: The Oak Grove Philharmonic Orchestra, the Oak Grove Ballet Company, Bixit Community College, Bixit Memorial Zoo, and the farm club Oak Grove Royals of the Class AA Mountain Baseball League.

No one faults the results of a "social audit" to be taken at Bixit. But the corporation's dividend policy reflects very clearly that corporate profits are not going in the two standard directions-- retained earnings and dividends. Instead, much of the net income after taxes goes to civic endeavors. And this public-spirited approach has elicited another remark from the analysts. The latter feel that stockholders of the firm could easily be resentful of the stingy dividend policy and might even bolt the firm by unloading their shares of stock. The analysts say that the figure of $14 a share on the market reflects the stockholders' negative attitudes and that a share of Bixit could easily be worth $20 or more under different corporate conditions.

Although many of the stockholders of Bixit live in the greater Oak Grove area, a vast majority do not. The Oak Grove stockholders group contains many executives, plant employees, and their relatives. Serious investors within the "far away" group have become increasingly disenchanted by the Bixit management's lackadaisical approach to the fortunes of the firm. When annual stockholder meetings are held in Oak Grove, owners in the immediate vicinity attend, and the other larger contingent is usually unrepresented. However, the voices of the "unrepresented" are about to be heard.

Ashley J. Phelan is a "corporate raider." This means that he and his associates go around the country looking for corporations to gobble up through "hostile takeover." We'll soon see exactly how they do it. Meantime, it must be pointed out that Phelan thinks of himself as a "raider in a white hat." This means that he intends to go into a corporation that is resting on its laurels and treating its stockholders shabbily. Once he gains control, he makes changes for the better, raises corporate profits, finds funds to expand the firm, and makes dividends to stockholders more generous. In addition, his moves are such that stock price goes up--a sign of renewed faith in a fresh, revamped firm. Now the "raid" on Bixit begins.

Noting, as we have, that Bixit common stock is selling for $14 a share, Phelan spread the word that he will be buying such shares at $22 each! He works through his brokers to acquire shares on the open market. He sends letters to Bixit's stockholders and places ads in financial journals that will be read by Bixit shareholders. Although Bixit's board has devised several "poison pills" (devices to make buying into Bixit most unattractive), Phelan forges ahead with a goal of achieving 70 percent of the stock--ensuring rulership of the board of directors. In his mailers and advertisements, Phelan points out that he will make the company more efficient, by cutting out excess executives and money-losing projects, and that shareholders who sell to him will want to get back into the dynamic, new company soon. Phelan will welcome them back, and he has promised that such "returnees" can repurchase their stock at a most favorable price. Phelan promises that he will restore "stockholders rights" and that vast civic undertakings by Bixit will occur only if the stockholders concur.

Apparently, Phelan's move has been awaited by many Bixit stockholders and the attack is welcome. Within three weeks, Phelan and his associates have been able to garner over 12 million Bixit shares, with more falling into their hands daily. As a surprise to all, laid back Bixit launches a savage counterattack--even getting on several national TV news programs to say its piece: "This is a cowardly attack on Bixit Corporation aimed at ruining not only a great greeting-card firm but also tearing down the pride of a fine community, Oak Grove. What will become of our town? We say to all stockholders not to sell to this raider but to pull together and save the corporation. We can't let the corporation go down the drain. The very life of the corporation is at stake. We must save her!"

A reporter for one of the nation's leading financial magazines, upon hearing the statement relayed above, wrote these lines for his column:

"The Bixit Corporation is saying that the way to save the firm is for stockholders to refrain from selling their shares to raider Ashley J. Phelan. To hear Phelan tell it, selling shares to him and his cohorts IS THE WAY to save the corporation. Who can we believe? First of all, we must make it clear that when 'The Bixit Corporation' speaks, as it has so eloquently and cryingly on national TV, we are not indeed hearing BIXIT; we are hearing Bixit MANAGEMENT pleading that their jobs be saved! Get the difference? According to all finance books, the corporation is those 20,000 shareholders. And maybe they know what is best for their corporation--despite the bleating of the near-sighted executives in Oak Grove."

1.   Now that you have several interpretations of just WHO is the Bixit Corporation, what is your interpretation?

2.   Will a Phelan "takeover" be good for Bixit? Why or why not?

3.   Comment on the Bixit case from the angle of stockholder rights.

4.   Based on what you have read here, would you sell your $14 shares to Phelan for $22? Would you later attempt to get back into the corporation by rebuying your stock at a "most favorable price"? Explain why or why not.

ANSWERS TO TRUE-FALSE QUESTIONS

1.	T	(p. 27)	6.	F	(p. 36)
2.	F	(p. 29)	7.	T	(p. 36)
3.	T	(p. 30)	8.	F	(p. 37)
4.	F	(p. 34)	9.	T	(p. 39)
5.	T	(p. 34)	10.	T	(p. 40)

ANSWERS TO MULTIPLE-CHOICE QUESTIONS

1.	D	(p. 27)	11.	B	(p. 35)
2.	C	(p. 27)	12.	A	(p. 35-36)
3.	B	(p. 30)	13.	D	(p. 36)
4.	A	(p. 31)	14.	C	(p. 36)
5.	D	(p. 31)	15.	B	(p. 37)
6.	C	(p. 31)	16.	A	(p. 39)
7.	B	(p. 33)	17.	D	(p. 39)
8.	A	(p. 33)	18.	C	(p. 39)
9.	D	(p. 34)	19.	B	(p. 39)
10.	C	(p. 34)	20.	A	(p. 43)

CHAPTER THREE

RECOGNIZING BUSINESS TRENDS AND CHALLENGES

CHAPTER OVERVIEW

The Bureau of Labor Standards defines a high-technology firm as one that spends twice as much on research and development and employs twice as many technical employees as the average U.S. manufacturing firm. The service sector consists of jobs that involve providing a service rather than creating a tangible product. There has been in recent years a gradual population shift to the Sunbelt. The American business scene has witnessed in recent years increased mergers, acquisitions, and alliances. Government regulates business and one of the main reasons for this regulation is to ensure the presence of competition in the marketplace. Deregulation, or the elimination of rules that restrict business activity, has been accomplished by the government in several industries with differing results. Business can influence government through lobbyists and political action committees. Some changes in the nation's labor force in recent years have been: the graying of the work force; more women; more immigrant influence; declining unionization; and more worker participation in company decisions. Businesses have had to adjust to a steady increase in the power of the consumer. Some challenges of the 1990s will be: productivity; international trade; pollution; and technology.

LEARNING OBJECTIVES

1. Describe five major trends that affect U.S. business today.

2. Explain why the U.S. government sometimes regulates business and how business seeks to influence the government.

3. Discuss changes in the U.S. labor pool and their effects on business.

4. Describe the changes in demographics and consumer rights and their impact on U.S. business.

5. Identify and discuss four major challenges for U.S. business in the 1990s.

DISCUSSION OF THE OPENING CASE

To make a major marketing impact, a firm needs money. Such funds, we are taught in finance, can be borrowed. Another source of funds is to sell portions of ownership in the business. That is, to sell shares of stock. If a firm must sell so many shares that the new stockholders control more of the company than the founder, then the new stockholders can theoretically vote through the board of directors to determine what the directions of the firm will be. That's what happened in the motion picture <u>Tucker</u>. To obtain money to manufacture a brand new concept in automotive transportation, the founder had to obtain millions of dollars. With the dollars came people whose money had bought them the right to make corporate decisions. Founder Tucker found himself at their mercy. A large board of directors operates somewhat like a democracy--reaching decisions by discussing and haggling. Sometimes, board members are not the best-qualified persons for making key decisions. But if they have the votes, they make the corporate decisions. That is what Robert D. Haas saw happening in the firm that Levi Strauss founded. Sometimes, you can't run a business like a democracy. Even in today's complex world, a firm needs a sense of direction that just one keen mind can provide. Here, we scuttle the democratic idea and go for a dictatorship. So, Haas set out to get all of those <u>other</u> stockholders out of the firm. He and his family slowly set about buying as many shares of stock in Levi Strauss as they could get their hands on. The result was that the Haas family came to hold 90 percent of the firm's stock-- clearly giving them control. This meant Haas could chart a clear course for the firm and see that it was implemented--without being hung up by wrangling and discussing and other forms of interference by board members. At this stage in the firm's saga, a clear signal as to where the firm was going was required. But getting back the shares of stock cost great bundles of borrowed money that could lay a heavy debt on the shoulders of the firm for a long time to come. Fortunately, the firm has been able to whittle away at much of that debt. At this writing, the big push to "buy back" the firm was a wise move indeed.

1.   What are some of the risks that go along with a buyout program such as Haas attempted?

2.   Evaluate this statement: "No doubt about it, Haas felt he knew what the public wanted from Levi Strauss better than all those other stock-holders did."

3.   Why did board members of the old Levi Strauss organization (prior to the buyout) feel hesitant about getting involved in "temporarily unprofitable" activities?

4.   What message does the Levi Strauss story send to you about bringing in the money of new co-owners to get a company launched?

ANNOTATED KEY TERMS

<u>High</u> <u>Technology (High-Tech)</u> <u>Firm</u> - A firm that spends twice as much on research and development and employs twice as many technical employees as the average U.S. manufacturing firm.

<u>Service</u> <u>Sector</u> - The sector of the economy consisting of jobs that involve providing a service, rather than creating a tangible product.

<u>Informational</u> <u>Services</u> - Service industries that provide information for a fee. Examples include law, accounting, and data processing.

Acquisition - The purchase of one company by another company.

Merger - The union of two companies to form a single new business.

Alliance - An agreement between companies in which the individual companies retain their independence, but agree to work together in one or more areas.

Horizontal Merger - A merger between two companies in the same industry.

Vertical Merger - A merger in which one of the companies is a supplier or customer to the other.

Conglomerate Merger - A merger of two firms in completely unrelated businesses.

Friendly Takeover - An acquisition in which the acquired company welcomes the merger.

Hostile Takeover - An acquisition in which the acquiring company buys enough of the other company's stock to take control, even though the other company opposes the takeover.

Raiders - Investors who acquire a large block of a company's stock and initiate a hostile takeover.

Greenmail - A buyback of a company's stock at a large profit from one or more investors who are threatening a hostile takeover of the firm.

Regulation - The establishment of governmental rules that restrict business activity.

Deregulation - The elimination of governmental rules that restrict business activity.

Lobbyist - A person hired by a company or industry to represent its interests with government officials.

Trade Association - An organization dedicated to assisting and promoting the interest of its members.

Political Action Committee (PAC) - A political fund-raising group that accepts contributions and distributes them to candidates for political office.

Consumer Movement - Activism on the part of consumers seeking better value from businesses.

Consumer Rights - The legally protected rights of consumers to purchase the products they desire, the right to safety from the products they purchase, the right to be informed about what they are buying, and the right to be heard in the event of problems.

Trade Deficit - The situation in which a country imports more than it exports; sometimes called a negative trade balance.

Trade Surplus - The situation in which a country exports more than it imports.

TRUE-FALSE QUESTIONS

1. In recent years, the manufacturing sector in the United States has increased as an employer of workers.

2. Ford's purchase of Jaguar was a vertical merger.

3. Kodak's acquisition of Sterling Drugs is an example of a conglomerate merger.

4. One of the reasons that government regulates business is to ensure competition.

5. Social goals promote the general well-being of society.

6. Since deregulation, the overall structure of the airline industry has changed.

7. Increased regulation has contributed to hard times in the savings and loan industry.

8. All lobbyists are required to register with the government as paid representatives of interest groups or particular businesses.

9. The influence of organized labor has begun to decline in recent years.

10. By the end of the twentieth century, there will be no landfills in the United States.

MULTIPLE CHOICE QUESTIONS

1. According the the Bureau of Labor Standards, a firm that spends twice as much on research and development and employs twice as many technical employees as the average U.S. manufacturing firm is defined as a

   a. conglomerate.
   b. service company.
   c. merger.
   d. high-technology company.

2.   Bank, restaurant, retail, transportation, and entertainment businesses are all examples of

     a. high-technology firms.
     b. mergers.
     c. service firms.
     d. speculative ventures.

3.   In 1991, what percent of U.S. jobs were service jobs?

     a. 28 percent
     b. 78 percent
     c. 40 percent
     d. 45 percent

4.   Lawyers, accountants, office personnel, and insurance agents provide

     a. informational services.
     b. high-tech jobs.
     c. unskilled labor.
     d. greenmail.

5.   A consolidation of two firms is called a(n)

     a. acquisition.
     b. joint venture.
     c. takeover.
     d. merger.

6.   When one of the companies in a merger is a supplier or customer to the other, it is called a

     a. horizontal merger.
     b. conglomerate merger.
     c. vertical merger.
     d. takeover.

7.   The term used to describe the situation in which investors acquire large blocks of a company's stock, threaten a hostile takeover, then let the target company buy back its stock at a price that gives the raiders a substantial profit is called

     a. a friendly takeover.
     b. greenmail.
     c. rescue by a white knight.
     d. a poison pill.

8. The establishment of rules by government that restrict business activity is called

   a. regulation.
   b. competition.
   c. greenmail.
   d. a takeover.

9. Which of the following is not a reason that the government regulates business?

   a. to help meet social goals
   b. to protect competition
   c. to ensure a safe workplace
   d. to prohibit market activity

10. The primary government agency charged with assuring worker safety is

    a. the EPA.
    b. the SEC.
    c. OSHA.
    d. the FTC.

11. The elimination of rules that restrict business activity is called

    a. regulation.
    b. deregulation.
    c. greenmail.
    d. government intervention.

12. Continental, Eastern, and Pan Am are examples of firms that have not been able to successfully compete since

    a. deregulation.
    b. the early 1800s.
    c. the SEC was established.
    d. CAB set fares and assigned routes.

13. A person hired by a company or industry to represent its interests with government officials is a

    a. CEO.
    b. CFO.
    c. competitor.
    d. lobbyist.

14. Special political fund-raising groups are called

    a. lobbyists.
    b. trade associations.
    c. PACs.
    d. demographers.

15. The National Rifle Association is an example of a

    a. corporate raider.
    b. PAC.
    c. firm meeting a social goal.
    d. government organization.

16. The statistical makeup of the U.S. labor force is called

    a. demographics.
    b. a PAC.
    c. a union.
    d. a census.

17. By 1990, the percent of the female population in the workforce exceeded

    a. 34 percent.
    b. 29 percent.
    c. 72 percent.
    d. 57 percent.

18. According to the author of your textbook, Xerox, Federal Express, Westinghouse, and Apple are a few of the many examples of firms in which many managerial functions are being

    a. controlled by government.
    b. centralized.
    c. turned over to teams of workers.
    d. shifted overseas.

19. Activism on the part of consumers seeking better value from businesses is referred to as the

    a. concept of changing demographics.
    b. consumer movement.
    c. graying of America.
    d. increase in cultural diversity.

20. Which of the following was not mentioned by the authors of your textbook as one of the business challenges of the 1990s?

    a. increased merger activity
    b. increased productivity
    c. the opportunities of technology
    d. pollution

WRITING TO LEARN

1. What has been the impact of high technology on the business world? Are there certain industries that can benefit more than others through the use of technology?

2. Will the growth in the service sector continue? What has driven the demand for informational services?

3. Are mergers, acquisitions, and takeovers beneficial to business and society? Describe several types of mergers. Are all takeovers friendly?

4.Why does government regulate business? Are government regulations beneficial to the consumer and society? Has deregulation been beneficial to business in general?

5.What challenges do businesses face in the 1990s?

DISCUSSION OF THE CLOSING CASE

In the Opening Case, we saw the Haas family attempting to get rid of existing stockholders at Levi Strauss who were holding the company back. In the Closing Case, we see Bob Rosenberg, chairman of Dunkin' Donuts, struggling to shut the door on stockholders who wanted to get in. Either task can, at times, be extremely difficult. Rosenberg used several tactics that proved to be successful. One of these involved recruiting General Electric Corporation. Here's how it happened. When a "corporate raider," such as George Mann, starts out to effect a "hostile takeover" of your firm by buying up as many shares of stock as possible, a strong defense is to quickly line up what is called in finance a "white knight"--a friendly firm that will purchase shares of your stock, thus making said shares unavailable for purchase by the "raider." When a group of hostile stockholder cavalry is galloping for your fortress, it is comforting to know that they will be intercepted and routed by your own allies--the white knight forces. A second ploy of Rosenberg's was to make shares of stock available to employees of Dunkin' Donuts. The end result was that the percent of shares available for sale to the "raider" was too small to allow the latter to gain control of the firm. The "raider" retreated. Before we become too satisfied and "comfy" with how things have worked out for Rosenberg and Dunkin' Donuts, perhaps we should recall the ancient tale of the Trojan horse. Remember it? A gift to the people of Troy in the form of a sculptured horse was accepted into the city. It contained, the poor Trojans were to later discover, enemy soldiers who exploited their ability to infiltrate the walls of Troy. How does the tale relate? What kind of effect will the presence of the "white knight" in the Dunkin' Donuts camp have on corporate decisions? Will General Electric's ownership of stock in the firm lead to pressures on Rosenberg to alter his way of operating?

1. Usually in an attempt at a hostile takeover, the "raider" offers high prices for shares of stock in the target company. Is this good for the current stockholders? Why or why not?

2. General Electric is not noted as a succesful marketer of doughnuts. Will this fact necessarily keep GE from giving advice to Dunkin' Donuts, assuming that GE presence on the board of directors is significant?

3. To enable him to fend off the "raider," Rosenberg took on additional debt. To be able to repay the debt, he cut staff. Do you feel that the latter move can hurt the organization? Why or why not?

4. Do you think the "satellite" shops are a good idea? Will Mr. Rosenberg soon see their folly and drop them? Why or why not?

AN ADDITIONAL CASE

If you live in the eastern half of the United States, chances are good that you've never heard of Johnny Hoopy. Actually, Johnny Hoopy is not a human being; it's a fast-food concept that has swept the west in the past seven years. Be patient, for Johnny Hoopy will soon be in your neighborhood!

Lloyd Diskin grew up in Homestead, Florida in the 1930s. A memory that stayed with him from that era was the giant county fair and a particular delicious treat that could be found in Homestead only at fair time. It was the french-fried potatoes booth. For a nickel, you could buy a small cup of piping-hot french-fried potatoes and sprinkle them with vinegar. It may not sound appetizing to you, but Lloyd Diskin loved the combination-- and so did all the fairgoers in Homestead. South Florida in those days was populated by a lot of people who, for various reasons, would eventually move on to other parts of the country. That happened to Lloyd.

In 1986, in Pueblo, Colorado, Lloyd brought the Homestead french fry back to life. He opened his first Johnny Hoopy stand. The facility, no bigger than the north half of a mobile home, would sell several varieties of fries, including, of course, the "Homestead Special" (fries in vinegar). The secret to a Johnny Hoopy was perhaps not so much in the taste as in the fact that the fries would always be <u>hot</u>. Whatever it was that Lloyd and his four assistants did to the Johnny Hoopy fries, the people of Pueblo loved them. Now, you're probably wondering how a fast- food establishemnt selling only french fries could survive. Well, the first Johnny Hoopy sat next-door to a frozen yogurt parlor. Just an accident. But the local people made use of the combination. Go get a yogurt, then get a Johnny Hoopy. Within six months, Lloyd had seven Johnny Hoopys in Pueblo, and each one of them next to a frozen yogurt parlor.

It soon became obvious to Lloyd that he had a product that might make it on a franchise basis. With the help of legal, nutritional, and technical experts, Johnny Hoopy became a franchisor. By 1990, there were 783 Johnny Hoopys in 9 western states. By January 1, 1992, the figure was 1,319 Johnny Hoopys in 27 states. In as many cases as possible, a Hoopy was located next to a frozen yogurt stand. Quite frankly, we can't tell you what the attraction was in a Johnny Hoopy; all we can say is that people came to the stands in droves, day after day. With that technical and nutritional advice as part of the central Johnny Hoopy payroll, Lloyd Diskin was able to maintain his original quality over every french fry that was served by a Hoopy. Lloyd never compromised on his staffing pattern: a manager and four assistants at each Johnny Hoopy stand constantly making fries.

Now, remember that Lloyd grew up in the 1930s. So, he was no kid as 1992 dawned. Johnny Hoopy had been financially good to him and his family. Good, you say? Hoopy had been fabulously good for the Diskins. As a result, Lloyd was open to someone buying the operation so that he could retire. Fortunately, the era of mergers and acquisitions had not yet run its course, and AJ Industries was interested in taking over Johnny Hoopy.

AJ Industries was headquartered in Tulsa, Oklahoma, and still carried some of the characteristics of a conglomerate firm--although the conglomerate craze had peaked and dipped. AJ was originally a waste-treatment cooperative, but had joined forces with a national frozen yogurt franchise network, a major soccer-equipment supplier, a small publishing house, and a respectable chain of 71 daily newspapers in the Southwest. AJ was noted for sharp and crisp management and for turning waning enterprises into financial winners. The executives at AJ Industries were very impressed with the instant and almost-unexplained popularity of Johnny Hoopy. Certainly Johnny Hoopy was no sick enterprise, but AJ felt it could do even more for Hoopy, perhaps marketing its product on a nationwide scale, maybe even into Canada.

AJ Industries paid Lloyd Diskin and his financial associates a generous sum to purchase all rights to Johnny Hoopy. AJ would now take a business that was already succesful and turn it into a resounding achievement.

The secret to AJ's new success with Johnny Hoopy would be what AJ executives called "financial integrity." No Johnny Hoopy employee knew what the term meant, but they would soon find out. AJ field representatives quickly visited each and every Hoopy franchise.

After surveying the chain, AJ headquarters made a few changes. First, ingredient formulas were altered for more economically-astute operation. Second, there would be only a manager and 2 assistants at any given Johnny Hoopy stand. Since such savings were to be effected, payouts to franchisees were altered downward. Hours of operation were curtailed so that overtime pay could be avoided. To bring about a more general menu, hamburgers and hot dogs would be added at all Johnny Hoopys along with old-fashioned milkshakes. Frozen yogurt was also added to the menu. Since the renovations of the Hoopy chain showed such signs of promise, 500 more outlets were quickly opened by AJ Industries and the state count rose to 39.

The undeniable savings from cost-cutting were reflected in the first income statement published for Johnny Hoopy on the AJ Industries letterhead. Hoopy profits were thus allowed to rise significantly. It wasn't until the third income statement for AJ that it was noticed that sales volume was dropping--especially in the original 1,319 stands. By the fourth income statement, the drop in sales was alarming, but mostly in the 1,319 original stands.

Carlos Finter, director of marketing for AJ Industries, placed a call to Lloyd Diskin to get the latter's input on the temporarily sinking fortunes of Johnny Hoopy.

"Mister Diskin. Carlos Finter here. I'm director of marketing at AJ. Have you been keeping up with the improvements we've been making with Hoopy? Good. Looks like you sold out at a perfect time, because the french-fries fad is starting to fade. Sales have been dropping on us. We'll shape it up quickly. Just wondered if you have any ideas on what's happening to our sales?"

1. What answer would you give to Carlos Finter if you were Lloyd Diskin?

2. Although AJ Industries owns a frozen-yogurt chain, how much french-fry expertise to you feel they brought into Johnny Hoopy? Explain.

3. What can AJ Industries do to put Johnny Hoopy back on the track?

4. Was acquiring Johnny Hoopy a good idea for AJ Industries? Why or why not?

ANSWERS TO TRUE-FALSE QUESTIONS

1.	F	(p. 51)	6.	F	(p. 57)
2.	F	(p. 54)	7.	F	(p. 58)
3.	T	(p. 54)	8.	T	(p. 58)
4.	T	(p. 55)	9.	T	(p. 61)
5.	T	(p. 55)	10.	T	(p. 67)

ANSWERS TO MULTIPLE-CHOICE QUESTIONS

1.	D	(p. 51)	11.	B	(p. 56)
2.	C	(p. 51)	12.	A	(p. 57)
3.	B	(p. 51)	13.	D	(p. 58)
4.	A	(p. 51)	14.	C	(p. 59)
5.	D	(p. 52)	15.	B	(p. 60)
6.	C	(p. 53)	16.	A	(p. 61)
7.	B	(p. 54)	17.	D	(p. 61)
8.	A	(p. 55)	18.	C	(p. 64)
9.	D	(p. 55)	19.	B	(p. 64)
10.	C	(p. 56)	20.	A	(p. 65)

CHAPTER FOUR

CONDUCTING BUSINESS ETHICALLY AND RESPONSIBLY

CHAPTER OVERVIEW

Ethics are an individual's beliefs about what is right and wrong or good and bad. Ethical behavior is behavior that conforms to generally accepted social norms while unethical behavior does not. The most common influences on an individual's ethics and behavior are family and peers (and the values they convey), situations, and experiences. Within the workplace, the company itself can influence ethical bahavior, if not always beliefs. Formulating a code of corporate ethics is not an easy task but it must be done. While ethics affect how an individual behaves within a business, social responsibility affects how a business behaves toward other businesses, customers, investors, and society at large. There are several major areas of social responsibility: responsibility toward the environment, responsibility toward customers, responsibility toward employees, and responsibility toward investors. There are three approaches to social responsibility: the social-obligation approach; the social-reaction approach; and the social-response approach, with the latter approach representing an attitude of actively seeking opportunities to contribute to the well-being of society. Small businesses face many of the same social responsibility questions as large corporations.

LEARNING OBJECTIVES

1. Explain how individuals develop their personal codes of ethics and why ethics are important in the workplace.

2. Distinguish social responsibility from ethics and trace the evolution of social responsibility in U.S. business.

3. Describe how the concept of social responsibility applies to environmental issues and to businesses' relationships with customers, employees, and investors.

4. Identify the four general approaches to social responsibility and the four steps a firm needs to take to implement a social responsibility program.

5. Explain how issues of social responsibility and ethics affect small businesses.

DISCUSSION OF THE OPENING CASE

It is far beyond the scope of this study guide to explicitly determine, for international consumption, what were the original motivations behind the establishment of the Bank of Credit and Commerce International (BCCI). If the idea from the very beginning was to operate outside the law, then BCCI is hardly an appropriate commentary on business ethics within the typical American firm. However, if BCCI was first established as a thoroughly-legitimate banking institution and then later sank into questionable operations, then we have an example of what can happen to any business firm--the gradual erosion of integrity. When a firm finds itself in deep trouble, an executive of the firm can be expected to ask at some point: "Where did it all begin?" Often, the answer to the executive's question is hard to find. People in business, as a rule, want to be thought of as ethical. As a result, many such persons conduct themselves in a completely ethical manner. However, at some point an action may be taken that is not clearly wrong. Perhaps that action in unfamiliar territory makes easier a future action that is clearly wrong. From then on, improper acts may follow swiftly, and unethical behavior is rampant. A prudish observation could be that once an unethical act feels comfortable, plenty of additional such acts will follow freely. A secret may be to avoid that first act that is of doubtful virtue. The motion picture Judgment at Nuremberg dealt with the war crimes trials held in that German city after World War II. In a scene near the end of the picture, Burt Lancaster (playing a former German judge who is on trial for crimes against humanity) asks an American judge, who is presiding over the proceedings, how this whole terrible mess began. The American judge--played by Spencer Tracy--said, in so many words: "It started the very first time that you knowingly sentenced an innocent man to prison. That's exactly the moment when it started." A second question that resounds through all of the clamor is simply this: "How could BCCI's practices have continued for such a long period of time before the authorities knew that something was wrong?" Seeing BCCI thrive for so long on allegedly criminal practices could easily inspire within other parties the notion that corrupt practices will not be detected or punished. That is not the message we want transmitted around the world.

1.   Verdicts in theb BCCI trials could well reveal that true criminals were involved in operating the institution. But how do you explain that several people of high integrity were drawn into BCCI's many alleged illegal schemes?

2.   What are some reasons why the true nature of BCCI operations was not revealed until so late in the bank's history? Do you feel that some governmental agencies dealing with BCCI should have been a little more astute and alert? Why or why not?

3.   What are some ways that a firm, large or small, can avoid the pitfalls of an eroding sense of ethics?

4.   How much control do you feel that a chief executive officer has over the ethical behavior of his or her firm? Explain.

ANNOTATED KEY TERMS

<u>Ethics</u> - An indivudial's beliefs about what is right and wrong, good and bad.

<u>Ethical Behavior</u> - Behavior that conforms to generally accepted social norms.

<u>Unethical Behavior</u> - Behavior that does not conform to generally accepted social norms.

<u>Social Responsibility</u> - How a business behaves toward other businesses, customers, investors, and society at large. In effect, social responsibility is an attempt to balance different commitments.

<u>Pollution</u> - The injection of harmful substances into the environment.

<u>Acid Rain</u> - Rain mixed with sulphur that has been injected into the air by manufacturing and power plants.

<u>Recycling</u> -The reconversion of waste materials into useful products.

<u>Toxic Waste</u> - Dangerous chemical and radioactive byproducts of various manufacturing processes.

<u>Superfund</u> - A special fund set up by Congress to help clean up heavily polluted land.

<u>Consumerism</u> - A form of social activism dedicated to protecting the rights of consumers in their dealings with businesses.

<u>Collusion</u> - An illegal agreement between two or more companies to agree on ("fix") prices.

<u>Whistle Blower</u> - An employee who detects an unethical, illegal, or socially irresponsible action within a company and tries to put an end to it.

<u>Check Kiting</u> - The illegal practice of writing checks against money that has not yet arrived at the bank on which a check has been drawn.

<u>Insider Trading</u> - The use of confidential information to gain from the purchase or sale of stocks.

<u>Social-Opposition Approach</u> - An approach to social responsibility in which the company does as little as possible and often makes decisions that most people would recognize as not being in the best interests of society.

<u>Social-Obligation Approach</u> - An approach to social responsibility in which the company just meets minimum legal requirements.

Social-Reaction Approach - An approach to social responsibility in which the company goes beyond the bare legal minimums if specifically asked to do so.

Social-Response Approach - An approach to social responsibility in which the company actively seeks opportunities to contribute to the well-being of society.

Social Audit - A systematic analysis of a firm's success at using funds earmarked for its social-responsibility goals.

TRUE-FALSE QUESTIONS

1. Ethics are based on individual beliefs that vary widely from person to person and situation to situation.

2. Ethics have little affect on how an individual behaves within a business.

3. Much of the damage to forests and streams in the eastern United States and Canada has been attributed to land pollution.

4. According to the author of your textbook, not too many years ago, you could develop photos in the river beside an Eastman Kodak plant.

5. Altogether, U.S. manufacturers produce between one and two tons of toxic waste material each year.

6. A company that does not behave responsibly toward its customers will ultimately lose their business.

7. Firms differ in their level of concern about responsibility to customers.

8. "Gentlemen's agreements" that block competition are legal today.

9. If managers of a firm abuse its financial resources, the ultimate losers are the owners.

10. All corporations must conform to generally accepted accounting practices (GAAP) in maintaining and reporting their financial status.

MULTIPLE CHOICE QUESTIONS

1. An individual's beliefs about what is right and wrong or what is good and bad is defined as

   a. behavior.
   b. social responsibility.
   c. legal authority.
   d. ethics.

2. Behavior that conforms to generally accepted social norms is called

   a. social responsibility.
   b. unethical behavior.
   c. ethical behavior.
   d. legal policy.

3. Which of the following are not mentioned by the authors of your textbook as the most common influences on an individual's ethics and behavior?

   a. family and peers
   b. books
   c. situations
   d. experiences

4. The belief and practice that hard work brings rewards is called

   a. the work ethic.
   b. social responsibility.
   c. business ethics.
   d. religion.

5. Which of the following affects how a business behaves toward other businesses, customers, investors, and society at large?

   a. behavior
   b. legal sanctions
   c. ethics
   d. social responsibility

6. The second phase in the evolution of social responsibility occurred

   a. in the 1960s.
   b. in the late nineteenth century.
   c. during the Great Depression.
   d. in the 1980s.

7. The injection of harmful substances into the environment is called

    a. behavior.
    b. pollution.
    c. business tactics.
    d. social responsibility.

8. Much of the damage to forests and streams in the eastern United States and Canada has been attributed to

    a. acid rain.
    b. clear cutting.
    c. land polution.
    d. overpopulation.

9. Strip mining is an example of

    a. corporate social responsibility.
    b. water pollution.
    c. air pollution.
    d. land pollution.

10. The reconversion of waste materials into useful products is called

    a. pollution.
    b. ethics.
    c. recycling.
    d. reclamation.

11. Dangerous chemical and/or radioactive byproducts of various manufacturing processes are called

    a. recycled materials.
    b. toxic wastes.
    c. substantitive wastes.
    d. cost-efficient commodities.

12. Which of the following agencies is charged with administering the Superfund program?

    a. EPA
    b. SEC
    c. FTC
    d. EEOC

13. A form of social activism dedicated to protecting the rights of consumers in their dealings with businesses is

    a. a protest.
    b. a strike.
    c. a lockout.
    d. consumerism.

14. Free and open competition among companies is an example of which of the following rights of the consumer?

    a. the right to safe products
    b. the right to be informed about all relevant aspects of a product.
    c. the right to choose what to buy
    d. the right to be heard

15. When firms get together to agree on ("fix") prices, it is called

    a. competition.
    b. collusion.
    c. consolidation.
    d. a price support.

16. Employees who detect an unethical, illegal, and/or socially irresponsible action within the company and try to put an end to it are called

    a. whistle blowers.
    b. trouble shooters.
    c. trouble makers.
    d. "scabs."

17. E.F. Hutton and Company was noted by the authors of your textbook as a firm that was convicted of violating

    a. antitrust laws.
    b. the Superfund regulations.
    c. air pollution laws.
    d. check kiting laws.

18.   Ivan Boesky and Dennis Levine were found to be engaging in

        a. air pollution violations.
        b. EPA regulation violations.
        c. insider trading.
        d. ethically correct behavior.

19.   Tobacco companies exemplify which of the following social responsibility approaches?

        a. the social-reaction approach
        b. the social-obligation approach
        c. the social-response approach
        d. the international-response approach

20.   The systematic analysis of a firm's success at using funds earmarked for its social-
        responsibility goals is called a

        a. social audit.
        b. pollution control hearing.
        c. legal indictment.
        d. social-reaction approach.

WRITING TO LEARN

1. What is ethical behavior? What influences our ethical behavior?

2. Is ethical behavior important in business relationships? What can a business do to influence its employees ethical behavior?

3. What is meant by the term "social responsibility"? Discuss the evolution of social responsibility. What social responsibility issues need to be addressed by businesses?

4. Does business have a responsibility to employees and/or customers? What rights do consumers have?

5. Is there a consensus on how business firms should behave? Which social responsibility approach is best? Do small businesses have social responsibilities?

DISCUSSION OF THE CLOSING CASE

The final case presents some intriguing reading on the subject of worldwide mud-slinging. We see here a macrocosmic view of such practices--a view that few recent college graduates will have a chance to orchestrate with a giant corporation right away. But such petty backbiting is common fare in a microcosmic sense, and it calls for an exercise of everything that a person has learned about ethical conduct. As someone must have said at some time or other, the trouble with organizations is that they are made up of humans. Even in the smallest firm, there can be personalities that clash with one another. Most of these clashes are lateral in nature. A young college graduate accepts the fact that a boss will hand down some unsavory comments and assignments. The college graduate accepts that his or her subordinates may grumble now and then. Particularly shocking and even threatening, however, is a lateral colleague who may lash out at you with surprising bitterness. You're first shocked because you weren't aware that the colleague even knew you were on the staff. Sometimes you become a target of attack just because you are new or because you are a college graduate. It could be that the guy in the black hat is testing you. Often, that person's campaign is conducted strictly through memorandums--always with a copy going to your boss. [Such memos can take the most modern of forms--Fax, E-Mail, Voice Mail, etc.] The idea is to thoroughly discredit you and your performance. Now, some supervisors will not tolerate these little memorandum games, and will smash such cheap tirades immediately. However, and here's the part that is hard to understand, some supervisors encourage such competition. They feel it keeps the warring employees on their toes. Small-minded managers who like to observe these gladiatorial combats do not realize that the conflicts take away valuable time from corporate objectives. If a lateral colleague attacks you with a condemning memo, an answer in kind only escalates the struggle, and enlarges the caliber of the poison-pen artillery. But there's a cowardly variation on the central theme: a lateral colleague who sends memos to your boss or makes phone calls with the same malevolent intent--all without your having the slightest inkling that someone is (to put it in genteel terminology) acting in a way that does not serve your best interests.

1.   Your name is Patricia and you get a copy of a memo containing this line: "Patricia has shown herself to be totally uncooperative with me and threatening to both of my secretaries. Hiring her has been a major mistake of the corporation." What action--if any--will you take in response to this memo?

2.   A lateral colleague condemns you in a memo to your boss by using several absolute falsehoods. Can you set the record straight? If so, how will you do it?

3.   As a head of a firm, what moves can you make to establish an   atmosphere that will not tolerate such petty carrying on? Draft a memo designed to put a stop to such backbiting.

4.   Can a memo alluded to in #3 above really change the environment in a firm? Explain.

AN ADDITIONAL CASE

Terry Baskerville is up for promotion for the position of Assistant-to-the-President at Thronkin Industries. President Steve Wilson, in a meeting of section heads, proclaims that he wants to be sure that Terry Baskerville is indeed the man for the job. The spot calls for a sharp young man who is willing to spend long hours with the President working on a variety of projects. In addition, the new Assistant-to-the-President (ATTP) must have the respect of everyone in the firm because he will be interacting with them all in various ways. In short, good human relations are required. When given an assignment, the new ATTP must act swiftly and conscientiously to fulfill it so that the President is not held up in any way. Punctuality is of prime importance to President Wilson, and he also admires a man who is willing to report for work as early as 6:30 A.M. Ethical behavior is also a prerequisite for the new ATTP.

President Wilson seeks input from each of the section heads. Their response is generally quite positive concerning young Baskerville. Why shouldn't they be positive in response? None of them know anything about Baskerville's capabilities. As a rule, however, ignorance does not necessarily keep section heads from sounding off! But it must be kept in mind that the section head who knows the most about Baskerville would have to be Esther Marvin, currently the supervisor of Terry Baskerville. President Wilson explains to Esther that her input will be the key to some determination on Baskerville's appointment.

Before Esther sits down to develop an objective analysis of the performance of Terry Baskerville, she picks up several sets of vibrations. First of all, she notes that President Wilson and his two top vice-presidents, Arthur Blank and Geoff Laird, have a strong personal bond with Terry Baskerville. In short, the three of them want Terry in the ATTP spot and Esther's strong recommendation will give the move a smooth white gown of legitimacy. In any organization, it is helpful to know--if one can determine it--what the _true_ atmosphere is. Having worked in several quirky organizations, Esther is better than most at picking up vibes and clues. She never takes a statement on face value. Accordingly, when President Steve Wilson said he wanted Esther's full input on Baskerville as a means of determining Baskerville's worthiness, she didn't fully believe what she was hearing. And when her intuition declared loud and clear that the people in the executive suite _wanted_ _Baskerville_ to join them, she knew that her input was not really very important and, further, that Baskerville would probably get the position regardless of what she wrote.

Nevetheless, Esther sat down to seriously draft a memorandum evaluating Terry Baskerville. In it, she would address the "needs" expressed by President Wilson. Esther did not want to derail Baskerville's career express in any way. At the same time, however, she owed it to her boss to tell the truth of what she knew about young Baskerville. Here's what she wrote:

"Although Terry Baskerville is a fine young man, I have not observed that he is overly eager to work beyond the plant's normal workday of 8:00 to 4:30. Maybe it is the nature of the work in this section, but on several occasions he has quite openly stated that he will not stay late for any reason. You need a person who can relate favorably to every person in the plant. May I say that Terry is about average in this capacity. There have been a few human relations mishaps on

Terry's part in this section, but I have normally just blamed it on his youth. Surely he will mature under your nurture. Admitting again that the work in my section is certainly not inspiring, I have found that Terry often is late in completing tasks assigned to him. Let me put it this way: He is not the most efficient worker in my section. Surely, for an exciting job as Assistant-to-the-President, Terry will rise early and be at his desk in your complex as early as you want him. I'm sure of it! But, while he was with us in this section, his arrivals by 8:00 A.M. were rare. You said you valued ethical behavior. Surely you know what the whole plant knows: Married Terry Baskerville has been having an affair with one of the steno pool secretaries. Terry Baskerville will make you a great Assistant-to-the-President. However, as a loyal employee of Thronkin Industries, I felt that I owed it to you to offer these important insights I have gained regarding Terry. If you are depending on my input in reaching a final decision, I must tell it like it is. Should you wish to talk further, please do not hesitate to give me a call."

Esther had a good relationship with another section head, Lois Stephens. They were dedicated workers, ethically solid, who could trust one another. The plant moved far smoother because Esther and Lois had this bond. Esther asked Lois to take a look at the memo Esther was ready to send to President Wilson. Esther, by the way, was familiar with Terry Baskerville's impact on Thronkin Industries to this point. When she finished reading the draft, Lois said:

"You're committing professional suicide with this note. Everybody knows that Baskerviille is a shoo-in. The last thing that the top boys want is real honesty from you. He'll get the job, for sure, and you'll not only look foolish, but you'll have three, maybe four, of the executive suite inhabitants thinking less of you. Tell them what they want to hear! Baskerville is a superman; in the process you'll get rid of him."

"But, that wouldn't be honest. I owe it to President Wilson to let him know he's making a mistake!"

"Mistake? This is the kind of mistake he wants to make. He wants Baskerville. Regardless of what you write in that memo, Esther, Baskerville will get the job. Don't you see, your words won't make any difference."

"But when Baskerville starts having trouble getting along with people on the line--as we've witnessed so many times before-- President Wilson could say to me that I should have told him about Baskerville's human relations problems."

"That's crazy. The President likes Baskerville. As a result, if there are human relations problems, Wilson will blame them on the people on the line, not Baskerville. My advice, old friend, is tell them what they want to hear."

1.   Did Esther send to President Wilson the memo you have just read? Why or why not?

2.   Should Esther send that memo to President Wilson? Why or why not?

3.   If the   memo goes forward as written above, do you feel it could affect Esther's

effectiveness as a section head in the future with Thronkin Industries? Why or why not.

4. Although the case gives no hints, do you think the ATTP position has existed for years at Thronkin or is it a NEW position created just for Baskerville? Explain.

ANSWERS TO TRUE-FALSE QUESTIONS

1.	T	(p. 77)	6.	T	(p. 86)
2.	F	(p. 81)	7.	T	(p. 86)
3.	F	(p. 83)	8.	F	(p. 86)
4.	T	(p. 83)	9.	T	(p. 88)
5.	F	(p. 85)	10.	T	(p. 89)

ANSWERS TO MULTIPLE-CHOICE QUESTIONS

1.	D	(p. 77)	11.	B	(p. 85)
2.	C	(p. 77)	12.	A	(p. 85)
3.	B	(p. 77)	13.	D	(p. 86)
4.	A	(p. 77)	14.	C	(p. 86)
5.	D	(p. 81)	15.	B	(p. 86)
6.	C	(p. 82)	16.	A	(p. 87)
7.	B	(p. 83)	17.	D	(p. 88)
8.	A	(p. 83)	18.	C	(p. 88)
9.	D	(p. 85)	19.	B	(p. 89)
10.	C	(p. 85)	20.	A	(p. 92)

CHAPTER FIVE

MANAGING THE BUSINESS ENTERPRISE

CHAPTER OVERVIEW

Management is the process of planning, organizing, leading, and controlling an organization's financial, physical, human, and information resources in order to achieve its goals. The three basic levels of management are top, middle, and first-line management. Managers may be found within a large company in a variety of areas, including marketing, finance, operations, human resources, and information. Companies acquire managers from three main sources: the academic world, the company itself, and other companies. Effective managers need to develop several types of skills: technical, human relations, conceptual, decision making, and time management. Technical skills are especially important for first-line managers. Important at all levels, human relations skills are especially important for middle managers. Top managers depend most on conceptual skills. Corporate culture is the shared experiences, stories, beliefs, and norms that characterize an organization. Corporate culture helps everyone work toward the same goals. It helps newcomers learn accepted behaviors. A strong corporate culture gives each organization its own identity. Managers need to carefully consider the kind of culture they want for their organization and must work to nourish it and communicate it to everyone.

LEARNING OBJECTIVES

1.   Describe the four activities that comprise the management process.

2.   Differentiate types of managers by level and explain how individuals acquire managerial skills.

3.   Define and discuss the five basic managerial skills.

4.   Describe the development and importance of corporate culture.

DISCUSSION OF THE OPENING CASE

Numerous business theoreticians have written about the Disney organization. With such a glorious history, with so many facets, and so many shifts in focus over the years, the Disney story can be made to superbly illustrate so many points in management and in other spheres of business as well. In the opening narrative, there is an emphasis on the internal workings of the firm. But a glance at the world outside the studios of Disney can provide an equally valid lesson to be learned. Implicit in what you have read in the Disney case in your textbook is the fact that the organization has had to continually adapt to its environment; external changes forced changes within Disney. A glance at an American institution called "vaudeville" may help to illustrate the point. Around the turn of the century, theaters across the land featured five or six acts of live entertainment--singing soloists, dancers, magicians, ventriloquists, gymnasts, comedians, musicians. Even with the great popularity of the "talkies" in the 1930s, live entertainment shared the stage with movies. With the coming of the 1950s, vaudeville's place in the entertainment scheme of things began to erode. Some blamed the demise on television. It could have just been that America's tastes were changing. A vaudeville performer could have said: "I'll work harder on my act. I'll perfect the high notes in my songs. I'll rehearse longer on each of the dance routines. I'll get a larger orchestra to back me up. I'll commission new songs and buy new costumes." None of these internal efforts would have made any difference. The American environment that was once so receptive to vaudeville was becoming apathetic, perhaps even hostile. Shrinking audiences at movie-vaudeville houses prevented theater managers from hiring the five or six acts as before. Nothing that vaudevillians could do could save the dying institution. Individual vaudevillians were able to survive only by moving to new media still popular with the American public-- radio, television, motion pictures, nightclubs, Las Vegas-- leaving the corpse of vaudeville behind. The Disney organization had learned the lesson early. From animated shorts, they moved to full-length cartoon features. From full-length cartoon features they moved to theme parks, television, movies with real- life actors, and a plethora of other novelties--always adapting to changing American tastes.

1.   Could anything have been done to save American on-stage vaudeville? Explain your answer.

2.   If you were running the Disney organization, what devices would you employ to test new ideas with the American public? Is a sharp think-tank sufficient for such testing?

3.   What do you feel are some new areas into which the Disney organization--keeping its finger on the public's pulse--may successfully venture?

4.   Looking at the Disney saga going back at least as far as your lifetime, did Disney respond to public tastes or did Disney play a major role in shaping and nurturing those tastes?

ANNOTATED KEY TERMS

Management - The process of planning, organizing, leading, and controlling an organization's financial, physical, human, and information resources in order to achieve its goals.

Planning - That part of a manager's job that includes determining what the organization needs to do and how best to get it done.

Organizing - That part of a manager's job that includes determining how best to arrange a business's resources and the jobs it needs to get done into an overall structure.

Leading - That part of a manager's job that includes guiding and motivating employees to meet the firm's objectives.

Controlling - That part of a manager's job that includes monitoring a firm's performance to make sure that it is meeting its goals.

Top Managers - Managers responsible to the board of directors and stockholders for the firm's overall performance and effectiveness.

Middle Managers - Managers responsible for implementing the strategies, policies, and decisions made by top managers.

First-Line Managers - Managers responsible for supervising the work of employees.

Marketing Managers - Managers responsible for getting products and services to buyers.

Financial Managers - Managers responsible for planning and overseeing the firm's financial resources.

Operations Managers - Managers responsible for production control, inventory control, and quality control.

Human Resource Managers - Managers responsible for hiring, training, evaluating, and compensating employees.

Information Managers - Managers responsible for the design and implementation of systems to gather, process, and disseminate information.

Headhunters - Professional recruiting firms.

Technical Skills - The skills associated with performing specialized tasks within a company.

Human Relations Skills - The skills associated with understanding and being able to get along with other people.

Conceptual Skills - The skills associated with being able to think in the abstract, to diagnose and analyze different situations, and to see beyond the present.

Decision Making Skills - The skills associated with being able to define problems and to select the best course of action.

Time Management Skills - The skills associated with being able to use time wisely and productively.

Corporate Culture - The shared experiences, stories, beliefs, and norms that characterize an organization.

TRUE-FALSE QUESTIONS

1. By definition, managers have the power to give orders and demand results.

2. The power of managers and the complexity of their duties decrease as they move up the ladder.

3. Top managers tend to spend most of their time working with and supervising the employees who report to them.

4. Firms dealing in consumer products often have large numbers of marketing managers at a variety of levels.

5. Promotion from within tends to perpetuate current practices and ideas, providing more opportunity for innovation.

6. Stroh's Brewing Company and International Paper Company often use headhunters.

7. Technical skills are especially important for top managers.

8. Top managers depend the most on conceptual skills.

9. Managers must manage their time spent on paperwork, the telephone, and in meetings effectively.

10. Every company has its own corporate culture.

MULTIPLE CHOICE QUESTIONS

1. The process of planning, organizing, leading, and controlling an organization's financial, physical, human, and information resources in order to achieve its goals is defined as

   a. experience.
   b. Maslow's Hierarchy of Needs.
   c. organizational structure.
   d. management.

2. Determining what the organization needs to do and how best to get it done requires

   a. leading.
   b. controlling.
   c. planning.
   d. advertising.

3. Determining how best to arrange a business's resources and the jobs it needs to get done into an overall structure is called

   a. planning.
   b. organizing.
   c. leading.
   d. controlling.

4. A graph of a firm's structure with boxes representing jobs and lines between them showing reporting relationships is called a(n)

   a. organizational chart.
   b. flow chart.
   c. PERT chart.
   d. work-flow analysis.

5. The portion of a manager's job concerned with guiding and motivating employees to meet the firm's objectives is called

   a. controlling.
   b. planning.
   c. organizing.
   d. leading.

6. The component of the managerial process that involves monitoring a firm's performance to make sure that it is meeting its goals is called

   a. planning.
   b. directing.
   c. controlling.
   d. organizing.

7. President, CEO and CFO are common titles for

   a. supervisors.
   b. top managers.
   c. middle managers.
   d. first-line managers.

8. Plant Manager and Division Manager are typical titles for

   a. middle managers.
   b. supervisors.
   c. middle managers.
   d. staff functions.

9. Generally, responsibility for implementing strategies, policies, and decisions fall on

   a. supervisors.
   b. first-line managers.
   c. top managers.
   d. middle managers.

10. Direct supervision of the work of employees is usually the responsibility of

    a. top managers.
    b. the staff.
    c. first-line managers.
    d. middle managers.

11. Getting products and services to buyers is the responsibility of

    a. production managers.
    b. marketing managers.
    c. financial managers.
    d. human resource managers.

12. The investment and accounting functions are usually under the managerial area of

    a. finance.
    b. marketing.
    c. production.
    d. human resources.

13. Responsibility for production control, inventory control, and quality control is usually accomplished by the firm's

    a. financial managers.
    b. marketing managers.
    c. human resource manager.
    d. operations managers.

14. Managers responsible for the design and implementation of systems to gather, process, and disseminate information are

    a. production managers.
    b. development managers.
    c. information managers.
    d. financial managers.

15. Which of the following is not noted by the authors of your textbook as a main source of new managers?

    a. the academic world
    b. newspaper advertisements
    c. the company itself
    d. other companies

16. Professional recruiting firms are commonly referred to as

    a. headhunters.
    b. advertising companies.
    c. production firms.
    d. talent agencies.

17. A secretary's ability to type and an animator's ability to draw a cartoon are examples of

    a. human relations skills.
    b. conceptual skills.
    c. decision making skills.
    d. technical skills.

18. The ability to think in the abstract, to diagnose and analyze different situations, and to see beyond the present are

    a. technical skills.
    b. decision making skills.
    c. conceptual skills.
    d. human relations skills.

19. How productively a manager uses his time is referred to as the manager's

    a. decision making skills.
    b. time management skills.
    c. conceptual skills.
    d. information skills.

20. The shared experiences, stories, belief, and norms that characterize an organization make up its

   a. corporate culture.
   b. history.
   c. organizational chart.
   d. selection criterion.

WRITING TO LEARN

1. What is meant by the management process? Describe the activities that make up the management process. Do all managers perform these activities?

2. What are the three levels of management? What responsibilities does each level have?

3. Within a large company, what functional areas do managers work in?

4.	Describe the skills that are important to managers. Which of these skills is important to the first-line manager; to the middle manager; and to the top manager?

5.What is meant by the term corporate culture? How can managers create corporate culture? What determines corporate culture? Can corporate culture change?

DISCUSSION OF THE CLOSING CASE

In 1984, when oil was selling for $28 a barrel, Royal Dutch Shell planners sketched out a scenario that included an oil price of $15 per barrel. The notion probably seemed pretty silly at the time, but it was an implementation of a management planning concept that must not be disregarded. The concept deals with the "worst case scenario"--drawing up the worst possible turn of events that can transpire. Why be so negative in planning; why not stress the positive approach? The answer seems to be that planning for the "worst case scenario" allows a firm to have some devices available for coping with adversity. To play around with words a bit, we could say that adversity can be unexpected, but it must not be unanticipated. The "worst case scenario" is a way to anticipate. The case points out that such anticipation enabled Royal Dutch Shell to cope most admirably when oil prices did indeed drop to $15--and lower--in 1986. It is the opinion of some that a key instance of a "worst case scenario" NOT being sketched occurred in 1941. Although wars had raged in Europe and the Orient for several years, the American public just did not want to acknowledge that American involvement in these wars was a possibility--a strong possibility. Even in the several weeks just prior to December 7, 1941, there were high hopes that negotiations in Washington between two special Japanese envoys and Secretary of State Cordell Hull would result in a resolution of differences between the United States and Japan. In an editorial of December 4, 1941 on page 24, The New York Times said in essence that now would be a foolish time for Japan to extend its war-like operations. The editorial, "The Siege of Japan," made good sense, and readers of it perhaps were comforted, knowing that Japan would not do anything so foolish as to attack the United States. Even after all the revelations of the fiftieth anniversary of the Pearl Harbor attack, we still cannot be totally sure just how much the military knew of Japanese plans. However, it is relatively safe to opine that the American public had never really come to grips with a "worst case scenario" concerning relations in the Pacific in late 1941. Few, if any, news commentators of the era were openly saying: "My friends, there is a better than 50-50 chance that we will soon be at war with Japan." As a result, that fateful Sunday made us a nation in shock. A nation should not be in a state of shock. For the purposes of this case, a corporation should not be in shock. And Royal Dutch Shell is to be commended for avoiding the shock of low oil prices in 1986 by playing a "what if" game two years earlier.

1. Why is it that there is such a strong temptation among businesses to avoid plotting the "worst case scenario?"

2. Evaluate this statement on the part of a businessperson: "I don't believe in planning more than a year or so ahead. If I don't solve the problems of TODAY, my business may not be here tomorrow for me to worry about."

3. If it is true that no one can truly predict the future, then is planning twenty years down the line a little foolish? Why or why not?

4   How do takeover laws in Great Britain and the Netherlands make long range planning a more realistic venture than would be the case in the United States? Should such statutes make any difference at all?

69

AN ADDITIONAL CASE

Melvin W. Crester, founder, CEO, large-majority stockholder, and thus Chairman of the Board at Butte Electronics knew he had to do something about the feud within the firm between Nathan Nelson and Bry Hiltonn. Resolving the petty animosity between Nathan and Bry was particularly important right now because--if we can believe rumors around the plant--one of the two is to be chosen to succeed Crester when the latter retires in a few months. Who will wear the crown?

Butte Electronics never cared much about the accuracy of the terms it used. First of all, the firm was engaged in numerous activities that had nothing to do with electronics. Their most successful venture, by the way, was the marketing of autographed footballs to fans of the National Football League. The word "Butte" certainly suggests the wide open spaces of the Great West; Butte Electronics was actually headquartered in North Flemington, New Hampshire. And the same promiscuity in devising terminology carried over into titles. For example, "Chairman of the Board" was not an elective position. Although Butte had a small but conscientious board of directors, it was always understood that the chairman would be Melvin Crester or a person of his personal choosing. In the same vein, Nathan Nelson was called "Operations Coordinator," while Bry Hiltonn's door carried the title "Technical Manager." Actually, Nathan was in charge of future planning while Bry was the executive who kept production rolling.

Nathan Nelson had earned bachelor's and master's degrees in Ivy League institutions and had majored in sociology while minoring in accounting. A commissioned officer during the Vietnam conflict, he held a spot on the staff of a two-star general commanding an infantry division. Although supposedly far from the "front"--if indeed there ever was a front in Vietnam--Nathan's headquarters had been bombed twice by Viet Cong infiltrators and Nathan was wounded in the left ankle. Upon return from the war, he took a position in scheduling with a mammoth electrical appliance firm in Pennsylvania. This background made him ideal in the eyes of Butte's chairman, Melvin Crester, when the latter was seeking someone to give a sophisticated sense of direction to Butte Electronics.

Bry Hiltonn's military experience was just as exciting but a bit earlier than that of Nathan's. Bry was a 17-year-old U.S. Marine stationed in peaceful, pastoral South Korea in 1950 when the North Koreans began rolling south in the steamy month of June. For combat exploits, he was highly decorated and came back to the States as a drill instructor at San Diego to finish out his hitch with the Marines. Starting on the assembly line at Hawks Tool in Encino, Bry, over the years, worked his way up to foreman and then to plant manager. Failing health of an aging mother-in-law in New Hampshire brought him to Butte Electronics. From virtually his first day at Butte, he has been the force that "gets the product out the door."

When Butte's chairman, Melvin Crester, talked to the CEO at Hawk tool by way of checking references on Hiltonn, one thing that he <u>didn't</u> find out was that Hiltonn had a rather arrogant way. He got things done by subtle (and sometimes no-so-subtle) intimidation of the workers. In fact, behind his back, the first-line crew members at Butte call Bry "Hitler." A new secretary at Butte, having heard Bry referred to in that manner so regularly, mistakenly sent a memo to him addressed: "Mr. Bry Hitler." A big joke to the "boys in the back room," the gaffe was not at all comical to Hiltonn. As the years went by, however, Melvin Crester accepted Bry's style, often saying: "If Satan himself could get the results that Bry gets, we'd put him on the payroll. Bry's tough, but he has never let the company down."

Nathan Nelson spent much of his time up in the executive suite mapping out realistic directions for the future of Butte. It was his research, feeling of the public mood, planning, and insistence that moved the firm to supply the super-hard composition base used in the running shoes manufactured by the leading sportswear purveyors. It took a trip to Taiwan to seal the deal, but company profits have soared ever since. Thanks to Nathan's looking ahead and sensing a very narrow window of opportunity, Butte was just about the first firm to manufacture and broadly distribute those white caps with college logos on them that can be seen in great profusion all over college campuses of America.

What a perfect combination Nathan and Bry seemed to be; one finding in the future some exhilarating new breakthroughs and the other following through with ultra-dependable production. But Nathan and Bry were not harmonious brothers. Nathan resented Bry's consistent resistance to anything new. Whatever was proposed, Bry was against it. Bry, on the other hand, resented the fact that Nathan showed little concern for production problems and continued his "pie in the sky" dreaming about what the future could hold for Butte Electronics.

Although Melvin W. Crester, Butte's Chairman of the Board, had a highly-specific timetable for his retirement, the timetable was never revealed or hinted at for consumption of Butte employees. As the deadline neared, Crester knew he could not bring peace to the "sibling rivalry" under his nose. He realized that he would have to appoint one to be the new chairman of the board. The losing candidate would have to choose, then, whether to stay on with Butte or not.

Who knows what thoughts lurk in the minds of company executives. Whether he intended to or not, Melvin Crester stretched the suspense far beyond reasonable limits. At a banquet that was supposed to be the scene of the great announcement, Melvin had this dull proclamation to make: "Effective October 1, I'll be in retirement in Punta Gorda, Florida. My first official act there in my new home will be to write a letter back to you all. That letter will contain the official appointment of the new chairman of the board. Be watching the mail guys and gals."

Sure enough, the letter arrived in North Flemington, New Hampshire at the Butte plant on October 4. The secretary who had been instructed to open it did so, and then took copies of it to both Nathan Nelson and Bry Hiltonn.

1.   Who received the appointment to chairman of the board? Explain your answer. Make frequent reference to the kinds of managerial skills discussed in this chapter.

2. If Bry Hiltonn had been the nephew of Melvin Crester, should this have made a difference in the final choice of chairman of the board? Why or why not?

3. Predict the future of Butte Electronics if the new chairman of the board is Bry Hiltonn. Designate his greatest strengths and weaknesses.

4. What kind of condition will Butte Electronics be left in if Nathan Nelson becomes the chairman and Bry Hiltonn resigns immediately?

ANSWERS TO TRUE-FALSE QUESTIONS

1.	T	(p. 110)	6.	T	(p. 117)
2.	F	(p. 111)	7.	F	(p. 118)
3.	F	(p. 113)	8.	T	(p. 119)
4.	T	(p. 113)	9.	T	(p. 120)
5.	F	(p. 117)	10.	T	(p. 121)

ANSWERS TO MULTIPLE CHOICE QUESTIONS

1.	D	(p. 109)	11.	B	(p. 113)
2.	C	(p. 109)	12.	A	(p. 114)
3.	B	(p. 110)	13.	D	(p. 114)
4.	A	(p. 110)	14.	C	(p. 115)
5.	D	(p. 110)	15.	B	(p. 117)
6.	C	(p. 110)	16.	A	(p. 117)
7.	B	(p. 111)	17.	D	(p. 118)
8.	A	(p. 111)	18.	C	(p. 119)
9.	D	(p. 113)	19.	B	(p. 120)
10.	C	(p. 113)	20.	A	(p. 121)

CHAPTER SIX

RUNNING THE SMALL BUSINESS

CHAPTER OVERVIEW

Small business defies definition. The U.S. Department of Commerce considers a business small if it has fewer than 500 employees; the Small Business Administration, however, considers some companies with 1,500 employees to be small. Small business is a strong presence in the nation's economy through job creation, innovation, and importance to big business. There are five major small-business industry groups--service, retailing, wholesaling, manufacturing, and agriculture. Small businesses have a better success rate now than in years past. Reasons for failure have been: managerial incompetence or inexperience; neglect; weak control systems; and lack of sufficient capital. Reasons for success are: hard work, drive and dedication; demand; managerial competence; and luck. Getting into small business can occur by buying out an existing business, starting from scratch, or going into franchising. Either way, sufficient funding is necessary and it comes from several sources: the businessperson's personal resources; money borrowed from friends and relatives; banks; independent investors; venture capital firms; SBICs; incubators; and government funding of varying degrees and types. There are many sources of management advice for the small business.

LEARNING OBJECTIVES

1. Define small business and explain its importance in the U.S. economy.

2. Explain which types of business enterprise best lend themselves to small business.

3. Identify key reasons for the success and failure of small business.

4. Describe the start-up decisions of small businesses and identify sources of financial aid and management advice to such enterprises.

5. Identify the advantages and disadvantages of franchising.

DISCUSSION OF THE OPENING CASE

The saga of Howell and Syme carries a strong message that is often neglected in business courses. Unless a student listens very carefully, there is a chance that he or she will receive a business degree under the assumption that mastering business procedures will lead to success in commerce. Howell and Syme, especially Syme, brought something more to their enterprise than mere administrative mastery. They offered knowledge of <u>what makes a great stove</u>! So far as we know, there is not a business school in the world that offers courses in how to build a good stove. This expertise concerning the product an enterprise will attempt to market could be considered the starting point for any successful business. From this point, this particular story is the standard struggle between "vision" and "professional management." In a continually successful firm, however, it is not a matter of "struggle" but rather a case of one phenomenon complementing the other. As a glowing example, in the days when the Disney organization was run by brothers Walt and Roy, no one questioned the need for the creative genius of Walt. But fewer observers in the general public are aware of just how important a role was played by the business acumen of Roy. It's hard to imagine Walt saying: "I don't care about the financial implications here; I say we risk the whole organization on this project." Or can you hear Roy saying: "We don't have the funds to hire a staff to develop a new character such as Donald Duck. You'll just have to be content with Mickey Mouse and Minnie." Notice how, in trying to save the firm, the "corporate types" took what the case has called "standard moves." These standard moves may have been the perfect prescription for troubled firms in <u>other industries</u>. But Duncan Syme soon concluded that what they were doing was not appropriate for the stove industry. Although firms still diversify freely with solid rationales for doing so, the age of the conglomerate eventually showed us that branching out into unfamiliar industries can often be a mistake of gargantuan proportions. The narrative does not tell us, so one is left to wonder just how much the "corporate types" knew about stoves.

1. Do you see the "corporate types" at Vermont Castings as villains in this case? Give several solid reasons why or why not.

2. Based on what you have experienced in reading this case, do you see an entrepreneur as someone primarily bent on becoming prosperous from operating a business or someone determined to put a burning idea into action?

3. What one main ingredient would you single out as the cause of the initial success of the Defiant Stove? Explain why.

4. Compare Vermont Castings under the "corporate types" to a local newspaper that is more interested in making a profit than in adequately covering the news.

ANNOTATED KEY TERMS

<u>Small Business Administration (SBA)</u> - A federal agency charged with assisting small businesses.

<u>Small Business</u> - A business that is independently owned and managed and does not dominate its market.

<u>Retail Business</u> - A business that sells products manufactured by other firms directly to consumers.

Wholesale Business - A business that buys products from manufacturers or producers and then sells them to retailers.

Lifestyle Business - A business formed for the specific purpose of allowing its owner to live a certain lifestyle.

High-Growth Venture - A business that has rapid growth as its fundamental goal from the start.

Venture Capital Firms - Collections of small investors that invest money in companies with rapid growth potential.

Small Business Investment Companies (SBICs) - Federally licensed companies that borrow money from the SBA and invest it in or loan it to small businesses.

Minority Enterprise Small Business Investment Company (MESBIC) - Federally sponsored companies that specialize in financing businesses owned and operated by minorities.

Guaranteed Loans Program - An SBA loan program in which small businesses borrow from a commercial lender, with the SBA guaranteeing to repay 75 to 85 percent of the loan up to $750,000.

Immediate Participation Loans Program - An SBA loan program in which small businesses are loaned funds put up jointly by banks and the SBA.

Local Development Companies (LDCs) Program - An SBA loan program in which the SBA works with a profit or nonprofit corporation founded by local citizens who want to boost their community's economy.

Incubator - A "sheltered environment" for new businesses that generally includes cost-sharing and other subsidies.

Management Consultant - An independent specialist, hired from outside the company, who helps managers solve business problems.

Service Corps of Retired Executives (SCORE) - An SBA program in which retired successful executives work with small businesses on a volunteer basis.

Active Corps of Executives (ACE) - An SBA program in which currently employed executives work with small businesses on a volunteer basis.

Small Business Institute (SBI) - An SBA program in which students and instructors at colleges and universities work with small businesspeople to help solve specific problems.

Small Business Development Company (SBDC) - An SBA program designed to consolidate information from various disciplines and to make this knowledge available to new and existing small businesses.

Networking - Interactions among businesspeople for the purpose of discussing mutual problems, solutions, and opportunities.

Franchising - An arrangement in which a buyer (the franchisee) purchases the right to sell the good or service of the seller (the franchiser).

TRUE-FALSE QUESTIONS

1. Most U.S. businesses employ fewer than 100 people.

2. Over the last twenty years, most new jobs have come from big business.

3. Most automobile dealerships that sell Ford or Chevrolet automobiles are independently owned and operated.

4. Wholesalers need more employees for a given volume of business than do manufacturers, retailers, or service providers.

5. According to your textbook, the failure rate among small businesses has been declining in recent years.

6. Black-owned businesses are increasing at a rate two and a half times that of all new businesses.

7. Because the odds of success are better, lawyers and bankers often advise small businesspeople to start a new business from scratch, rather than to buy out an existing business.

8. A businessperson's personal resources are the least important source of financing for starting a small business.

9. Venture capital firms supply money to small businesses in return for stock in those companies.

10. According to the U.S. Department of Commerce, over fifty percent of all franchises in the country were discontinued in 1990.

MULTIPLE CHOICE QUESTIONS

1. According to the authors of your textbook, a company that is independently owned and managed and does not dominate its market is the definition of a

    a. corporation.
    b. partnership.
    c. government agency.
    d. small business.

2. As a general rule, which of the following forms of businesses is the hardest to start?

    a. a service business
    b. an information services business
    c. a manufacturing business
    d. a wholesale business

3. A firm that sells products manufactured by other firms directly to consumers is a

    a. service business.
    b. retail business.
    c. manufacturer.
    d. wholesaler.

4. A firm that buys products from manufacturers or producers and then sells them to retailers is a

    a. wholesale business.
    b. service business.
    c. manufacturing business.
    d. agricultural business.

5. Perhaps the oldest small business enterprise is

    a. bricklaying.
    b. manufacturing.
    c. banking.
    d. agriculture.

6. MicroSoft Corporation was started by

    a. Neil Boggs.
    b. Steven Jobs.
    c. Bill Gates.
    d. Robert Stempel.

7.   Which of the following was not mentioned by the authors of your textbook as a reason that small businesses fail?

a. managerial incompetence or inexperience
b. market demand
c. neglect
d. weak control systems

8.   A firm formed for the specific purpose of allowing its owner to live a certain lifestyle is sometimes called a

a. lifestyle business.
b. service business.
c. wholesale business.
d. primary business.

9.   Sun Microsystems is an example of a

a. wholesaler.
b. service business.
c. lifestyle business.
d. high-growth venture.

10. According to the authors of your textbook, approximately what percent of new businesses started in the 1980s were bought from someone else?

a. ten percent
b. seventy-six percent
c. thirty percent
d. sixty-four percent

11. Collections of small investors seeking to make a profit on companies with rapid growth potential are called

a. high-tech firms.
b. venture-capital firms.
c. SBICs.
d. manufacturing firms.

12. Which of the following was created by the Small Business Investment Act of 1958 and is federally licensed to borrow money from the SBA and to invest it in or loan it to small business?

   a. SBICs
   b. SCORE
   c. LDCs
   d. incubators

13. Under which of the following programs can small businesses borrow from a commercial lender with the SBA guaranteeing to repay 75 to 85 percent of the loan amount, not to exceed $750,000?

   a. the immediate participation loans program
   b. the LDC program
   c. the incubator program
   d. the guaranteed loans program

14. Under which of the following programs does the SBA work with a profit or nonprofit corporation founded by local citizens who want to boost their community's economy?

   a. the immediate participation loans program
   b. the incubator program
   c. the LDC program
   d. the SCORE program

15. A form of small business assistance in which a sheltered environment is created for new businesses that generally includes cost sharing and other subsidies is a(n)

   a. ACE.
   b. incubator.
   c. LDC program.
   d. franchise.

16. Someone who specializes in helping managers solve problems is called a

   a. management consultant.
   b. bank.
   c. business associate.
   d. headhunter.

17. The talents and skills of students and instructors at colleges and universities are used through the SBA's

   a. ACE program.
   b. SCORE program.
   c. SBDC.
   d. SBI.

18. Businesspeople who meet regularly with each other to discuss common problems and opportunities are engaging in

   a. competitive restraint.
   b. industrial espionage.
   c. networking.
   d. grapevining.

19. GM, Rexall, McDonald's and Howard Johnson's are examples of

   a. wholesalers.
   b. franchisers.
   c. manufacturers.
   d. suppliers.

20. According to the NFIB, approximately what percent of U.S. businesses now run under some kind of franchise agreement?

   a. twelve percent
   b. eighty-one percent
   c. thirty-seven percent
   d. twenty-one percent

WRITING TO LEARN

1. Discuss the importance of small business in the U.S. economy. What small businesses are operating in your home town? Why were these businesses started?

2. Why are some small businesses harder to start than others? What trends are evident in small business start-ups? Why do some small businesses fail while others seem to thrive?

3. What does it take to be a successful entrepreneur? Are all entrepreneurial goals the same?

4. How does one go about starting a small business? What are some ways that the start-up firm can finance the small business? What financial and managerial help is available from the SBA and other agencies and institutions?

5. What is a franchise? What are the advantages and disadvantages of franchising? Should franchising be considered as a small business alternative by every potential owner?

DISCUSSION OF THE CLOSING CASE

Often we think of a small business getting a start because of a totally new and creative idea. Ironically, the more creative the idea, the more difficult it can be to market to prospective clients. But alongside new ideas, there is the approach of taking an <u>old</u> idea and applying it in spots that heretofore had seemed inappropriate. Nanny service seems to fit the latter category. Nannies have been, if we can believe what we read of polite English society, a staple of well-to-do British life for many years. The concept has made progress in the United States among what are often referred to as upper-class families. But to market nannying to middle-class families was a new challenge. Young couples with children have hired maids, have hired baby- sitters, have engaged tutors for special academic problems, and have utilized the services of day-care facilities. A nanny, it must be made clear, is different from all of these. Some students from southern families may have heard their elders talk of outstanding "maids" who worked long hours and often stayed overnight--cooking, laundering, cleaning, waxing, picking up children at school, helping children with school work, helping with music lessons, and performing as chief disciplinarian in the absence of parents. Is that the same as a nanny? Perhaps! But purveyors of "new concepts" such as nannying must be ready to establish that "what we have to offer is something totally different!" Believing the old Roman adage **Nihil novi sub sole** (There is nothing new under the sun), we know that no concept is "totally different." However, it is incumbent upon purveyors of such services to convince prospective clients of the complete novelty of the idea. Old or new, nannying seems to be coming into its own because the time is right among middle-class Americans. Demographics show that the two-career family is becoming an American standard. And when both of the parents are away from the home for long periods of time, a niche is being created that could well be filled by the nanny.

1.   As a client of a nanny service, would you expect your nanny to do the family laundry? Why or why not?

2.   Having gained from the case some notion of how a nanny operates, give some reasons why you feel that a family could easily become disenchanted with a particular nanny.

3.   Assume that you are running a nanny agency. Explain to a prospective client the difference between a nanny and a baby-sitter.

4.   If your venture into small business were to be the establishment of a nanny agency in your community, what would be your first moves?

AN ADDITIONAL CASE

With a major metropolitan area just forty miles away, there was no need for a television station in Augusta. But <u>radio</u> flourished. There were seven stations aggressively jockeying for top position and combing the town of 43,000 for advertisers. Probably one of the biggest names in the business was Thurston Baker who had been a radio personality in Augusta for some twenty years. Thurston had a super voice for reading the news and he intoned sensitive poetry during the late evening hours. Oddly enough, he was also immensely popular with the young set, who listened devotedly to "What's Hittin' in Augusta"--a countdown of the city's top rock hits. Thurston was a man of many facets. He was president of his civic club, a leader in his church, a colonel in the Army Reserve, and chairman of the county's planning and zoning board. With all these positive contacts, Thurston was ready to launch a small business in Augusta, a town he had hailed on his radio shows as "The Opportunity Center of the Great Southwest."

Thurston Baker had observed that despite the broad radio activity in Augusta, there was no advertising agency. He approached the radio station managers he knew well, and several expressed a willingness to work with such an agency were it to be formed. Those who were less enthusiastic would be willing to try such an arrangement if Thurston could prove to them that he would indeed be saving the station a lot of work. The standard practice in big cities, Thurston believed, was for a radio station to provide time on the air to an agency for 15 percent below the standard card rate. For the 15 percent consideration, the agency would write the commercials, produce tapes, devise jingles--whatever the advertising client wanted. In short, an advertising agency would be performing valuable services to earn that 15 percent rebate.

In actual practice in the ideal, Thurston Baker would go to a furniture store, for example, and say: "I'll be your advertising agency. I'll work with you to design radio spots that will bring a boom to your business. I'll handle all of the details. So long as we don't do anything terribly out of the ordinary, there will be no extra cost to you. You will pay the same fees to the radio station that you have always paid. My compensation will come from the radio station. There will be no cost to you for my services. I can see that we put on the air exactly what you want; I know I can take a more personal interest in you than the station has been able to do." If the furniture store bought a series of radio spot announcements with a total cost of $1,000, Thurston Baker would bill the store for $1,000 of advertising. He would then be obligated to pay the station $850--retaining for his agency the standard 15 percent. To Thurston Baker, the concept looked like a sure winner.

On January 1, Thurston opened Baker Advertising Agency.

He was aware that the agency idea would require a little "selling," but he was not prepared for so many local businesspeople to be so closed to the new idea. For example, there was Fred Arnold who managed the Collins Appliance Store at 1010 Broad Street. "You know, Thurston," Arnold began, "I've been on two of the top stations here in town for nearly every day since around 1946. Station personnel have changed hundreds of times over the years, but we've always had a great working relationship. As you know, we've sponsored Western Willie Baggs and the Golden Sodbusters ever since they went on the air; it's been great for business. And, to be blunt, I don't need any intermediary getting in between Collins Appliance Store and the stations. I'm sure you'll line up some good clients, but I'm not one to get on this bandwagon."

"But you don't understand, Fred," Thurston countered. "What I can do for you won't cost you a penny, and I can provide you and the store more personal attention than any radio station possibly could."

"Tell you what. Go call Western Willie Baggs and see what he thinks of the deal. If he thinks his show for Collins Appliance will benefit, then I'll sign on with you."

Well, we can forget about Fred Arnold and the Collins Appliance Store. Surely there are other enlightened advertisers in Augusta. Well, if there are, Thurston had difficulty in finding them! The antiquated thinking of Fred Arnold was echoed in Thurston's ear numerous times by the major advertisers already using radio in Augusta. Thurston was severely disappointed. He was happy that he had followed his wife's advice. She had counseled that he not resign from his various on-the-air duties until the agency was moving along briskly. Accordingly, Thurston maintained his full broadcast schedule and worked for the agency in whatever spare time he had.

Then a breakthrough occurred.

Fred Arnold retired as manager and principal owner of Collins Appliance, capping several years of negotiations over sale of the store. Majority ownership of the store went to a young Chicago man, Ted Tuten, who fully intended to come to Augusta and operate the store. To Thurston, this made Collins Appliance a whole new ballgame. And as soon as Ted Tuten had had the chance to get settled in at Collins, Thurston Baker paid him a call. As delightful to Thurston's ears as the final movement of Beethoven's Ninth Symphony were these words from the newcomer Tuten.

"Am I glad that you dropped by! Sure I can use your help! I'll be glad to have you handle all my advertising. Up in Chicago I discovered what good, targeted radio spots can do for an appliance store. I'm dumping some of the stuff Fred Arnold had on the air for years--coming out with a whole new approach. And I need your help in judging what will go over here in Augusta."

It was only a day or so later that Thurston happened by Dampel's Pest Control, a firm that had never used radio in Augusta. Marilyn Dampel was anxious to know how to get on the airwaves. "I won't do much advertising at first, and I won't make a high- volume client, but I'd be happy to have you handle my advertising."

Maybe Baker Advertising Agency will be a hit after all.

1.   It should be clear to Thurston Baker where he must search to find willing clients. Where? And why is this so?

2.   `On his wife's advice, Thurston has not devoted his full-time efforts at getting the agency started. Do you feel his wife's advice was wise? Why or why not?

3.   Before he opened Baker Advertising Agency, Thurston talked with several station managers concerning their willingness to work with him. Who else should he have contacted? Should these responses have been the main determining factor in whether or not Baker Advertising would open? Why or why not?

4.   Compare Thurston's task of selling what was for Augusta a new concept with the task of selling nannying to middle-class America.

ANSWERS TO TRUE-FALSE QUESTIONS

1.	T	(p. 130)	6.	T	(p. 134)
2.	F	(p. 130)	7.	F	(p. 137)
3.	T	(p. 131)	8.	F	(p. 139)
4.	F	(p. 133)	9.	T	(p. 139)
5.	T	(p. 134)	10.	F	(p. 146)

ANSWERS TO MULTIPLE-CHOICE QUESTIONS

1.	D	(p. 130)	11.	B	(p. 139)
2.	C	(p. 132)	12.	A	(p. 140)
3.	B	(p. 132)	13.	D	(p. 140)
4.	A	(p. 132)	14.	C	(p. 141)
5.	D	(p. 133)	15.	B	(p. 141)
6.	C	(p. 134)	16.	A	(p. 141)
7.	B	(p. 134)	17.	D	(p. 143)
8.	A	(p. 135)	18.	C	(p. 143)
9.	D	(p. 136)	19.	B	(p. 144)
10.	C	(p. 138)	20.	A	(p. 144)

CHAPTER SEVEN

SETTING BUSINESS GOALS AND STRATEGIES

CHAPTER OVERVIEW

The starting point of strategic planning is goal setting, and the primary purpose of setting goals is to provide direction and guidance. Goals also assist in allocation of resources, defining corporate culture, and assessing performance. Goals may be long- term, intermediate, or short-term. Goal optimization means balancing and reconciling different and sometimes contradictory goals. The steps in strategy formulation are: establishment of strategic goals; environmental analysis; organizational analysis; and matching threats and opportunities against corporate strengths and weaknesses. Many firms have three levels of strategy: corporate; business; and functional. Functional strategies correspond to areas of management: marketing; finance; production; human resources; and research and development. Implementation of strategies usually requires a series of tactical and operational plans. Tactical plans address local market conditions, government regulations, local competition, among others. Operational plans fall into at least three categories: single-use plans; standing plans; and standard operating procedures. Contingency planning hedges against changes that might or might not occur. Managing the planning process can involve management by objectives (MBO) and the surmounting of barriers to planning.

LEARNING OBJECTIVES

1. Identify the purposes of business goal-setting and the three levels of goals.

2. Describe the process by which successful strategic plans are formulated.

3. Discuss the three levels of strategic plans.

4. Distinguish between tactical and operational plans and indicate how each can be used to implement strategic plans.

5. Explain how management by objectives assists in the planning process and describe how the barriers to successful planning can be surmounted.

DISCUSSION OF THE OPENING CASE

To make a narrative exciting, it is necessary to pile one compelling and informative fact upon another in rapid-fire succession. As in the case of H.J. Heinz in recent years, it is exhilarating to see how Tony O'Reilly dramatically increased the firm's revenues and profits. So many happenings since 1979 have been crammed into several pages of copy, that it seems as if the firm was making drastic changes nearly every day of its existence. Well, that can't be true, because a firm can't keep control of itself if it makes too many changes too rapidly. Behind all these changes, although the narrative does not have time to tell us, there must have been a formulation of broad, long-term strategy. The energetic changes and impressive results, then, were merely the fruits of a sound strategy being implemented properly. Rather than helter-skelter, impromptu taking advantage of new opportunities, the upward movement of the company was actually a gradual, progressive advancement along lines that were carefully laid out beforehand. Said another way, there was "method in their madness." Here is a comment upon why O'Reilly "pared away the fat" in human resources. A glance at an income statement for many companies will reveal that the largest single item of operational expense is that of paying for the services of the firm's employees. So, if a cost-cutter such as Tony O'Reilly arrives on the scene, he is able to see that cutting payroll is a great way to lower expenses. You've probably heard of a firm that saves on paper, paper clips, pens, manilla folders, and copying expenses. Such minor savings are only a drop in the bucket compared to the terminating of one full-time employee. Tony O'Reilly was able to visualize a firm that could operate successfully with far fewer people than were on the bulging roster when Tony arrived. But Tony O'Reilly ran right into the buzzsaw that will nick you if you're not careful every time you run amuck with economizing: "Yet along the way, quality had begun to slip." Surely, some of the "fat" that had been "pared away" would love to have been around to tell O'Reilly: "I told you the quality of the product would drop with all your cutting, but you just wouldn't listen."

1.   In your own words, state the primary goal of H.J. Heinz under Tony O'Reilly.

2.   Should a firm place monetary success as its primary goal? Why or why not?

3.   Regardless of how you responded to Number 2 above, what are some other worthy goals for a large corporation that are completely unrelated to monetary success?

4.   Would you have liked being a right-hand assistant to Tony O'Reilly during the periods of greatest cost-cuttting at H.J. Heinz? Why or why not?

ANNOTATED KEY TERMS

Goal or Objective - Something a person or business hopes to achieve.

Long-Term Goals - Goals that are set for extended periods of time, typically five years or more into the future.

Intermediate Goals - Goals that are set for the period from one to five years into the future.

Short-Term Goals - Goals that are set for the very near future, typically less than one year hence.

Goal Optimization - The balancing and reconciling of different and sometimes contradictory goals.

Strategy Formulation - The creation of strategies to meet the company's goals at all levels.

Strategic Goals - Long-term goals derived directly from a firm's mission statement.

Environmental Analysis - The process of scanning the business environment for threats and opportunities.

Organizational Analysis - The process of analyzing a firm's strengths and weaknesses.

Corporate Strategy - A strategy that addresses the issue of what business or businesses a corporation wishes to enter.

Growth-Share Matrix - A tool for categorizing businesses into four categories according to their current market share and their market growth: stars (high market growth, high market share); cash cows (low market growth, high market share); question marks (high market growth, low market share); and dogs (low market growth, low market share).

Business Strategy - A strategy concerned with achieving the goals of a business or a related set of businesses within a corporation.

Retrenchment - A business strategy that involves cutting back on some aspects of a firm's operations.

Transformation - A business strategy that involves changing both the company's mission and its approach to doing business.

Functional Strategy - A strategy that deals with the major aspects of a company's operations: marketing, finance, production, human resources, and research and development.

Differentiation - A marketing strategy in which a company develops an image for its products or services that serves to distinguish it from those of its competitors.

Price Leadership - A marketing strategy that involves aggressive price- and cost-cutting.

Focus Strategy - A marketing strategy that targets a selected region, consumer group, or other market segment.

Debt Policy - A financial strategy that addresses a firm's method of paying for major operations.

Asset Management - A financial strategy that addresses a firm's plans for earning income on its assets.

Capitalization Strategy - A financial strategy that addresses the precise mix and different kinds of stock issued by a company, how that stock is backed, and related issues.

Time-Based Competition - Competition in which speed is an important element of success.

Tactical Plan - Specific short-run and intermediate plans that parallel strategic goals, but on a narrower scale. Tactical plans are more narrowly focused than strategic goals and are implemented by middle management.

Operational Plan - Highly detailed short-run plans that detail the activities that must be completed to further the firm's tactical and strategic plans.

Single-Use Plans - Operational plans that are used only once.

Standing Plans - Operational plans for carrying out activities that are performed on a regular basis.

Contingency Planning - Planning for change. Contingency planning attempts to identify important aspects of the business or its market that might change, and defines how the company will respond to those changes.

Crisis Management - A firm's methods for dealing with emergencies.

Management by Objectives (MBO) - A system of collaborative goal setting in which managers meet with each of their subordinates individually to establish goals against which the employee's performance is later evaluated.

TRUE-FALSE QUESTIONS

1. The primary purpose of setting goals is to provide direction and guidance.

2. Every enterprise has a purpose, a reason for being.

3. The level of the goal determines the person in the company who is responsible for setting that goal.

4. Mars's candy business, which features such mainstays as Snickers, M&Ms, and Milky Way, is a star.

5. The slow growth business strategy approach is most useful for stars.

6. The strong growth business strategy approach is generally called for when costs have gotten out of hand or when the market for a business's products has become stagnant.

7. The price leadership marketing strategy is appropriate for companies that sell chili in Texas and clam chowder in New England.

8.   Strategic goals are set by lower levels of management and take a shorter time to implement.

9.   Tactical plans imply action.

10.   By its nature, a contingency plan is speculative.

MULTIPLE CHOICE QUESTIONS

1.   Something a person or business hopes to achieve is called a

        a. strategy.
        b. plan.
        c. procedure.
        d. goal.

2.   A view of how a business will achieve its purpose is called a

        a. goal.
        b. objective.
        c. mission.
        d. regulation.

3.   Aiming for a three percent increase in return on investment in three years is an example of a

        a. long-term goal.
        b. intermediate goal.
        c. short-term goal.
        d. contingency plan.

4.   Top managers, working in conjunction with the board of directors, set the company's

        a. long-term goals.
        b. intermediate goals.
        c. short-term goals.
        d. growth-share matrix.

5.   Balancing and reconciling different and sometimes contradictory goals is referred to as

        a. contingency planning.
        b. environmental analysis.
        c. establishing single-use plans.
        d. goal optimization.

6. Long-term goals derived directly from the firm's mission statement are

   a. environmental goals.
   b. functional strategies.
   c. strategic goals.
   d. standing plans.

7. A popular tool developed by the Boston Consulting Group that allows managers to look at their company as a portfolio of different businesses is the

   a. financial leverage criterion.
   b. growth-share matrix.
   c. tactical plan.
   d. MBO approach.

8. The low market growth, high market share classification in the growth-share matrix, describes the type of firm called a

   a. cash cow.
   b. star.
   c. question mark.
   d. dog.

9. Which of the following is concerned with achieving the goal of each business or related set of businesses within the corporation?

   a. corporate strategy
   b. marketing strategy
   c. standing plans
   d. business strategy

10. When the company changes both its mission and its approach to doing business, it is called

   a. retrenchment.
   b. differentiation.
   c. transformation.
   d. time-based competition.

11. When a company develops an image of its products or services that serves to distinguish them from those of its competitors, the firm has adopted a

    a. functional strategy.
    b. differentiation strategy.
    c. price leadership strategy.
    d. financial strategy.

12. Debt policies, dividend policies, and asset management programs are

    a. financial policies.
    b. marketing policies.
    c. production policies.
    d. corporate objectives.

13. Companies that have borrowed large sums of money against their assets are

    a. developing their capitalization strategies.
    b. cash cows.
    c. devoting a large share of their profits to pay dividends.
    d. highly leveraged.

14. Productivity improvement and plant location are concerns addressed in a company's

    a. financial strategies.
    b. marketing strategies.
    c. production strategies.
    d. asset management strategies.

15. Personnel policies, labor relations, and executive development are issues found in a companie's

    a. research and development strategies.
    b. human resource strategies.
    c. financial strategies.
    d. marketing strategies.

16. Short-run and intermediate plans that parallel strategic goals, but on a narrower scale, are called

    a. tactical plans.
    b. functional strategies.
    c. corporate objectives.
    d. business goals.

17. Policies, standard operating procedures, and rules and regulations are all

    a. tactical plans.
    b. policies.
    c. goals.
    d. standing plans.

18. Planning for change is also called

    a. standard planning.
    b. setting policies.
    c. contingency planning.
    d. establishing corporate objectives.

19. Management that centers around an organization's methods for dealing with emergencies is called

    a. contingency planning.
    b. crisis management.
    c. standard planning.
    d. a focus strategy.

20. A system of collaborative goal setting that extends from the top of the organization to the bottom is called

    a. MBO.
    b. crisis management.
    c. contingency planning.
    d. barrier management.

WRITING TO LEARN

1. What is the starting point of strategic planning? Why should a business set goals? What are the different levels of goals?

2. What are the steps involved in strategy formulation? What is the heart of strategy formulation?

3. Discuss the three levels of strategic planning. How can a manager use the growth-share matrix as a tool? What alternative business strategies might a firm consider?

4. Discuss the differences between tactical and operational plans. What are the two main types of operational plans? Are contingency plans important to managers?

5.   How are goals and objectives set under the management by objectives approach? Discuss the barriers that might disrupt plans and how to overcome them.

DISCUSSION OF THE CLOSING CASE

We can coin a phrase, and say that at several levels, Rubbermaid does a lot of <u>throwing away</u>. Further, we might express the opinion that this <u>throwing away</u> is a key to the firm's success. First of all, at a lower level of the organization, high quality control standards dictate that products with the slightest flaws will be cast aside and will never be seen by the buying public. Under Stanley Gault, quality became a high value for the firm. In terms of this chapter, high quality was very much a part of the formulation of corporate strategy. Knowing that Rubbermaid would be charging a "premium price" for its products, it was important that such products maintain high levels of quality. Second, there was <u>throwing away</u> at a much higher level in the organization. Since the company introduces 100 new products per year, it is necessary that the firm quickly determine which of these products will make it and which won't. We say "quickly," because to give a failing product several years to catch on means taking valuable resources (of various kinds) away from products that will be a success. So, it is important that Rubbermaid be willing to <u>throw away</u> that small percent of new products that are not a "hit" with the public. Although, at present, a high percent of new products are successful, there may be years in which that is not the case. That's when the <u>throwing away</u> should be of high magnitude. Perhaps the secret to having warmly- received new products is the R & D effort--a key element in Rubbermaid's strategy. There may have been a time when a poor, young inventor could slave away in a dimly-lit laboratory to produce something that would alter the lot of mankind for centuries to come. Without surveying the potential consumers of that invention, the inventor would one day emerge from his dark lab into the sunlight of a bright spring day, head for the U.S. Patent Office to register his brainchild, and then seek to market it. It's not that simple anymore. [Actually, it was not that simple in the old days, either.] To develop a product that is needed by masses of people, research and development are necessary. Apparently, Rubbermaid is willing to make that effort. So far, the effort has paid off admirably.

1. What would you say to a plan whereby Rubbermaid was able to sell, under a <u>different brand name</u>, all of its units rejected by quality control. Would this be a viable method for compensating for the costs of high quality standards?

2. Compare Mr. Gault's leadership of Rubbermaid with that of Mr. O'Reilly with H.J. Heinz.

3. Explain how the fluctuating prices of petrochemicals is a severe challenge for planners at Rubbermaid.

4. Do you feel that the departure of Mr. Gault from Rubbermaid means the firm will experience less favorable fortunes? Why or why not?

AN ADDITIONAL CASE

Achiavendelli Shoes are now available, at last, in America! Noble Watson wants to market them exclusively in Evanston. Noble is a psychologist at a community mental health center in nearby Warrenton, and he has always wanted to phase himself out of psychology into retail sales. Achiavendelli seems to be his best chance.

The ladies' shoes of Achiavendelli are made in Italy and have been popular items for years throughout Europe and the British Isles. They have the ideal combination of high quality and moderate price. For a retailer, they have the advantage of a healthy markup, leading to substantial gross profit. The Achiavendelli agent for the eastern United States, Paddy Gagliardi, has awarded the Evanston dealership to Noble Watson-- if Noble can achieve an annual volume level of 10,000 pairs of shoes by the time the firm has completed its <u>second</u> year of operation. Noble figures that this means he must sell 27 pairs of Achiavendellis per day for 365 straight days. To reach such a goal, Noble begins to envision a large store with about the same floor space as a McDonald's restaurant. Before any more "envisioning," Noble stops by to see an old management professor at the University.

After the professor hears the situation as sketched by Noble Watson, he has a comment or two.

"Seems to me, Noble, that you are mixing long-term goals and short-term goals. What we need to do is sort them out and then arrive at a strategy. You want a store as big as a McDonald's, and that makes good sense--but <u>not</u> <u>right</u> <u>away</u>. Regardless of that ambitious goal Achiavendelli has set for you of 10,000 pairs, you have to start out slowly. To establish the store you've been thinking about and stock it with Achivendellis will take plenty of capital. You'll be drowning in debt, while we have no guarantee of how much revenue the shoes will generate in your early stages. Let me tell you a story about how I see your Achivendelli store progressing."

"Okay. That's why I've come to see you."

"When I was a freshmen in college, just after World War Two, we had on campus an exchange student from Austria named Heintz. Heintz came to all the Greek organization dances and took pictures of the couples. Several days later, he would show up at the fraternity or sorority house to sell those photographs. They were a popular item. That first year, the quality of the pictures was barely acceptable. As the years went by, however, the quality steadily improved. It just seemed to me that Heintz was investing in better and better equipment as his revenues permitted. Speaking of revenues, his markups were substantial. He could produce a photo for several cents and then sell it for $1.50 to $2.00. By the time I was a junior, Heintz had an assistant. In my senior year, he had three assistants. You see, as he improved his equipment, he also added to staff."

"I'm getting a picture here of start small, and grow slowly."

"Right. But there's more to the Heintz saga. When I was a freshman, Heintz walked to all the dances and Greek houses; we were a small campus in a small town. When I was a sophomore, he rode a bike. When I became a junior, Heintz had a motor scooter, and in my final year there, he had a Chevrolet. Had I stayed around another year or two, Heintz, I am positive, would have been driving a Cadillac or a Mercedes! His slowly-growing business allowed him these increasing evidences of success."

"Well, Doctor, what does this say to me specifically as I start my life with Achiavendelli?"

"Set a long-term goal for five years from now of a large Achiavendelli store, as big as you've been dreaming, with an annual sales volume of 27,250 pairs of shoes. With the average markup you've been telling me about of $17 a pair, your gross profit (before administrative expenses, etc.) would be $463,250-- that's close to half a million!"

"Wow! It's a success!"

"But wait. You need to establish an intermediate goal to be reached at the end of your second year of operation. That goal-- as required by Achiavendelli--is annual volume of 10,000 pairs of ladies' shoes for that second year. If you fail to meet this one, then you're out as the Achiavendelli store of Evanston. A reasonable short-term goal for the first year would be 5,000 pairs of Achiavendellis--or around 14 pairs of shoes sold per day. Progress toward that first-year goal is something you want to monitor almost moment by moment. If you have difficulty selling 5,000 pairs in the first year, then achieving 10,000 in year two may be impossible. If year one falls way below the 5,000 pairs, you may want to consider staying in psychology and kissing the shoe business goodbye."

"What kind of facility should I plan on for that first year?"

"Remember Heintz who walked to all the dances that first year? In light of Heintz's experience, I'd recommend that you need no more space than the size of a one-car garage. You could even share space with a dress shop, pharmacy, card shop, florist, or dry cleaners. The last thing you need in that first year is a lot of rental expense for your struggling new business."

"You used to talk about contingency planning when I took your courses. Should we build some of that in here?"

"Noble, I think the contingency we have to plan for is the unhappy circumstance of your store not getting anywhere near its sales-volume quota for the first year. We need to map out some emergency measures to still reach that 10,000 pairs for the second year, given that first-year figures are far below 5,000. You know, we can reach the volume if we are willing to sacrifice profit per pair and have some two-for-one sales. A contingency plan should include alternatives such as this."

"A first step--an extremely short-range goal--is to find a hole- in-the-wall to use for my first year as the exclusive Achiavendelli representative for Evanston."

1.   Do you find any advice by the professor that is unrealistic? Explain.

2. Let us suppose that the first year's volume of pairs sold totals to 4,500. What are some drastic measures that Noble Watson can use to still achieve that goal of 10,000 pairs sold for the second year?

3. We are familiar with Noble Watson's emphasis on that 10,000 pairs in year two. Tell why you think Achiavendelli Shoes has set such a requirement.

4. What is the main lesson of the story of Heintz, the campus photographer? Exactly what does the Heintz tale say to Noble Watson in his plans for the Achiavendelli store?

ANSWERS TO TRUE-FALSE QUESTIONS

1.	T	(p. 155)	6.	F	(p. 162)
2.	T	(p. 155)	7.	F	(p. 163)
3.	T	(p. 157)	8.	F	(p. 166)
4.	F	(p. 160)	9.	T	(p. 167)
5.	F	(p. 161)	10.	T	(p. 168)

ANSWERS TO MULTIPLE-CHOICE QUESTIONS

1.	D	(p. 155)	11.	B	(p. 163)
2.	C	(p. 155)	12.	A	(p. 164)
3.	B	(p. 156)	13.	D	(p. 164)
4.	A	(p. 157)	14.	C	(p. 164)
5.	D	(p. 157)	15.	B	(p. 164)
6.	C	(p. 158)	16.	A	(p. 166)
7.	B	(p. 160)	17.	D	(p. 167)
8.	A	(p. 160)	18.	C	(p. 168)
9.	D	(p. 161)	19.	B	(p. 168)
10.	C	(p. 162)	20.	A	(p. 169)

CHAPTER EIGHT

ORGANIZING THE BUSINESS ENTERPRISE

CHAPTER OVERVIEW

The need to fit structure to operations is common to all companies. Organizational charts depict the company's structure and show employees where they fit into the firm's operations. Job specialization and departmentalization represent the basic building blocks of all businesses. Departmentalization may occur along customer, product, process, geographic, or functional lines. The decision-making hierarchy answers the question: Who makes which decision? Responsibility is the duty to perform an assigned task. Authority is the power to make decisions necessary to complete the task. Delegation begins when a manager assigns a task to a subordinate. In a centralized organization, most decision-making authority is held by upper-level managers. In a decentralized organization, a great deal of decision-making authority is delegated to lower-level management. Decentralized companies require few layers of management; this results in a flat organizational structure. A firm with many layers of management has a tall organizational structure. In a line organization, there is a simple chain of command. Span of control is the number of people that one supervisor manages. Staff departments are made up of specialists such as lawyers, engineers, accountants, and human resources personnel. One of the most powerful informal forces in any firm is the grapevine. Some alternative organizational structures are divisional, matrix, and international. Intrapreneuring means creating the innovative atmosphere of a small business within a large firm.

LEARNING OBJECTIVES

1.   Discuss the elements that influence a firm's organizational structure.

2.   Identify and describe the building blocks of organizational structures.

3.   Distinguish between responsibility and authority and describe how authority is delegated.

4.   Define the informal organization and explain its importance.

5.   Explain the differences among divisional, matrix, and international organization structures and the reasons for encouraging intrapreneurship.

DISCUSSION OF THE OPENING CASE

A good portion of the current chapter is devoted to the matter of forming units within an organization. The optimal scheme of such departmentalization should lead to the greatest efficiency of the firm, and also the greatest profits. The Borden case shows us that departmentalizing can become quite complicated. Now, if Harry and Joe are going to open a service station, they can agree that Harry will handle the gas pumps and do all the paper work while Joe will be strictly a full-time mechanic. Even if Harry and Joe add five or six new employees, it is rather simple to explain to each which "department" they will be assigned to. However, when the organization in question employs many thousands of workers and has facilities all over the world, the forming of units within the organization becomes terribly complex. Adding to the complexity is the fact that the larger the total organization, then the greater will be the number of ways to organize. We see, in this installment of the Borden story, two different corporate presidents coming on board and each dreaming of changes that must be made. It should be pointed out that a new CEO will probably not arrive at his or her new office with a whole new organizational chart in hand. Ideally, we would suppose, a new CEO with organizational changes in mind will engage some experts to draw up some possibilities for improvement. In a doctoral program in business at a major university, it is easy for students to make changes on the paper version of a firm's organizational chart. It is equally easy to do so in the comfortable executive suite of a huge firm. However, putting such alterations into implementation in the worldwide facilities of a multinational firm can be a monumental undertaking. For example, a new CEO at Borden could say: "Scratch off our operations in France." We can change the chart in a matter of seconds. In France, however, "scratching off" can become very involved: notifying several thousand people they no longer have a job; facing the violence of demonstrations by unhappy French union workers; trying to get out of long-term leases on offices all over Paris; shutting down and trying to sell manufacturing equipment; trying to be released from long- term rentals on sprawling production facilities at several locations in France.

1.   Explain why you feel or do not feel that the reorganizing of a firm as large as Borden has to involve "experts" in such matters.

2.   Is it possible that the true effects of an organizational change cannot be fully known until the change is actually made? Why or why not?

3.   Is there anything wrong with Borden drastically cutting operations in its original endeavor--dairying? Why or why not? Should "dairying" be treated differently than other candidates for abandonment or cutback?

4.   Some commentators have indicated that the golden age of the conglomerate has passed. Should this statement affect Borden's planning for the future? Why or why not?

ANNOTATED KEY TERMS

<u>Organizational</u> <u>Structure</u> - The specification of the jobs to be done within an organization and how those jobs relate to one another.

<u>Organizational</u> <u>Chart</u> - A diagram that depicts a company's structure and shows employees where they fit into the firm's operations.

<u>Chain</u> <u>of</u> <u>Command</u> - The reporting relationships within a company.

<u>Job</u> <u>Specialization</u> - The process of breaking jobs down into individual components to permit concentration in performing each component of the task.

<u>Departmentalization</u> - The process of grouping jobs into logical units.

<u>Customer</u> <u>Departmentalization</u> - Departmentalization according to the type of customer likely to buy a given product or service.

<u>Product</u> <u>Departmentalization</u> - Departmentalization according to the specific product or service being created.

<u>Process</u> <u>Departmentalization</u> - Departmentalization according to the production process used to create a good or service.

<u>Geographic</u> <u>Departmentalization</u> - Departmentalization according to the area of the country or the world that is served by the business.

<u>Functional</u> <u>Departmentalization</u> - Departmentalization according to a group's function or activities.

<u>Profit</u> <u>Center</u> - A unit of a corporation that is responsible for its own costs and profits.

<u>Responsibility</u> - The duty to perform an assigned task.

<u>Authority</u> - The power to make the decisions necessary to complete an assigned task.

<u>Delegation</u> - The assignment of a task, responsibility, or authority by a manager to a subordinate.

<u>Accountability</u> - The liability of subordinates to accomplish the tasks they are assigned by their managers.

<u>Centralized</u> <u>Organization</u> - An organization in which most decision-making authority is held by upper-level management.

Decentralized Organization - An organization in which a great deal of decision-making authority is delegated to lower-level management.

Line Organization - An organizational structure in which all authority flows in a direct chain of command from the top of the company to the bottom.

Line Departments - Departments that are directly linked to the production and sales of specific products.

Span of Control - The number of people that one supervisor manages.

Staff Members - The advisors and counselors in a company. Staff members aid line departments in making decisions, but do not have the authority to make final decisions for line departments.

Line-and-Staff Organization - An organization that includes not only line departments, but also staff members who advise line managers.

Functional Organization - A form of business organization that uses the functional approach to departmentalization; commonly used by smaller and medium-sized firms.

Formal Organization - The specified relationship between individuals, their jobs, and their authorities as shown in a company's organizational chart.

Informal Organization - The network of everyday social interactions among the employees of a company; unrelated to the firm's formal authority structure as depicted in the organizational chart.

Grapevine - An informal communication network that carries gossip and information throughout an organization.

Networking - Interactions, often informal, among businesspeople for the purpose of discussing mutual problems, solutions, and opportunities.

Mentoring - The process by which younger, less experienced employees are taught and sponsored by older, more experienced employees.

Divisional Organization - An organizational structure in which each division of a corporation maintains its own identity and operates as a relatively autonomous business within the larger corporate umbrella.

Matrix Organization - An organizational structure in which teams are formed, with the individuals on each team reporting to two or more managers.

International Organization Structures - A variety of approaches to organizational structure developed to respond to a business's need to manufacture, purchase, and sell in global markets.

Intrapreneuring - The process of creating and maintaining the innovation and flexibility of a small business environment within the confines of a large, bureaucratic organization.

TRUE-FALSE QUESTIONS

1. Organizations frequently need to make changes in their structure.

2. Job specialization is a natural part of organizational growth.

3. Process departmentalization makes customer shopping easier by providing identifiable store segments.

4. Delegation involves a specific relationship between a manager and a subordinate.

5. There is a tendency for companies to adopt a more and more centralized organization as they grow.

6. Decentralized companies require multiple layers of management.

7. When several employees perform the same simple task or interrelated tasks, a narrow span of control is possible and often desirable.

8. Staff employees are the doers and producers in a company.

9. According to Peters and Waterman, many successful companies encourage the informal exchange of information.

10. Matrix organization is particularly appealing to firms that want to slow down the decision making process.

MULTIPLE CHOICE QUESTIONS

1. The specification of the jobs to be done within an organization and how those jobs relate to one another is defined as

   a. the chain of command.
   b. job specialization.
   c. MBO.
   d. organizational structure.

2. The solid lines connecting boxes in the organizational chart that show the reporting relationships within the company defines the

   a. informal organization.
   b. grapevine.
   c. chain of command.
   d. intrapreneuring relationship.

3. The process of determining what jobs need to be done and who will perform them leads to

   a. departmentalization.
   b. job specialization.
   c. productivity assessment.
   d. organizational responsibility.

4. Sears and Macy's are grouped into logical units according to

   a. customer departmentalization.
   b. product departmentalization.
   c. process departmentalization.
   d. geographic departmentalization.

5. In the United States, utility companies are organized according to

   a. customer departmentalization.
   b. product departmentalization.
   c. process departmentalization.
   d. geographic departmentalization.

6. Departmentalization allows the firm to hold each separate unit responsible for its own costs and profits as a

   a. functional department.
   b. separate activity.
   c. profit center.
   d. matrix organization.

7. The duty to perform an assigned task is called

   a. authority.
   b. responsibility.
   c. specialization.
   d. organization.

8. Most decision-making authority is held by upper-level management in a

   a. centralized organization.
   b. decentralized organization.
   c. matrix organization.
   d. flat organizational structure.

9. General Electric and Xerox have a strong tradition of

   a. centralization.
   b. tall organizational structures.
   c. a wide span of control.
   d. decentralization.

10. Departments that are directly linked to the production and sales of specific products are

   a. staff departments.
   b. tall structures.
   c. line departments.
   d. research and development departments.

11. The number of people that one supervisor manages is referred to as the

   a. chain of command.
   b. span of control.
   c. profitability matrix.
   d. personnel mix.

12. Lawyers, engineers, accountants, and human resources personnel are examples of

   a. staff members.
   b. line managers.
   c. departmentalization representatives.
   d. research and development personnel.

13. The most common form of business organization in small to medium-size firms is the

   a. line-and-staff organization.
   b. line organization.
   c. matrix organization.
   d. functional organization.

14. An informal communication network that carries gossip and information throughout the organization is the

   a. telephone.
   b. company newsletter.
   c. grapevine.
   d. organizational structure.

15. Teams are formed in which individuals report to two or more individuals, usually a line manager and a staff manager in a(n)

   a. divisional organization.
   b. matrix organization.
   c. geographic departmentalized organization.
   d. functional structure.

16. The National Aeronautical and Space Administration (NASA) pioneered the

   a. matrix organization.
   b. divisional organization.
   c. departmental organization.
   d. tall organization structure.

17. Creating and maintaining the innovation and flexibility of a small business environment within the confines of a large, bureaucratic structure is called

   a. research and development.
   b. divisional structuring.
   c. product structuring.
   d. intrapreneuring.

18. Most innovations have historically come from

   a. large corporations.
   b. matrix organizations.
   c. individuals in small businesses.
   d. staff members.

19. An approach to organization in which aspects of the product form of departmentalization and the business portfolio management approach to corporate strategy are used is the

   a. profit center.
   b. divisional approach.
   c. tall organization structure.
   d. matrix organization.

20. Everyday social interactions among employees occur in the

   a. informal organization.
   b. divisional organization.
   c. product-oriented organization.
   d. tall organizational structure.

WRITING TO LEARN

1.Why do companies need an organizational structure? How is the chain of command depicted on an organizational chart?

2.What are the basic building blocks of all businesses? Is job specialization beneficial to the employee and the business? How do companies departmentalize?

3.Are responsibility and authority important in business? Should a manager delegate authority and responsibility?

4.What is the difference between centralization and decentralization? Should a manager have a broad or narrow span of control? Can the firm benefit by encouraging the informal exchange of information?

5.What are the advantages and disadvantages of the matrix form of organization?   What is intrapreneuring? How can intrapreneuring be beneficial to a large organization?

DISCUSSION OF THE CLOSING CASE

There is an old saying still heard in science classrooms: "Matter can neither be created nor destroyed." Said another way, this means that there is a limited amount of matter available. The same could be said of professional energy in an organization. There is, for any organziation-- everything else kept constant--a limited amount of professional energy. This statement itself tells us very little that has any practical value. But something we can gather from the statement can mean a lot. Indirectly, the statement tells us that in order to allocate unusually large pockets of that professional energy to a specific aspect of the firm, you simultaneously must deny pockets of professional energy to other aspects of the firm. Said still another way, when you designate one aspect of the firm as "top priority," you must then downgrade all other aspects to lower priority ratings. In an ideal world, everything a firm does would have top priority. But that's foolish and absolutely unrealistic. It's just a law of nature: when a firm becomes "gung ho" for a particular aspect of operations, other aspects will suffer. That is exactly what happened at Florida Power and Light Company. Surely, at some board meeting or some informal gathering of the firm's executives, someone must have said: "With all this emphasis on upgrading quality standards, I'm afraid we're neglecting some other very important aspects." Often, in a typical organization, such a voice is written off as a trouble-maker with a negative attitude. Nevertheless, such voices will continue to speak up and perhaps their message may be heard in time. Beware of new CEOs who say they plan to make major improvements in all areas of the firm. For example, let's look at the faculty members with whom you react on a daily basis at your college or university. A new president might say: "I want more out of the faculty. I will see that faculty members are better prepared for each daily lecture. I will see to it that all faculty members do far more research than at present. It will be mandatory that each faculty member serve on more committees than at present." All of this sounds fine. The only problem is that fully accomplishing any one of the president's new goals will mean a deemphasis of one or both of the other goals. There is only just so much professional energy in any given organization.

1.   If Florida Power and Light Company had made quality just one of several goals of the organization, could the firm have won the Deming Award? Why or why not?

2.   To put it mildly, there has been rapid population growth in the state of Florida. Does the case indicate that Florida Power and Light was adequately planning for such growth? Why or why not?

3.   How has the purchase of Colonial Penn Life Insurance affected the fortunes of Florida Power and Light Company?

4.   Based on what you have learned from reading the Florida Power and Light Company case, how would you assess the firm's image currently with the general public of Florida?

112

AN ADDITIONAL CASE

Dr. J. Worthington Caudill is superintendent of schools for Maupine City. In addition to a bulging central bureaucracy, Dr. Caudill oversees three high schools, six junior highs, and fifteen elementary schools. Although school districts across the nation are considering such concepts as the middle school and the magnet school, Dr. Caudill considers them "frivolous," and is not willing to "contaminate" Maupine City with such "nonsense."

When an opening as principal at Howard Elementary School occurs, Dr. Caudill brings in an experienced teacher from nearby Albany to fill the spot. She is Evelyn Jergens. Evelyn has a master's degree in education along with some 35 credit hours toward a doctorate at the state university. Before moving into her office, Evelyn is subjected to Dr. Caudill's normal welcoming speech.

"Ms. Jergens, you are in full control of Howard School. After our talk today, you will hear nothing from me, because I hand the reins of Howard to you. I expect you to be fully capable of handling matters there at the school and I know that you will bring to my attention any happenings that need my assistance. Welcome to Maupine City, and the best of luck at Howard Elementary School."

Evelyn was appreciative of the confidence that Dr. Caudill had placed in her ability to handle whatever might come up at Howard School. Evelyn found her faculty of teachers--eleven women and a man--to be most friendly and helpful, and quite excited that such a sharp young lady was taking over from the grouchy old Mr. Clivins, who was retiring. Even though the beginning atmosphere seemed quite rosy, Evelyn encountered some problems. Let's take a look at three of them.

Evelyn Jergens was three days into the resumption of classes in early September when Dr. Caudill paid her a surprise visit. Always a man on the go, Caudill introduced the first item of business as the two walked up the hall to Evelyn's office.

"Ms. Jergens, I noticed on the bulletin board your schedule for the day's activities. Starting lunch at 11:45 is far too late for best results. The children are grumpy and out of sorts, the kitchen staff will resent working later, and the lunch area will remain messy all the longer. Besides, the janitors will resent it. Start lunch at 11:00."

"Dr. Caudill, the entire faculty and I worked out the best possible schedule and we have lunch at 11:45 because morning kindergarten has not cleared the building until that time. The cooks don't mind because they get to sleep a little later in the morning. In fact, they love the new schedule."

"Let's not argue, my dear. Lunch is at 11:00. How is your new reading book working out in second grade--you know, Timmy and Buffy See Europe?"

"After several days of conferring with my first and second grade teachers and the school district's elementary curriculum specialist, we decided to shelve Timmy and Buffy and to pick from the list the curriculum specialist offered us, Fun with Words, Part II. It is working out beautifully!"

"I have no idea why the specialist allowed you to go with Fun with Words. Better talk to her and make the switch to Timmy and Buffy no later than Thanksgiving. I don't want pressure from parents over their little darlings reading mediocre material. Well, I'm in a hurry. Glad to see you're doing well. Make those changes quickly. Bye."

Almost in a cloud of smoke, Dr. Caudill was gone.

Despite this taking of wind out of her sails, Evelyn continued to innovate and administrate-- usually with excellent results. A move that she felt students and teachers alike would applaud was lengthening morning recess by 7 minutes. Recess would run from 10:00 to 10:22. Evelyn's research told her that kids need a long break, especially in the morning. After about a week on the new recess schedule, Evelyn gazed out her window at the happy children on the playground and noticed that they all began trooping back in at the old time of 10:15, even before the bell had sounded. This was happening every day of the week. When she very subtly investigated the matter, several teachers all said the same thing: "Well, Mrs. Thomas began bringing her pupils in at 10:15."

Without ever mentioning recess, Evelyn made an attempt to get well acquainted with Mrs. Thomas. The latter was a tall, distinguished woman in her fifties. She had some 40 hours beyond her master's degree and had been an elementary principal in a neighboring town some years back. A gracious, cultured and articulate woman, Mrs. Thomas had the respect of every teacher in the school. Mrs. Thomas, however, seldom if ever exploited that respect for her own gain. By the way, two of the younger teachers had run around with Mrs. Thomas's children when they all were younger. For the future, Evelyn knew that any innovations she had in mind should be very informally run by Mrs. Thomas. Once this lesson was learned, things went smoothly at Howard School. That is, until the afternoon when Dr. Caudill came bursting into the principal's office.

"Ms. Jergens, I've had several parents complaining about the halls not being kept clean here at Howard School. We can't have that. We must have clean halls at all times!"

Evelyn Jergens was not going to be intimidated very easily, and today was the day that Dr. Caudill would find that out.

"Dr. Caudill, you are well aware," she began, "that I have no authority over the janitors. Thus I am not responsible for the way they keep the building. Under your system, janitors receive their orders from your central office, not from me. My complaints to your director of maintenance over this very matter of trashy hallways have availed me nothing. If the halls are dirty today, it is your system that is at fault. If you want to change your system and make ME responsible for the janitors in this building, I shall accept that responsibility. My first act will be to fire them all and rehire people who care about what they are doing. Is that clear?"

"Why, uh, yes...Ms. Jergens."

1.   What can we say about Dr. Caudill's ability to effectively delegate?

2.   Based on what you have just read, explain the workings of the <u>informal</u> organization at Howard School. Here's an easy question: Who is the informal leader?

3.   Why does Dr. Caudill have no right to hold Evelyn responsible for the work of janitors at her building?

4.   Do you feel that this last conversation with Evelyn Jergens will cause Dr. Caudill ro change his system on janitorial responsibilities? Explain.

ANSWERS TO TRUE-FALSE QUESTIONS

1.	T	(p. 179)	6.	F	(p. 186)
2.	T	(p. 180)	7.	F	(p. 187)
3.	F	(p. 181)	8.	F	(p. 187)
4.	T	(p. 186)	9.	T	(p. 189)
5.	F	(p. 186)	10.	F	(p. 193)

ANSWERS TO MULTIPLE-CHOICE QUESTIONS

1.	D	(p. 179)	11.	B	(p. 187)
2.	C	(p. 179)	12.	A	(p. 188)
3.	B	(p. 180)	13.	D	(p. 189)
4.	A	(p. 181)	14.	C	(p. 189)
5.	D	(p. 183)	15.	B	(p. 191)
6.	C	(p. 183)	16.	A	(p. 191)
7.	B	(p. 184)	17.	D	(p. 194)
8.	A	(p. 186)	18.	C	(p. 194)
9.	D	(p. 186)	19.	B	(p. 191)
10.	C	(p. 187)	20.	A	(p. 189)

CHAPTER NINE

MOTIVATING, SATISFYING, AND LEADING EMPLOYEES

CHAPTER OVERVIEW

The foundation of good human relations in business is a satisfied work force. Just as the rewards of high worker satisfaction and morale are great, so are the costs of poor morale and job dissatisfaction. Motivation is the set of forces that cause people to behave in certain ways. According to the classical theory of motivation, workers are motivated solely by money. Following ideas of Frederick Taylor, time-and-motion studies were performed widely in the United States, but the Hawthorne studies revealed that action on the part of management that made workers believe they were receiving special attention caused worker productivity to rise. Managers in the Theory X category believe people are naturally lazy; managers in the Theory Y category believe people are naturally energetic. Abraham Maslow has developed a hierarchy of needs, going from physiological needs up to self-actualization needs. Herzberg separated employee motivation into two categories of factors--hygienic and motivating. Expectancy theory suggests that people are motivated to work toward rewards they believe they have a chance of obtaining. Leadership is the process of motivating others to perform specific objectives. Some managerial styles are: autocratic, democratic, and free-rein. Students should be familiar with: management by objectives, participative management, quality circles, job enrichment, and modified work schedules.

LEARNING OBJECTIVES

1. Discuss the importance of job satisfaction and employee morale and summarize their roles in human relations.

2. Identify and summarize various theories of employee motivation.

3. Discuss different managerial leadership styles and their roles in human relations.

4. Describe some of the strategies used by organizations to improve employee motivation and job satisfaction.

DISCUSSION OF THE OPENING CASE

If you have read through the opening case and found yourself a little bewildered by it all, then maybe you're not as adaptable and flexible and as ready for the future as you had thought. Don't worry about it; such loose procedures may never be appropriate for the firms for which you will work. Your reaction, after reading the situation at Steelcase, might have been: "Good Heavens, how can any manager keep all of this mishmash straight. How will anything get done with every employee ministering to himself or herself first and, if intellectual energy remains, devoting some thought to the welfare of the company. Who's running the show here?" First of all, it must be kept in mind that, although we always want happy and fulfilled employees, the mission of the corporation must come first. The leaders of a company will engage in all of those "flexibilities" cited in the Steelcase narrative only so long as such a tactic benefits the company and helps the firm to reach its objectives successfully. As you will soon see, this chapter introduces the concepts of Theory X and Theory Y. Remember that Theory X managers see workers as basically lazy and ready to cheat the company at every turn, while Theory Y managers see workers as conscientious people who want to do the best possible job for the firm. With this differentiation in mind, listen to a THEORY X MANAGER commenting on Steelcase's program: "As you can see, you can't go flexible with just any set of employees. Some employees would definitely take unfair advantage of such a situation--unless the system had a series of authoritarian controls, like a time-clock to be punched in and out. For example, let your employees switch from a 40-hour work week of 5 days and 8 hours a day to a 4 day, 10 hours a day format. If you're not careful, the employees will come in a <u>little</u> early and stay a <u>little</u> later under the 4-10 plan, but you'll probably never get your full 40 hours out of them." On the other hand, a THEORY Y MANAGER would observe: "Since our employees are all highly-motivated, good-spirited workers who want to help me put this company on top, they'll work even harder with these flexible programs. Do I trust them? What an absurd question! If I couldn't trust them, I'd never have thought up this flexible plan for them."

1.   Is the Steelcase flexibility a realistic program in your eyes? Why or why not?

2.   Can you fully accept either of the statements above by the two types of managers? Which one? Why? If neither statement expresses your feelings, take a few moments to draft your own statement.

3.   Would you install a time-clock for punching in and out if you managed a firm using flexible hours or would you leave the matter on the consciences of the workers? Why?

4.   Of the flex plans revealed in the Steelcase narrative, which seems least workable to you? Explain.

ANNOTATED KEY TERMS

<u>Human</u> <u>Relations</u> - The interactions between employers and employees and their attitudes toward one another.

<u>Job</u> <u>Satisfaction</u> - The degree of enjoyment a person derives from performing his or her job.

<u>Morale</u> - The overall feeling that employees have about their workplace.

Motivation - The set of forces that causes people to behave in certain ways.

Classical Theory of Motivation - A theory of motivation that holds that people are motivated solely by money.

Time-and-Motion Studies - Studies that use industrial engineering techniques to analyze each facet of a job in order to determine how to perform it most efficiently.

Piecework System- A system of compensation in which individuals are paid a set rate per piece completed.

Scientific Management - A system of management that uses scientific analysis of individual jobs to increase productivity and efficiency.

Hawthorne Effect - The tendency for workers' productivity to increase when they believe they are receiving special attention by management.

Theory X - A theory of motivation that holds that people are naturally lazy, irresponsible, and uncooperative.

Theory Y - A theory of motivation that holds that people are naturally energetic, responsible, and growth-oriented.

Hierarchy of Human Needs - A theory of motivation developed by Abraham Maslow that describes five levels of human needs-- physiological, security, social, esteem, and self-actualization--it argues that basic needs must be fulfilled before people can seek to meet higher-level needs.

Two-Factor Theory - A theory of motivation developed by Frederick Herzberg that concludes that job satisfaction depends on two types of factors: hygienic and motivating.

Hygienic Factors - Factors that must be present to an acceptable degree in order for employees not to be dissatisfied with their jobs.

Motivating Factors - Those factors that, if increased, lead employees to work harder.

Expectancy Theory - A theory of motivation that holds that people are motivated to work toward rewards that they want and that they believe they have a reasonable chance of obtaining.

Leadership - The process of motivating others to perform specific objectives.

Managerial Style - A pattern of behavior that a manager exhibits in dealing with subordinates.

Autocratic Style - A managerial style in which managers simply issue orders and expect those underneath them to obey unquestioningly.

Democratic Style - A managerial style in which managers ask their subordinates for suggestions prior to making decisions but retain final decision-making power.

Free-Rein Style- A managerial style in which managers serve as advisors but allow subordinates to make most decisions.

Contingency Approach - A managerial philosophy that holds that the appropriate managerial behavior in any situation is dependent (contingent) on the unique characteristics of that situation.

Participative Management - A method of increasing job satisfaction by giving employees a voice in how they do their jobs and how the company is managed.

Quality Circle - A group of employees that meets regularly to consider solutions to problems in their work area.

Job Enrichment - A method of increasing job satisfaction by adding one or more motivating factors to a job.

Job Redesign - A method of increasing job satisfaction by restructuring work to achieve a more satisfactory worker-job fit.

Telecommuting - A version of flextime that allows people to do some or all of their work away from their office.

Flextime - A method of increasing job satisfaction by allowing workers to choose their working hours.

Worksharing (Job Sharing) - A method of increasing job satisfaction by allowing two or more people to share a full-time job.

TRUE-FALSE QUESTIONS

1.   Low morale often results in low turnover.

2.   The overall level of job satisfaction and morale in the United States is not very positive at this time, especially among middle managers.

3.   Employees at small firms are generally less content with their lot.

4.   According to Maslow, higher-level needs must be met before a person will seek to meet lower-level needs.

5.   Only a very low percentage of individuals meet self- actualization needs.

6. Theory X works especially well in groups that are culturally diverse.

7. Extensive rewards work best when people are learning new behavior, new skills, and new jobs.

8. Job redesign can motivate individuals with strong needs for career growth or achievement.

9. Job enrichment allows people to choose their working hours.

10. Regardless of its duration, job sharing benefits both employees and employers in most cases.

MULTIPLE CHOICE QUESTIONS

1. The interactions between employers and employees and their attitudes toward one another is defined as

   a. morale.
   b. motivation.
   c. a hygiene factor.
   d. human relations.

2. The overall feeling that employees have about their workplace is referred to as

   a. job satisfaction.
   b. motivation.
   c. morale.
   d. human relations.

3. Workers are motivated solely by money according to the

   a. two-factor model.
   b. classical theory of motivation.
   c. hierarchy of needs.
   d. contingency theory.

4. The classic book Principles of Scientific Management was written by

   a. Frederick Taylor.
   b. Elton Mayo.
   c. Abraham Maslow.
   d. Peter Drucker.

5. Managers in this category believe that people are naturally energetic, responsible, and growth-oriented, and are self- motivated and interested in being productive.

    a. Theory Z managers
    b. Theory A managers
    c. Theory X managers
    d. Theory Y managers

6. The most basic level in Maslow's hierarchy of human needs are the

    a. social needs.
    b. security needs.
    c. physiological needs.
    d. self-actualization needs.

7. The firm's pension plans and job security help to satisfy the

    a. physiological needs.
    b. security needs.
    c. esteem needs.
    d. social needs.

8. A challenging job can help satisfy a person's

    a. self-actualization needs.
    b. security needs.
    c. esteem needs.
    d. physiological needs.

9. The two-factor theory was developed by

    a. Abraham Maslow.
    b. Elton Mayo.
    c. Glen Rinker.
    d. Frederick Herzberg.

10. According to the two-factor theory, what factors affect worker motivation and job satisfaction only if they are absent or fail to meet workers' expectations?

    a. security needs
    b. social needs
    c. hygienic factors
    d. motivating factors

11. Which of the following theories suggest that people are motivated to work toward rewards that they want and that they believe they have a reasonable chance of obtaining?

    a. contingency theory
    b. expectancy theory
    c. Maslow's hierarchy of needs
    d. McGregor's Theory X and Theory Y

12. The process of motivating others to perform specific objectives is called

    a. leadership.
    b. motivation.
    c. management style.
    d. entrepreneurship.

13. Managers who adopt this style ask their subordinates for suggestions prior to making decisions but retain final decision-making power.

    a. autocratic style
    b. contingency style
    c. free-rein style
    d. democratic style

14. The military commander on the battlefield best exemplifies the

    a. democratic style of managing.
    b. free-rein style of managing.
    c. autocratic style of managing.
    d. security style of managing.

15. Managers that view appropriate managerial behavior in any situation as dependent on the elements of the situation have adopted a(n)

    a. free-rein managerial style.
    b. contingency approach to managerial style.
    c. autocratic managerial style.
    d. democratic managerial style.

16. Pay, praise, promotions, and job security are

    a. rewards.
    b. punishment.
    c. participative.
    d. negative sanctions.

17. Employees are given a voice in how they do their jobs and how the company is managed in

   a. autocratic management.
   b. free-rein management.
   c. democratic management.
   d. participative management.

18. A group of employees that meets regularly to consider solutions to problems in their work area is called a

   a. committee.
   b. board.
   c. quality circle.
   d. job redesign group.

19. A job rotation program is an example of a

   a. job redesign program.
   b. job enrichment program.
   c. flextime arrangement.
   d. job sharing program.

20. Combining tasks or establishing client relationships are ways of

   a. redesigning a job.
   b. enriching the job.
   c. sharing the job.
   d. telecommuting.

WRITING TO LEARN

1. What serves as the foundation of good human relations in business? What roles do employee satisfaction and morale have in job satisfaction?

2. Discuss the theories of employee motivation in organizations. Is there a relationship between Maslow's hierarchy of human needs and Herzberg's two-factor theory? What is expectancy theory?

3. Are there common traits of a leader? Discuss the different managerial styles commonly found in the workplace. Why is the contingency approach to managerial style important?

4.   Discuss the five common types of programs designed to make jobs more interesting, rewarding and pleasant.

5.   Why is participative management so popular among employees and employers alike? When are job enrichment and job redesign programs the most effective? What are the two most common forms of modified work scheduling?

DISCUSSION OF THE CLOSING CASE

No doubt about it, the Sam Walton account is inspiring. Reading through the Wal-Mart narrative just once makes one want to be a part of such an organization. It appears that individuals are not only respected but are rewarded for their efforts. There is a feeling throughout the entire organization that the late founder was a caring individual who realized the importance of happy, motivated people. Certainly, Wal-Mart is not the very first organization to take such an approach to its employees. Your teacher can provide other examples. In some of those other such firms, the picture was not totally rosy for every employee signed on. In an organization where people are respected for the tremendous contributions they can make, it is necessary to limit the roster to those people who are really capable of contributing and who understand how to play the game established by the firm. To be more blunt, if you don't fit in, you won't be staying around long! This is to say that you can build a strong organization with good people. But you can't do the job with bad people. It then becomes important for a growing organization to carefully filter its supply of employees, ensuring that only the "good" people remain. What we see here is a manager who must, at certain stages, be a THEORY X manager and at other stages adopt the THEORY Y strategy. As employees are added and put through their probationary periods, the manager must be saying--in harmony with THEORY X: "There is a good chance that some of these people may not want to take the initiative here in the organization, who may be uncomfortable when their supervisors expect them to perform in admirable ways. It is important that I discover such people and then weed them out." Once the probationary period has ended and final selection of new employees has been made, the manager switches to THEORY Y, saying: "Isn't it great? We have sharp employees and I can count on them to really move this organization to be the most successful in its field. I'm motivated, but some of these employees can show even me a thing or two about real motivation. It's great to be surrounded by such sharp people!" Being surrounded by sharp people, as was the case of Sam Walton with Wal-Mart, doesn't just happen. You have to carefully make it happen.

1.   Will every employee looking for a job find satisfaction at Wal-Mart? What are some types of people who might NOT find Wal-Mart their perfect setting?

2.   Overall, which did Sam Walton espouse--Theory X or is it Theory Y? Explain.

3.   Comment upon the kind of energy and enthusiasm that Sam Walton displayed. Is this approach rubbing off on Wal-Mart employees? Why or why not?

4.   Would you like to work for Wal-Mart? Why or why not?

AN ADDITIONAL CASE

Gideon Bennett has assumed the position of director of marching bands at Elijah W. Bowden High School in Iowa. It seems like a match made in heaven. Bowden High has had very good bands over the past thirty years and Gideon Bennett has had a fabulous career of marching band accomplishments with schools in Alabama and Georgia. The principal at Bowden has been warned that Gideon Bennett will "run a tight ship," but the principal also knows that Bennett's bands at Bowden will gain regional and national recognition.

In the middle of August, Mr. Bennett called a meeting of all "first team" band members, and he told the 160 students just how glorious an era was about to begin at Bowden.

"I know you're all going to be proud of what we're going to do here at Bowden in the next few months. I studied the personnel of the bands here, and I can assure you that you are fully capable not only of winning state competition in marching band but also national recognition. You are going to put Bowden on the map; I promise you that. Now, we're going to have to make a few changes. We'll rehearse before school each day at 7:15 A.M. as well as after school at 3:30. This is the way to develop a finely-tuned instrument--lots of practice."

After explaining that there was lots of work ahead, Bennett told of some of the fruits of this labor.

"Your principal tells me that the band has always formed a big 'B' on the field for Bowden. Well, as far as I'm concerned, letters are a thing of the past. From now on, we'll form words. Fortunately, for purposes of paying tribute to our football opponents, the first four schools on the schedule have short names--Lee, Taft, Tech, and East. But I know a way to spell out all of B-O-W-D-E-N, and what's more, we'll make it move down the field just the way they do it at Ohio State! In fact, anything they do at Ohio State or Michigan or Northwestern, we can do it here at Bowden. We're going to double the size of the trombone section and get the size of the band up to 200. Your principal tells me that new band uniforms are already on order. And those new uniforms will look great as we march in the Rose Bowl Parade or the Orange Bowl Parade. Yes, we're going to places like that--where Bowden bands have never gone before!"

However, Gideon Bennett never lost sight of the price to be paid for all these accomplishments.

"To get where we all want to go, it will take lots of work, and plenty of discipline on your part. I'll demand punctuality for every practice and perfect attendance. This is especially true for section leaders. During rehearsal, I will demand your complete attention. Although you may want to warm up before a rehearsal in the band room and you may want to talk things over with your section members, when I step on the podium I must have complete silence. Those who cannot go along with this feature will receive a demerit. I already have a demerit secretary ready for each rehearsal. When we rehearse outside, I shall expect complete attention--no giggling, chatting, or playing without being directed to play. All of this I call the Bennett Plan. It has developed championship marching bands for me in Alabama and Georgia, and the Bennett Plan can work here at Bowden. If you find the Bennett Plan oppressive, then turn in your uniform today. I told you I want a band of 200. But I'll settle for a brass quartet of properly-disciplined musicians instead of 200 yahoos who don't know and don't care what they're doing out on that field."

As Gideon Bennett had expected, his opening proclamation was a bombshell. None of the Bowden band members were ready for this kind of authoritarian discipline. But quite a few were willing to give the Bennett Plan their best efforts. Things went beautifully for the first few days, and students accomplished more in one Bennett rehearsal than they would have in a week under the former band director. Then it hit! Biff Buckley, head of the 12-member trombone section, was late for rehearsal three days in a row. Mr. Bennett, in a totally private conversation, said to him: "Biff, you are no longer section head. You are now the number 12 trombone. Two more tardies and you're out of the band." Biff spread the word all over school: Bennett is for real. The result was a more serious approach to bandsmanship by most members. Biff, by the way, resigned two days after his talk with Mr. Bennett.

Parents were less than happy with the two rehearsals per day. Mr. Bennett's goal of a band of 200 seemed far from reach, especially when key musicians resigned. Gideon Bennett called up eager new personnel from the "second team" band. But by the middle of the football season, a band of 160 had dwindled to 110. The remaining members, it must be pointed out, could be said to be still quite enthusiastic about the Bennett Plan, and the smaller band was a precision unit. Some parents felt the Bennett Plan was a tremendous challenge for young people to experience. Other parents were openly critical of his drill sergeant methods. One parent, Dr. Regen J. Tarsh, who had three children in the band, flatly told Bennett: "You told the kids you'd rather have a good brass quartet than a sloppy band of 200, didn't you? Well, that's what you're going to get eventually. I'm taking my kids out of the band."

Gideon Bennett had no intention of changing his tactics. He knew that eventually the students and their parents would come around to seeing things his way. And Bennett worked like a plantation slave. One night, around supper time, Gideon was still in his office behind the band room writing out a special trumpet part for a Bennett arrangement of the national anthem. A tall visitor appeared in the doorway.

"Hello, Mr. Bennett. I'm Jed Wilson. I'm an attorney in Atlanta. I had some business over in Des Moines, and I wanted to stop by to look you up. There's no way that you can remember me, but I was in your band at Athens about 25 years ago. I hated you; I fought your strict regime every step of the way. I quit the band, then begged to be let back in. You gave me that second chance. Even as late as my graduation from college I still detested the way you forced us into your 'Bennett Plan.' But as the years have gone by, I have come to respect you and what you did for me more and more and more. You gave me the discipline that got me through college and then law school. I shall always be grateful to you for that."

"Well, thank you, Jed. That's very kind of you."

"I'm not just being kind, Mr. Bennett. It's the truth. Say, how's your Bennett Plan doing here?"

"I'd have to say that I really don't know for sure."

1.   What is your opinion? How is the Bennett Plan Working?

2.   Support the contention that Gideon Bennett is a Theory X manager.

3.   Support the contention that Gideon Bennett is a Theory Y manager.

128

4. If we are assessing the success of Gideon Bennett, what help is provided to us by the appearance of attorney Jed Wilson?

ANSWERS TO TRUE-FALSE QUESTIONS

1.	F	(p. 211)	6.	F	(p. 219)
2.	T	(p. 211)	7.	T	(p. 222)
3.	F	(p. 212)	8.	T	(p. 224)
4.	F	(p. 217)	9.	F	(p. 225)
5.	T	(p. 218)	10.	T	(p. 227)

ANSWERS TO MULTIPLE-CHOICE QUESTIONS

1.	D	(p. 210)	11.	B	(p. 219)
2.	C	(p. 211)	12.	A	(p. 220)
3.	B	(p. 215)	13.	D	(p. 220)
4.	A	(p. 215)	14.	C	(p. 220)
5.	D	(p. 216)	15.	B	(p. 222)
6.	C	(p. 217)	16.	A	(p. 222)
7.	B	(p. 217)	17.	D	(p. 223)
8.	A	(p. 218)	18.	C	(p. 223)
9.	D	(p. 218)	19.	B	(p. 224)
10.	C	(p. 218)	20.	A	(p. 224)

CHAPTER TEN

PLANNING FOR AND DEVELOPING HUMAN RESOURCES

CHAPTER OVERVIEW

Human resources management is the development, administration, and evaluation of programs to acquire new employees and enhance the quality and performance of people in an organization. Human resource planning involves job analysis and forecasting. From job analysis, managers make up job descriptions and job specifications. Several things to be considered in forecasting are: projected growth; turnover; the number of older employees nearing retirement; number of candidates available; and sources of employees. The purpose of the recruitment phase is to generate a pool of potential employees. Recruiting assistance may be offered by firms called "headhunters." Internal promotion systems can be open or closed. The purpose of an orientation for new employees is to help these employees learn about and fit into the company. Employee training and development can take the form of: on-the-job training; off-the-job training; and management development systems. Performance appraisals are formal efforts to evaluate how well workers are doing their jobs. Written appraisals are extremely important in the event that workers must be terminated or demoted. Various incentive programs can be utilized. Legal and ethical issues in human resources management are: equal employment opportunity; affirmative action; reverse discrimination; equal pay; worker safety; cultural diversity; and employment at will.

LEARNING OBJECTIVES

1. Define human resource management and explain why businesses must consider job-relatedness criteria when managing human resources.

2. Discuss how managers plan for human resources.

3. Identify the steps involved in staffing a company.

4. Describe how managers can develop workers' skills and handle workers who do not perform well.

5. Explain the importance of wages and salaries, incentives and benefits programs, in attracting and keeping skilled workers.

6. Describe the legal and ethical issues involved in hiring, compensating, and managing workers.

DISCUSSION OF THE OPENING CASE

Some things defy explanation. Why some American CEOs make outrageous salaries cannot be reduced to rational reasoning. Why do professional athletes make such high salaries? Don't try to justify it; just accept it. Maybe there is a common thread running through salaries of certain CEOs and professional athletes. Here it is: a professional athlete has a limited time span in which to play games. Consequently, it is incumbent upon that athlete to make as much money as possible right now. In the same way, many a corporation's administrative framework is such that a CEO can be released without a moment's warning. Thus, such a CEO may well plot to garner as many dollars as possible while still in the good graces of the board of directors. In salary administration matters, few human resources specialists, however, will ever have to handle salaries such as those revealed in the opening case. But human resources personnel are charged with designing equitable levels of pay for persons in ordinary firms. Ironically, when it comes to executive's salaries, human resources administrators are often shut out of the process and top executives handle the matter. In so doing, the top executives often establish a most unwholesome atmosphere in which salary levels for middle managers and executives reflect a manager's **chutzpah** (nerve) more than abilities. Although salary levels are "strictly confidential," such figures quite frequently escape into the wrong venues. Then, it is normal to hear comments such as: "That nobody makes $83,000 a year for doing virtually nothing, while I put in all this extra effort for $47,000. Is that fair?" A far more wholesome atmosphere will exist when salary administrators--as well as the executives who also get into the act--can justify why certain managers make more money than others. The opposite extreme is a school system where annual pay for teachers is based solely on years of seniority and number of college degrees. Creative executives often look at such a system and sneer, opining that merit and ability are ignored. However, in the aforementioned school system pay structure, we have a ready explanation for why Mrs. Goodrich makes more money than Mrs. Franklin: Mrs. Goodrich has taught longer in the system and she has one more college degree. Explaining executive salary differences is seldom this easy.

1. What would be your reaction to learn that a colleague at work doing the same tasks as you perform received a salary that is double yours?

2. What do you think of this argument used by top executives and boards of directors: "We know we pay Mr. Carson more than his counterparts, but we had to offer that salary to get a man of his caliber."

3. Do you feel that top executives must have free rein in making salary offers to attractive middle managers from outside, or should this freedom be controlled by human resources staff members? Explain your stance.

4. What do you think of this order from the highest executive of the firm: "All middle managers, henceforth, will receive the very same salary and benefits."

ANNOTATED KEY TERMS

Human Resource Management - The development, administration, and evaluation of programs to acquire new employees and enhance the quality and performance of people in an organization.

Job-Relatedness - The principle that all employment decisions, policies, and programs should be based on the requirements of a position.

Person-Job Matching - The process of matching the right person to the right job.

Job Analysis - The detailed study of the specific duties required for a particular job and the human qualities required to perform that job.

Job Description - An outline of the objectives, key tasks, and responsibilities of a job.

Job Specification - The skills, education, and experience necessary to perform a job.

Recruitment - The process of generating a pool of applicants who are both interested in and qualified for an available position.

Headhunter - A firm that specializes in filling executive and top management positions.

Selection - The process of sorting through a pool of candidates to choose the best one for a job.

Closed Promotion System - A promotion system in which managers decide which workers will be considered for a promotion.

Open Promotion System - A promotion system in which available jobs and their requirements are posted on an employee bulletin board and in which all qualified employees are free to apply for the available positions.

Assessment Center - A multiple-day process of testing and interviewing that is used to identify candidates for promotion to higher-level executive positions.

Orientation - The initial acquainting of new employees with the company's programs, policies, and culture.

On-the-Job Training - Training that occurs while the employee being trained is at work.

Apprenticeship - A training program in which the apprentice must work at the trade for a certain amount of time before becoming a licensed specialist in that area.

Mentor - An older, more experienced employee who sponsors and teaches younger, less experienced employees.

Off-the-Job Training - A training program in which training is performed at a location away from the work site.

Vestibule Training - A form of off-the-job training in which employees work in a simulated setting under the observation of more experienced employees.

Management Development Programs - Programs that are aimed at improving the conceptual, analytical, and problem-solving skills of managers.

Performance Appraisal - A formal effort to evaluate how well a worker is performing his or her job.

Outplacement Counseling - Counseling designed to help workers cope with losing their jobs or to help workers find new jobs.

Disciplinary Action - An action taken to warn an employee that his or her performance or behavior is not meeting expectations.

Demotion - The process of moving an employee to a lower level position.

Transfer - The process of moving a worker to a completely new work setting.

Separation (Termination) - The dismissal of an employee.

Early Retirement - A program that gives older managers the option of retiring with full (or almost full) benefits before the normal retirement age.

Compensation System - The total package offered by a company in return for labor.

Wages - Money paid to workers on the basis of time worked.

Salary - Money paid to workers to get a job done.

Incentive Programs - Special pay programs designed to motivate high performance.

Merit Salary System - A compensation system that links raises to performance levels in non-sales jobs.
Bonus - A special payment, over and above wages and salaries, that is offered in return for meeting or exceeding certain goals.

Gain-Sharing Plan - An incentive program that distributes bonuses to all employees when a company's costs are reduced through greater work efficiency,

Profit-Sharing Plan - An incentive program that distributes profits earned above a certain level to employees.

Pay for Knowledge - An incentive program in which employees receive additional pay for each new skill or job they master.

Benefits - Those things, other than wages and salaries, offered by a firm to its workers.

Workers' Compensation Insurance - Insurance that provides compensation to workers injured on the job.

Employee Income Retirement Security Act ERISA - The federal law that controls how an organization manages its retirement fund and provides insurance protection for employees in the event their retirement program goes bankrupt.

Cafeteria Benefits - A flexible approach to providing benefits in which employees receive a set dollar amount to spend on benefits and are permitted to choose the package of benefits that best suits their needs.

Equal Employment Opportunity - Nondiscrimination on the basis of race, color, creed, sex, or national origin in any aspect of employment.

Affirmative Action Programs - Programs that involve the seeking and hiring of qualified or qualifiable employees from racial, gender, and ethnic groups that are underrepresented in an organization.

Reverse Discrimination - Discrimination against certain groups that occurs when an organization concentrates too much on hiring from certain minority groups.

Comparable Worth - The philosophy that different jobs requiring different levels of training and skills should be paid the same.

Occupational Safety and Health Administration (OSHA) - The federal agency that monitors firms to ensure compliance with the nation's worker health and safety laws.

Employment At Will - An organization's right to retain or dismiss employees at its discretion.

Cultural Diversity - The diversity of the population and workforce in terms of racial, ethnic, and religious background.

TRUE-FALSE QUESTIONS

1.   All managers deal with human resources.

2.   Selection is the first step in hiring workers from the outside.

3. The application blank is commonly used by people seeking managerial or professional positions.

4. In staffing the organization, requiring an applicant to take a physical exam and/or a drug test are tests whose purpose is to protect the employer.

5. Open promotion system decisions tend to be made in an informal and subjective manner, and tend to rely heavily on the recommendations of an employee's supervisor.

6. Every firm has some system for performance appraisal and feedback that helps managers and employees assess the need for more training.

7. Compensation systems are highly individualized.

8. Salaried workers are paid by the hour.

9. The use of incentive programs is decreasing in most U.S. firms.

10. The Occupational Safety and Health Act specifically forbids sex discrimination in pay.

MULTIPLE CHOICE QUESTIONS

1. All employment decisions, policies, and programs should be based on the requirements of a position according to

   a. human resource management.
   b. the EEOC.
   c. the Civil Rights Act.
   d. the principle of job-relatedness.

2. The skills, education, and experience necessary to perform a job make up the

   a. job description.
   b. job analysis.
   c. job specification.
   d. job forecast.

3. Generating a pool of potential outside employees is the purpose of the

   a. selection phase.
   b. recruitment phase.
   c. testing phase.
   d. interview phase.

4. Specialized recruiting firms used for finding applicants for executive positions are called

    a. headhunters.
    b. placement offices.
    c. recruiters.
    d. personnel departments.

5. A prepared statement of the applicant's qualifications and career goals used by people seeking managerial or professional positions is a(n)

    a. application blank.
    b. recommendation form.
    c. questionnaire.
    d. resume.

6. When available jobs and their requirements are posted on an employee bulletin board, the firm is maintaining a

    a. closed promotion system.
    b. variable promotion system.
    c. open promotion system.
    d. external promotion system.

7. A multiple-day selection process used to identify candidates for promotion to higher-level executive positions that was pioneered by AT&T is the

    a. closed promotion system.
    b. assessment center.
    c. orientation center.
    d. open promotion system.

8. New employees learn about the organization and how they "fit" into the firm through the process of

    a. orientation.
    b. training.
    c. testing.
    d. application.

9. Training that occurs while the employee is at work is called

    a. vestibule training.
    b. management development training.
    c. assessment training.
    d. on-the-job training.

10.   An older, more experienced person that provides on-the-job training is called a

      a. programmed trainer.
      b. boss.
      c. mentor.
      d. personnel specialist.

11.   Which of the following off-the-job training programs tries to enhance conceptual, analytical, and problem-solving skills?

      a. vestibule training
      b. management development programs
      c. assessment training
      d. apprenticeship programs

12.   Formal efforts to evaluate how well workers are doing their jobs are called

      a. performance appraisals.
      b. vestibule training.
      c. management development programs.
      d. compensation packages.

13.   Moving an employee to a lower level position, usually at reduced pay is a

      a. promotion.
      b. separation.
      c. transfer.
      d. demotion.

14.   Wages, salaries, incentives, and employee benefits programs are component of the firm's

      a. training program.
      b. separation agreement.
      c. compensation system.
      d. employee training and development program.

15.   Workers who are paid by the hour are receiving

      a. a salary.
      b. wages.
      c. a promotion.
      d. a profit-sharing plan.

16. Sales bonuses and gain-sharing plans are examples of

    a. incentive programs.
    b. wages.
    c. salaries.
    d. benefit programs.

17. Incentive programs that distribute bonuses to all employees when a company's costs are reduced through greater work efficiency are called

    a. profit-sharing plans.
    b. pay for knowledge plans.
    c. cafeteria benefits.
    d. gain-sharing plans.

18. A plan that provides a set dollar amount of benefits per employee and allows each employee to choose from a variety of alternatives is a(n)

    a. gain-sharing plan.
    b. merit salary system.
    c. cafeteria benefits plan.
    d. incentive program.

19. Probably the most important law in the equal employment opportunity area is the

    a. Age Discrimination in Employment Act of 1967.
    b. Civil Rights Act of 1964.
    c. Equal Pay Act of 1963.
    d. Employment-at-Will Act of 1928.

20. A policy that different jobs requiring equal levels of training and skills should be paid the same is a policy of

    a. comparable worth.
    b. employment-at-will.
    c. cultural diversity.
    d. reverse discrimination.

WRITING TO LEARN

1. What does human resource management entail? What is the principle of job-relatedness?

2. How can a manager plan for human resource needs? What are the steps involved in staffing the organization?

3. Discuss the various types of manager and employee training and development. How does a manager evaluate the performance of his workers? What steps are generally used by companies in demoting and terminating workers?

4. How does the firm compensate its workforce? What programs are used to motivate the worker toward high performance? What benefit programs are available to workers?

5. What are the major legal and ethical issues in human resource management? How can the manager effectively manage cultural diversity to achieve the companie's goals?

DISCUSSION OF THE CLOSING CASE

In an Introduction to Business course, some professors make the assumption that most of their students will, as a result of earning a college degree, wind up in a managerial role at some point after graduation. Such professors do not envision their students--with degrees--performing blue-collar functions. If there is merit to the thinking of such professors, then students in Introduction to Business should look at current problems from the vantage point of management. With that in mind, we would ask students to take this same vantage point in looking at the Johnson Controls situation in Milwaukee. What the Johnson case tells us is that even with management's best efforts to do what is right for the employee, some employees will <u>resent</u> those very efforts. To protect women with child-bearing capacity from lead contamination, Johnson Controls discontinued assigning such women to areas where lead contamination was a possibility. This move was seen by some groups as "discrimination" and not as "protection." The latest court ruling seems to be that Johnson cannot "discriminate" against women in this way; if women want to run the risk of an unsuccessful pregnancy, that is their right and privilege. Such a decision causes a great fear for Johnson Controls. A court of last appeal rules <u>TODAY</u> that Johnson Controls cannot "protect" women by keeping them away from lead contamination. The court has made Johnson powerless and has thus taken away Johnson's responsibility for the women's health. However, what is there to prevent these same women <u>TOMORROW</u> from suing Johnson Controls for their resulting unsuccessful pregnancies? A knowledge of how courts behave can lead one to conclude that a court of <u>TOMORROW</u> could very easily assess significant damages against Johnson Controls for allowing these women to work in areas of possible lead contamination. A court of <u>TOMORROW</u> could very easily be deaf to this plea from Johnson Controls: "But we were prevented <u>by the court</u> from providing any protection for these very same women. How can you now assess damages against us?" Whether we like it or not, being fair to all employees at all times in all ways is--make a note of it-- impossible!

1. Do you feel that the child-bearing-capable women of Johnson Controls, under the circumstances, should retain the right to sue Johnson Controls if they experience unsuccessful pregnancies as a result of lead contamination? Why or why not?

2. Relate the following entreaty to the Johnson Controls case and its possible aftermath: "What have they done for me lately?"

3. How would this have been as a policy at Johnson: "Any women who wish to be assigned away from the area of possible lead contamination will be so transferred--with pay in the alternate assignment being equal, now and in the future, to rates paid in the area of possible lead contamination."

4. Play the role of a company attorney. Would the proposal in Number 3 above free Johnson Controls from responsibility for the unhealthy pregnancies of the women involved?

AN ADDITIONAL CASE

(**WARNING TO OUR READERS: Many students may find themselves easily offended by the remarks to flow from the lips of Barshett Basket Company's CEO, Lothar Clark. The authors wish to emphasize that Mr. Clark is emblematic not of CEOs in general, but, instead, is symbolic of all that is wrong in a CEO, in regard to human resources decisions. The authors have created Lothar Clark to be especially offensive with the purpose in mind of underlining improper approaches to filling vacancies in corporate staffs. Get mad at Lothar if you wish, but also note the specific improper attitudes he represents.**)

Barshett Basket Company of Springfield, Missouri, has long been recognized as the largest manufacturer of wicker baskets in the world. Even before the Soviet Union broke up, the Republic of Russia imported several million Barshett Baskets per year. One of the keystones in the company's operations has been Roy Ruiz-Hernandez, Director of International Relations. It has been Roy, fluent in several languages, who has made Barshett a global firm. Now, Roy has announced his resignation so that he might assume an important position on the executive staff of the Secretary-General of the United Nations. It is up to Lothar Clark, CEO at Barshett, to select a successor. Lothar will begin the process by exploring several aspects of the search with his sidekick, Creighton Aarons, assistant to the CEO. Lothar speaks first.

"Now, Creighton, we want every middle manager in the firm to <u>think</u> that he or she has a chance at this opening that has been paying a salary of $125,000 annually. But you and I will know that this is not an open search. I already have someone in mind. But before we talk about him, I want to bounce a few basic ideas off of you. Okay?"

"Okay, Sir. But wait just a minute. Since we have government contracts that amount to some three to four million dollars every year, we are obliged to follow Affirmative Action guidelines. How can you conduct a <u>closed</u> search for a position that is this important?"

"For the record, it is NOT a <u>closed</u> search. We'll go through all the motions of a legitimate recruitment campaign that will have all the earmarks that Affirmative Action officers would love. And you can handle the smokescreen for me. We do it all the time here! Now, back to my ideas. First of all, I'm not replacing Ruiz-Hernandez with another Hispanic. That's out; no Hispanic!

In fact, I don't want any minority in this spot ever again. The very idea that to get a guy who speaks foreign languages we have to go with a foreigner is crazy. Also, we need to avoid getting some old geezer in here. Roy was 51 and starting to slow down a little."

"But, Sir, he had more energy than most people half his age."

"Not in my eyes, he didn't. I say he was slowing down. Besides, as a rule, if we bring in some young pup, we can get them for a much lower salary. These young kids don't know what to ask for. I don't want some juvenile punk in here. But if I did--and the kid had all the qualifications-- we could probably start him at half what we were paying Ruiz-Hernandez. Speaking of salary,

I'd say the spot is worth the $125,000 we had to pay Roy. If we hire a woman, we can get her to fill the spot for only $75,000-- just because she's a woman. Heck, If the girl's husband is a doctor or lawyer, and she's just out looking for 'fulfillment' in industry, we could give her $35,000 and she'd purr like a kitten. Besides, she won't know what the job is worth anyway. Yes, we could really save a bundle by getting a woman, but I won't put a woman in that job. No woman could handle it."

"But, Sir, did you know that Amy Flynn has traveled and studied abroad for many years and can speak French, Russian, German, Spanish, and Arabic, and has understudied Mr. Ruiz-Hernandez in the post of Director of International Relations. In addition, she knows the basket business."

"You didn't hear me. This time, read my lips: no woman in this job. What I want to do is bring in Fielding Riepel, the international guy at Rupert Tool and Gun. We're going to have to pirate him away from Rupert and that may take a bundle. I'm prepared to offer Riepel up to $200,000 to take the spot. He speaks only English, he has seldom traveled abroad, but he's a sharp cookie and I want him. That's it; I'm going after Riepel with a $200,000 bundle in my hand."

"You are aware, I am sure, Sir," Creighton countered, "that such a salary is way out of line when compared to what other executives in similar jobs are making here. If your director of international relations is worth $200,000, then so are the directors of production, sales, finance, and government relations. Not one of them is making over $120,000 currently."

"Don't you understand, boy? It's a matter of bargaining power. We have to pay what the market is asking for. And it's asking $200,000 for a Riepel."

"The Riepel you have sketched for me is not all that qualified for this position. You are not getting a super-star in Riepel. I know all about his performance with Rupert Tool. His secretary--a greatly-underpaid woman, by the way-- does all the

foreign correspondence for him because she knows several languages. Riepel by himself is not worth $200,000. And the drop in morale that his hiring will bring about will, I assure you, cost our firm dearly."

"Nonsense. However, in the event that Riepel doesn't fit in here--an eventuality that I do not foresee--we'll give him several weeks severance pay and send him on his way. He'll certainly be smart enough to understand that we don't have to give him a hundred reasons for letting him go. If I get to where I don't like the color of his neckties, he's out. By golly, a CEO still has some rights, you know."

"Yes, I know."

1.   In a short paragraph, give your general reaction to the staffing approach exhibited by Lothar Clark.

2.   Now, dealing in specifics, list the instances where Lothar Clark is violating some of the legal and ethical principles discussed in this chapter.

3.   Is there any truth to what Lothar Clark says about the hiring of young people for key positions such as the one being vacated by Roy Ruiz-Hernandez? Explain.

4.   How much, do you think, of the foregoing narrative is a reflection of reality in the typical workplace? Explain.

ANSWERS TO TRUE-FALSE QUESTIONS

1.	T	(p. 235)	6.	T	(p. 242)
2.	F	(p. 237)	7.	T	(p. 247)
3.	F	(p. 238)	8.	F	(p. 247)
4.	T	(p. 240)	9.	F	(p. 247)
5.	F	(p. 240)	10.	F	(p. 252)

ANSWERS TO MULTIPLE-CHOICE QUESTIONS

1.	D	(p. 235)	11.	B	(p. 244)
2.	C	(p. 236)	12.	A	(p. 245)
3.	B	(p. 237)	13.	D	(p. 247)
4.	A	(p. 238)	14.	C	(p. 247)
5.	D	(p. 238)	15.	B	(p. 247)
6.	C	(p. 240)	16.	A	(p. 247)
7.	B	(p. 240)	17.	D	(p. 248)
8.	A	(p. 242)	18.	C	(p. 249)
9.	D	(p. 244)	19.	B	(p. 249)
10.	C	(p. 244)	20.	A	(p. 252)

CHAPTER ELEVEN

UNDERSTANDING LABOR-MANAGEMENT RELATIONS

CHAPTER OVERVIEW

Labor unions are groups of individuals working together to achieve shared job-related goals, such as higher pay, shorter working hours, greater benefits, and better working conditions. The earliest formal organizations of U.S. workers emerged during the Revolutionary War with the formation of craft unions. The founding of the NTU in New York in 1834 marked the start of labor organizations with a national membership. The Knights of Labor was formed in 1869 and the American Federation of Labor in 1886. A group of industrial unions became known in 1938 as the Congress of Industrial Organizations. Since the mid-1950s, unions have experienced difficulties: falling percent of the total work force that is union; cutting back of work forces in steel and automaking; revelations of corruption within unions; givebacks; and management techniques for avoiding unionization. A shop steward acts as a liaison between union members and supervisors. In large locals, a business representative (an employee of the union) plays a similar role. Some important laws governing labor-management relations have been: Norris-LaGuardia Act, National Labor Relations Act, Fair Labor Standards Act, Taft-Hartley Amendments to the National Labor Relations Act, and the Landrum-Griffin Act. A bargaining unit of a union comes into being with the certification election. Some union tactics are: strike; picketing; boycott; and slowdown. Some management tactics are: lockout; injunction; and strikebreaking.

LEARNING OBJECTIVES

1.   Explain why workers unionize.

2.   Trace the evolution of unionism in the United States.

3.   Describe the major laws governing labor-management relations.

4.   Describe the union certification and decertification process.

5.   Identify the steps in the collective bargaining process.

6.   Discuss the future of unionism in the United States.

DISCUSSION OF THE OPENING CASE

In an earlier chapter, the textbook dealt with the Theory X manager and the Theory Y manager. The case of The New York Daily News could possibly be considered an illustration of the difference between the two. Charles Brumback apparently felt that the only way to deal with the unions at the newspaper was to get tough. Using the Theory X perception, workers are basically lazy and untrustworthy, and the only way to get them to move is to bully them. Then along came Robert Maxwell who gave all the outward signs of being a Theory Y manager. Looking from that angle, workers are highly-motivated people who want to do a good job, and both labor and management can endeavor together to establish a stable working relationship that will be pleasing to both sides. The matter of "trust" enters the picture. The Daily News union leaders perceived that they could trust Maxwell. Unfortunately, there was no similar feeling with Brumback. Leaving violence out of the picture, there is still room in labor-management relations for a plethora of dirty tricks-- perpetrated by both sides. Sometimes, however, people of character in the opposing camps can establish with one another an atmosphere of trust. If you don't believe it, just ask a high- ranking manager who must deal with the busines representatives of several unions. He or she will tell you that some relationships will just be on a higher plain than others. The manager might say of one union boss: "In over 20 years of working with her, I have never known her to misrepresent anything to me." On the other hand, you might hear: "I have learned the hard way that I cannot trust anything that Frank Brillix says to me." There may be cases in which Theory X thinking is so strong that a firm decides to break the union--get union representation out of the plant! Although union-busting is a practice of doubtful value to a firm and should not be taught as an alternative to labor peace, there have been instances in which it has been accomplished. The recent history of the Greyhound bus lines provides an example of such an effort. In these cases, a union leader might ask of his or her colleagues: "Could more clever negotiation on my part have saved our union, or had the company already determined to wipe us out regardless of how we reacted to their proposals?"

1. If a true goal of Charles Brumback was to achieve a realistic working relationship with the union employees at The New York Daily News, what advice would you have given him when he went into negotiations with the union?

2. What prevented Brumback from having even a remote chance of a successful series of negotiating sessions with the newspaper's unions? Explain.

3. Go back over the case and point out several instances of support for the unions on strike. What were some sources of aid for the company at the same time?

4. What was the biggest asset of Robert Maxwell as he began negotiating with the unions? Explain.

ANNOTATED KEY TERMS

Labor Union - A group of individuals working together to achieve shared job-related goals, such as higher pay, shorter working hours, greater benefits, or better working conditions.

Collective Bargaining - The process by which union leaders and managers negotiate common terms and conditions of employment for those workers represented by unions.

Craft Union - A union composed of workers in a specific craft or trade.

Knights of Labor - A labor union formed in the nineteenth century that used political lobbying to fight for shorter work days, better working conditions, worker-ownership of factories, and free public land for those who wished to farm.

American Federation of Labor (AFL) - A group of craft unions formed in 1866 that emphasized collective bargaining, economic action, and a pragmatic approach to union-management relations.

Industrial Union - The unionizing of employees by industry rather than by skill or occupation.

Congress of Industrial Organizations (CIO) - A group of industrial unions established in 1938 that rapidly organized the auto, steel, mining, meatpacking, paper, textile, and electrical industries.

Givebacks - Union sacrifices of previously won terms and conditions of employment.

Local Unions - Unions organized at the level of a single company, plant, or small geographic region.

Shop Steward - The employee in a unionized workplace who acts as a liaison between union members and supervisors, generally to resolve grievances.

Business Agent (Business Representative) - A person employed by a union to act as a liaison between union members and the supervisors of an organization, generally to resolve grievances.

Norris-LaGuardia Act - A federal law passed in 1932 that imposed limitations on the ability of courts to issue injunctions against union strikes and outlawed yellow-dog contracts.

Injunction - A court order prohibiting certain activities.

Yellow-Dog Contract - A contract stating that a worker does not belong to and will not join a union while employed by a firm.

National Labor Relations Act (Wagner Act) - A federal law passed in 1935 that gave most workers the right to form unions, bargain collectively, and engage in group activities to reach their goals. The law also forced employers to bargain with duly elected union officials.

National Labor Relations Board (NLRB) - The organization created by the National Labor Relations Act to administer its provisions.

Fair Labor Standards Act - A federal law passed in 1938 that set a minimum wage and prohibited child labor.

Taft-Hartley Amendments - A series of amendments to the Wagner Act that forbade closed shops, promoted open shops by allowing states to enact right-to-work laws, and provided for the settlement of strikes in certain key industries.

Closed Shop - A workplace in which only those who already belong to the appropriate union may be hired by the company.

Open Shop - A workplace in which union membership has no effect on the hiring or retaining of an individual.

Right-to-Work Laws - Laws that prohibit union shops and agency shops.

Union Shop - A workplace that requires employees to join the union within a specified period after being hired.

Agency Shop - A workplace that requires employees to pay fees to the union, even if they choose not to join the union.

Cooling-Off Period - A 60-day period in which workers in key industries are restrained from striking while negotiations with management continue.

Landrum-Griffin Act (Labor-Management Reporting and Disclosure Act) - A federal law passed in 1959 that imposed regulations on internal union procedures, requiring unions to hold elections at least every five years and to file annual financial disclosure statements with the Department of Labor.

Worker Adjustment and Retraining Notification Act of 1988 (WARN) (Plant-Closing Notification Act) - A federal law passed in 1988 stipulating that companies employing more than 100 people must give workers at least 60 days notification of a shutdown or mass layoff.

Bargaining Unit - The group of employees represented by a union.

Cost-of-Living Allowance (COLA) - A clause in an employment contract stating that wages will increase automatically in proportion to increases in the cost of living.

Strike - A labor union tactic in which workers temporarily walk off the job.

Economic Strike - A strike triggered by an impasse over mandatory bargaining items.

Sympathy Strike (Secondary Strike) - A strike by one union in sympathy with strikes initiated by another labor organization.

Wildcat Strike - A strike unauthorized by the union during the life of a contract.

Picketing - A union tactic in which workers march at the entrance to the company with signs explaining their reasons for striking.

Boycott - A union tactic in which members agree not to buy the products of a firm and may also encourage consumers to shun the firm's products.

Slowdown - A union tactic in which workers do not go on strike, but instead work at a much slower pace than normal.

Lockout - A management tactic in which employees are denied access to the workplace.

Strikebreaker - A temporary or permanent replacement for a striking employee.

Mediation - The process in which a neutral third party is called in to offer suggestions for resolving a dispute.

Voluntary Arbitration - The process in which a neutral third party dictates a settlement between two parties who have agreed to submit to outside judgment.

Compulsory Arbitration - The process in which two parties are legally required to submit to the outside judgment of a neutral third party.

Grievance - A complaint by a worker that a manager is violating the terms of an employment contract.

TRUE-FALSE QUESTIONS

1.   The earliest formal organizations of U.S. workers emerged during the First World War.

2.   The AFL-CIO is the largest union in the United States today.

3.   Fifty-four percent of wage and salary employees today are union members.

4.   The growth and decline of unionism in the United States can be traced by following the history of labor laws.

5.   The Fair Labor Standards Act established the National Labor Relations Board.

6. To date, twenty states, mostly in the South and Southwest, have enacted right-to-work laws.

7. Unions are not permanent.

8. Following union decertification, a new election cannot be requested for at least five years.

9. Most strikes in the United States are sympathy strikes.

10. Laws forbid companies from permanently replacing workers who strike because of the firm's unfair labor practices.

MULTIPLE CHOICE QUESTIONS

1. The process by which union leaders and managers negotiate common terms and conditions of employment for workers represented by the union is called

    a. negotiation.
    b. mediation.
    c. arbitration.
    d. collective bargaining.

2. The organization made up of craft unions formed in 1886 by Samuel Gompers was the

    a. Knights of Labor.
    b. CIO.
    c. AFL.
    d. AFL-CIO.

3. The organizing of employees by industry rather than by skill or occupation is referred to as

    a. collective bargaining.
    b. industrial unionism.
    c. craftism.
    d. mediation.

4. Sacrifices of previously won terms and conditions of employment are

    a. givebacks.
    b. paybacks.
    c. non-negotiable items.
    d. compulsory items.

5. Unions organized at the level of a single company, plant, or small geographic region are

   a. shop unions.
   b. closed shops.
   c. national shops.
   d. local unions.

6. A regular employee who acts as a liaison between union members and supervisors is the

   a. national representative.
   b. mediator.
   c. shop steward.
   d. arbitrator.

7. The act that set a minimum wage and outlawed child labor was the

   a. Norris-LaGuardia Act.
   b. Fair Labor Standards Act.
   c. Taft-Hartley Act.
   d. Landrum-Griffin Act.

8. The type of shop that requires employees to pay fees to the union, even if they choose not to join the union is the

   a. agency shop.
   b. union shop.
   c. closed shop.
   d. Wagner shop.

9. Laws that prohibit union shops and agency shops are called

   a. agency laws.
   b. Taft-Hartley Laws.
   c. Norris-LaGuardia Laws.
   d. right-to-work laws.

10. The act that imposes regulations on internal union   procedures is the

   a. Taft-Hartley Act.
   b. Norris-LaGuardia Act.
   c. Landrum-Griffin Act.
   d. Federal Service Labor-Management Relations Statute.

11. The law that stipulates that companies employing more than 100 people must give workers at least sixty days notification of a shutdown or mass layoff is the

   a. Taft-Hartley Act of 1947.
   b. WARN Act of 1988.
   c. Postal Reorganization Act of 1970.
   d. Norris-LaGuardia Act of 1932.

12. Workers interested in forming a union start by defining the

   a. bargaining unit.
   b. NLRB.
   c. contract terms.
   d. mediator.

13. Bargaining that involves several unions and a single organization is called

   a. union bargaining.
   b. supplemental bargaining.
   c. industry bargaining.
   d. coalition bargaining.

14. In collective bargaining, wages, working hours and benefits are referred to as

   a. permissive items.
   b. voluntary items.
   c. mandatory items.
   d. economic items.

15. Strikes triggered by impasses over mandatory bargaining items are called

   a. secondary strikes.
   b. economic strikes.
   c. sympathy strikes.
   d. boycotts.

16. When union members agree not to buy the products of the firm that employs them, they are engaged in

   a. a boycott.
   b. picketing.
   c. a slowdown.
   d. an economic strike.

17. Which of the following are not mentioned by the authors of your textbook as union tactics?

    a. economic strikes
    b. picketing
    c. a slowdown
    d. injunctions

18. Which of the following are not mentioned by the authors of your textbook as management tactics?

    a. lockouts
    b. injunctions
    c. a slowdown
    d. employing strikebreakers

19. A neutral third party dictates a settlement between the two sides, who have agreed to submit to outside judgment in

    a. mediation.
    b. voluntary arbitration.
    c. compulsory arbitration.
    d. negotiation.

20. A complaint by a worker that a manager is violating the contract is a(n)

    a. grievance.
    b. permissive item.
    c. mandatory item.
    d. boycott.

WRITING TO LEARN

1. Discuss the evolution of unionism in the United States. What are some of the difficulties that unions face today?

2. What is the organizational structure of unions? Who represents the employee or unit in collective bargaining?

3. Discuss the major federal laws governing labor-management relations. Do these laws generally favor labor or management? Have these laws had an impact on the rise and decline of unionism in the United States?

4.   How are unions organized? If conditions warrant, may a union be decertified?

5.   What is collective bargaining and how does it work? When demands are not met, what tactics are used by unions? How can management respond to a bargaining impasse? What is the difference between mediation and arbitration?

DISCUSSION OF THE CLOSING CASE

The heavy involvement of labor unions in politics brings to mind an incident many years ago on a university campus. Call this a parable, if you will. At this university, Greeks (members of fraternities and sororities) were far outnumberd by non-Greeks. As a consequence, non-Greeks <u>always</u> won such elective posts as student body president, senior class president, junior class president, etc. Then, one particular year, it occurred to the Interfraternity Council and the Panhellenic Association that Greek organizations had an advantage over the non-Greeks. This was it: "We can require each and every member of our groups to get out and vote." In the next election, <u>every</u> Greek on campus cast a ballot for a Greek candidate. You can guess what happened. The Greeks won all the positions up for election. And the last thing we heard, they were still winning every year. The Greeks, you see, had an organizational structure that allowed them to "get out the vote." The unions, too, have an organizational structure which can often translate into a solidified, unitary support for a given cause either at the polls or in other political milieus. The name of the Polish group says it all: Solidarity! Now, in the United States, individuals value their independence. We've been that way ever since 1776 and beyond. Americans, as a rule, don't like to be told how to vote. When Ronald Reagan was running for re-election as president, there were some labor unions that endorsed the opposition candidate. (There's an irony in this, since Mr. Reagan was for several years the president of a strong union, Screen Actors Guild.) Commentators in the mass media, however, indicated that when an individual member of such an anti-Reagan union got in the voting booth, that union member would vote as he or she pleased-- not necessarily the way the union had recommended to its members. In 1940, John L. Lewis, President of the Congress of Industrial Organizations (CIO) endorsed Wendell L. Willkie against Franklin Roosevelt. Although the CIO had become a strong body by 1940, Roosevelt still won by a landslide. Although labor unions have been a political force in America, have they had the impact of their comrades-in-arms in Poland and South Africa?

1.   Have labor unions in America had impact to match that in South Africa or Poland? Why or why not?

2.   How much control do you feel a labor leader has over the voting decision of an individual member of that union?

3.   In the United States as a rule, for which major party have labor unions shown an inclination? Why?

4.   Compare a Greek organization's control over its members with that of a union's control over its members--when it comes to voting.

AN ADDITIONAL CASE

**8 (a) It shall be an unfair labor practice
for an employer--**
**(1) to interfere with, restrain, or coerce
employees in the exercise of rights guaranteed
in section 7....**
(c) The expressing of any views, argument, or opinion, **or the
dissemination thereof...shall not constitute** **or be evidence of an unfair labor
practice under** **any provisions of this Act, if such expression** **contains no
threat of reprisal or force or promise** **of benefit.**

Excerpts from the Taft-Hartley Act

The necessary number of authorization cards had been signed at Feldstein Fancy Foods (FFF), and the 193 production employees would be taking part in an NLRB-controlled certification election on May 12. Supporters of both sides of the issue would be doing a limited amount of campaigning--hopefully observing limits placed on such activity by the Labor-Management Relations Act of 1947, better known as the Taft-Hartley Act. Arthur Feldstein, CEO and son of the founder, was rather disappointed that some employees felt they had to have a union to get a fair deal with FFF. Arthur knew most of the 193 production workers by name, but he was particularly well acquainted with Myrna Marbin. When Arthur was just getting started in his father's firm, serving in the human resources section, Myrna was the first job applicant he interviewed. Both were plenty nervous. But the interview went well, and Myrna was hired. Arthur thought Myrna would be willing to tell him something of the employees' motivation for seeking union representation. They talked over coffee.

"Myrna, would you mind telling me why our employees--at least some of them--feel that they have to bring a union aboard?"

"Not at all, Mr. Feldstein. Although working conditions here have always been super, our paychecks haven't gone up with the cost of living. Some of us used to complain to your father; it did no good. He'd throw in a raise when he was good and ready. Then, a year ago, when you took over, we thought things would be different. You remember I came to you on behalf of the assembly line workers, asking for a meeting on wages? You turned me down cold. I didn't know where to turn. When some union organizers got hold of Becky Threet, we all listened to his pitch. It made good sense, and here we are."

"This whole thing is over wages?"

"That's it."

"But you could have talked to me first."

"I did. You wouldn't listen."

"It's not too late. I'd like to hold a meeting of the production workers and give my side of the story."

"That would be fine with us."

In the past, production worker meetings were held just before the day's shift started. No overtime was paid for arriving extra early, but there was plenty of free coffee. This time, Arthur Feldstein, sensing that this was a sensitive issue, decided to hold the meeting on "company time." So, instead of having the shift start at its usual 7:30 A.M., the meeting came at 7:30 and the shift would start only after the meeting was over. Production time would be lost, but Arthur thought this new plan a good idea. Instead of just free coffee, there was an abundance of coffee rolls and doughnuts available, and all employees were encouraged to take as many as they liked. When the relatively happy group was settled, Arthur began. "I hear you've scheduled a union election here for May 12. I'm pretty disappointed in myself because I haven't given you the feeling that I was approachable on matters such as pay. Myrna Marbin and I started here just about the same time and Myrna still calls me Mr. Feldstein. Golly, folks, I'm Arthur, and I am approachable. I know you have financial problems just like everyone else. And because of that I am happy to announce that effective with your pay envelope this Friday, each of you will receive an 11 percent increase. I say effective this Friday; that's really a misuse of the term. You'll see the difference this Friday, but the change itself will be retroactive to 60 days ago. In addition, we're going to hold an election to let you pick a committee of five workers to come to me regularly with any and all complaints--including problems with your wages. I want to know what you think about things. I'm sorry it took this union shock to wake me up."

Arthur sat down to a standing ovation and shouts of "Arthur, Arthur, Arthur." The meeting was adjourned and the 193 production workers started to work for the day. At any spare moment, workers would be chatting about Arthur's new attitude.

"Will this attitude last, or when we turn down the union will he be just as sour as before? There have been times when I've passed him in the hall and he didn't even speak."

"I think he's sincere. I think he'll be fair, and that committee idea for complaints is great. I see no need for a union coming in here."

"I think he's trying to bribe us. He's saying, in so many words, 'I'll give you more money if you'll vote down the union.' I don't know if that's right. The office staff aren't getting a raise merely because they're not threatening to form a union bargaining unit."

"Don't worry about the office staff; they were overpaid anyway."

All of the talk ended on May 12. All 193 production workers voted, and the count was 83 FOR the union and 110 AGAINST. The very next morning, the business representative with the union local that had attempted to organize the FFF workers decided to file a complaint with the National Labor Relations Board. He cited a violation of Sections 8(a)1 and 8(c) of the Taft-Hartley Act.

1.   Has Arthur Feldstein really changed his ways or is this just a tactic to keep the union out of Feldstein Fine Foods? Explain.

2.   Specifically (getting down to individual words and phrases), which part of the Taft-Hartley Act has Arthur possibly violated?

3.   This new committee that Arthur is going to form, can it be as effective at negotiating with Arthur as a union representative would be? Why or why not?

4.   If the NLRB nullifies the election on grounds that Arthur violated Taft-Hartley, what can Arthur do--prior to the next election--to show the employees he is sincere in wanting to change his ways?

ANSWERS TO TRUE-FALSE QUESTIONS

1.	F	(p. 263)	6.	T	(p. 271)
2.	T	(p. 266)	7.	T	(p. 273)
3.	F	(p. 266)	8.	F	(p. 273)
4.	T	(p. 270)	9.	F	(p. 275)
5.	F	(p. 270)	10.	T	(p. 276)

ANSWERS TO MULTIPLE-CHOICE QUESTIONS

1.	D	(p. 263)	11.	B	(p. 272)
2.	C	(p. 264)	12.	A	(p. 273)
3.	B	(p. 265)	13.	D	(p. 274)
4.	A	(p. 268)	14.	C	(p. 275)
5.	D	(p. 268)	15.	B	(p. 275)
6.	C	(p. 269)	16.	A	(p. 276)
7.	B	(p. 271)	17.	D	(p. 276)
8.	A	(p. 271)	18.	C	(p. 276)
9.	D	(p. 271)	19.	B	(p. 276)
10.	C	(p. 272)	20.	A	(p. 276)

CHAPTER TWELVE

PRODUCING GOODS

CHAPTER OVERVIEW

Utility is want satisfaction, and there are four utilities that would be impossible without production. These are the utilities of time, place, ownership, and form. Production management is the systematic direction and control of the processes that transform resources into finished goods. We classify production in three ways: by transformation technology; by whether the process is analytic or synthetic; and by the pattern or product flow. Production managers have three very broad responsibilities: planning; organizing; and controlling. Qualitative forecasts come from experts who use their best judgment. Quantitative forecasts come from special statistical methods. Plant layout alternatives include process layout, product layout, fixed-position layout, and customer-oriented layout. A master production schedule shows which products will be produced, when production will occur, and what resources will be used in the coming months. Short-term, detailed schedules provide information and direction concerning daily and weekly activities. Materials management is the planning, organizing, and controlling of materials from purchase through distribution of finished goods. Some tools for production control are: the just-in-time inventory system; material requirements planning; Gantt and PERT charts; and quality circles. Mechanization and automation of production will involve, in the future, greater use of computers and robotics.

LEARNING OBJECTIVES

1. Classify a business's production processes in three ways and explain the role of production managers.

2. Identify three major areas of production planning and two levels of production scheduling.

3. Describe the activities of materials management in manufacturing, and list five tools for production control.

4. Characterize the kinds of automation currently in use in production operations.

5. Explain the advantages and risks of small versus large production companies.

DISCUSSION OF THE OPENING CASE

In numerous chapters of this textbook and student study guide, a paramount fact that will be stressed is that conditions outside the plant's gates will be in a constant state of change. This means that any firm, large or small, must be ready to adapt to such changes. Now, the secret to successful adapting does NOT consist in waking up one morning to discover a changed situation and then reacting quickly to it. No, the primary key to successful adapting is to be alerted that drastically-changed conditions are just over the horizon. ADVANCE preparations, then, must be made to adapt to them. The problem that ensues here is that those persons who are able to peer into the middle- distance future are usually neither believed nor trusted. When these specialists deal in unpleasant predictions, they are particularly suspect. In fact, forecasters, seers, futurists, planners (call them what you will), are often seen as a funny gaggle of researchers. Here's an example of a dire prediction that few wanted to accept. In 1980, the United States, for political reasons we shall not delve into through this commentary, did not send a team to the Summer Olympics in Moscow. The 1984 Olympics were scheduled for Los Angeles. As early as 1980, a statistics teacher at a Midwestern university (helping his students understand the concept of "probability"), predicted that for 1984 there would be no team from the Soviet Union present at Los Angeles! Most colleagues and students scoffed at such an idea. That statistics teacher never corresponded with the Olympic officials overseeing the Los Angeles preparation for the 1984 games. But surely, someone in that group must have allowed for such an unpleasant development, and made plans to cope with this eventuality. Because of such planning, despite the fact that the Soviets did indeed NOT come to L.A., the Olympics there were a tremendous financial success--something rare in such events. In like manner, someone within the Deere organization at some point must have said: "Projecting from economic conditions that are gradually worsening for farmers, I see in the intermediate future a terribly shrinking market for our standard products. We must develop other products for other markets." Such a gloomy prediction may have felt discordant upon the ears, but the benefit gained from this alert could have served the company well. And a continuing flow of predictions of the middle-distance future will always be as important to a firm as water to a camel.

1.   Again, what were some signs that planners at Deere could have used to predict that basic farm equipment sales could well be dropping?

2.   What did the Deere Company do to compensate for slackening demand for basic farm equipment?

3.   If success of a firm like Deere depends on some knowledge of agriculture as an industry, what do you say of the wisdom of hiring a planning specialist from General Motors to handle planning for John Deere? Is the difference in the industries likely to be a major problem? Explain.

4.   Why would people in 1980 not want to hear of the Soviets passing up the 1984 Olympics at Los Angeles? What does your answer to this first question say about people's general attitudes toward planners with bad news? Explain. How should a good executive react to "bad news?"

ANNOTATED KEY TERMS

Utility - A product's ability to satisfy a human want.

Time Utility - The satisfaction created when a product is made available at the time that consumers want it.

Place Utility - The satisfaction created when a product is made available at a place that consumers want it.

Ownership (Possession) Utility - The satisfaction created by ownership of a product.

Form Utility - The satisfaction created through the conversion of raw materials into finished goods.

Production (Operations) Management - The systematic direction and control of the processes that transform resources into finished goods.

Production Process - The set of methods and technology used in the production of a good.

Analytic Process - A production process in which resources are broken down into components.

Synthetic Process - A production process in which raw materials are combined to create a finished product.

Continuous Process - A production process in which the product moves through the plant in a fairly smooth, straight, and continuous manner.

Routing - The unique set of steps required to produce a product.

Intermittent (Job Shop) Process - A production process in which the product flows through the plant in a stop-and-go fashion and through a seemingly scattered arrangement of equipment and departments.

Forecasts - Estimates or predictions about the future.

Capacity - The amount of a good that a company can produce under normal working conditions.

Industrial Park - A planned site created by a city to attract new industry. These sites come with the necessary zoning, land, shipping facilities, utilities, and waste disposal outlets already in place.

Process Layout - A way of organizing production activities such that equipment and people are grouped together according to their function.

Product Layout - A way of organizing production activities such that the resources being processed move through a fixed, smooth sequence of steps to become finished goods.

Assembly Line - A type of product layout in which a partially finished product moves through a plant on conveyer belts or other equipment, often in a straight line.

U-Shaped Production Line - A type of product layout in which machines and workers are placed in a narrow U shape rather than in a straight line.

Methods Improvement - A technique that identifies and eliminates the wasted operations in a production process by examining each step of production in close detail.

Flexible Manufacturing - A type of manufacturing system that allows businesses to respond rapidly when demand changes or when new products must be introduced into the marketplace quickly.

Fixed-Position Layout - A way of organizing production activities such that labor, materials, and equipment are brought to the location where the work is done.

Customer-Oriented Layout - A way of organizing production activities such that the interactions between a firm's customers and its services are enhanced.

Master Production Schedule - A general, rather than highly detailed, schedule showing which products will be produced, when production will take place, and what resources will be used in the coming months.

Production Control - The managing and monitoring of production performance.

Follow-Up - In production control, checking to ensure that production decisions are being implemented.

Materials Management - The planning, organizing, and controlling of the flow of materials from design through distribution of finished goods.

Standardization - The use of standard and uniform components, where possible, in the production process.

Holding Costs - The costs of keeping extra supplies or inventory on hand.

Lead Time - The time between placing an order and receiving shipment of that order.

Inventory Control - The receiving, storing, handling, and counting of all resources, partly finished goods, and finished goods.

Just-in-Time (JIT) Production System - A method of production control that brings together all materials and parts needed at each production step at the precise moment when they are required for the production process.

Material Requirements Planning (MRP) - A method of production control in which a bill of materials is used to ensure that the right amounts of materials are delivered to the right place at the right time in the production process.

Bill of Materials - A "recipe" for the production of a batch of a good that specifies the necessary ingredients (raw materials and components), the order in which they should be combined, and how many of each ingredient are needed to make one batch of the product.

Manufacturing Resource Planning (MRP II) - An advanced version of MRP that ties together all parts of an organization into the company's production activities.

Gantt Chart - A diagram laying out the steps to be performed in the production process, and the time required to complete each step.

PERT (Program Evaluation Review Technique) - A method of diagramming the steps in the production schedule along with the projected time to complete each step, taking into account the sequence of those steps and the critical path of those steps.

Critical Path - The sequence of steps in the production of a good or service whose time is crucial to completing the job on time. Any delay in any activity on the critical path will delay the entire project.

Quality Control - The management of the production process so as to manufacture goods or supply services that meet specific quality standards.
Mechanization - The process of using machines to do work previously done by people.

Automation - The process of performing mechanical operations with either minimal or no human involvement.

Soft Automation (Flexible Automation) Systems - Automation systems that allow machines to be adaptable to perform several functions.

Hard Automation - Automation systems in which each machine is dedicated to performing just one specific function.

Dispatching - The issuing of work orders for the production of a particular item.

Robotics - The construction, maintenance, and use of computer- controlled machines in manufacturing operations.

Computer-Integrated Manufacturing (CIM) - Computer systems that drive robots and control the flow of materials and supplies in production. CIM can also manage material requirements planning and just-in-time production systems.

Computer-Aided Design (CAD) - Computer analysis that allows users to create a design and simulate conditions to test the performance of the design, all within the computer. Also called computer-aided engineering (CAE).

Computer-Aided Manufacturing (CAM) - Computer systems used to design and control the equipment needed in the manufacturing process.

Decision Support Systems (DSS) - Computer systems used to help managers consider alternatives when making decisions on complicated problems.

TRUE-FALSE QUESTIONS

1. Farmers are production managers.

2. Combining data on employee absences and machine breakdowns into a productivity report is a fabrication process.

3. Printing shops are an example of a continuous process operation.

4. Quantitative forecasts come from an expert (or group of experts) who use their best judgment to predict the future.

5. A firm's capacity depends on how many people it employs and the number and size of its facilities.

6. Machine shops, wood working shops, and dry-cleaning shops usually have product layouts.

7. High quality goods also have high warranty costs.

8. Standardization increases the number of different parts and materials.

9. JIT reduces the number of goods in process.

10. Manufacturing is the hardest industry for small businesses to break into because of the extensive resource requirements.

MULTIPLE CHOICE QUESTIONS

1. Economists refer to want satisfaction as

   a. supply.
   b. demand.
   c. equilibrium.
   d. utility.

2. By turning raw materials into finished goods, production creates

   a. time utility.
   b. place utility.
   c. form utility.
   d. ownership utility.

3. The set of methods and technology used in the production of a good is called

   a. utility.
   b. a production process.
   c. form utility.
   d. operations management.

4. The transformation process common in the aluminum, steel, fertilizer, petroleum, and paint industries is the

   a. chemical process.
   b. fabrication process.
   c. assembly process.
   d. transport process.

5. In which of the following processes are basic resources broken down into components?

   a. continuous process
   b. intermittent process
   c. transport process
   d. analytic process

6. Stroh's breweries, RJR Nabisco's tobacco and food divisions, and Ford all use

   a. intermittent processes.
   b. analytic processes.
   c. continuous processes.
   d. chemical processes.

7. The amount of a good that a company can produce under normal working conditions is its

   a. process.
   b. capacity.
   c. position layout.
   d. degree of automation.

8. Planned sites, created by cities interested in attracting new industry, that come with the necessary zoning, land, shipping facilities, utilities, and waste disposal outlets already in place are

   a. industrial parks.
   b. shopping centers.
   c. warehouses.
   d. residential districts.

9. Process layouts are well suited to

   a. slow periods.
   b. assembly lines.
   c. U-shaped production.
   d. job shops.

10. Automobile plants, food processing plants, and computer assembly factories use

    a. process layout.
    b. job shops.
    c. product layouts.
    d. chemical processes.

11. The Japanese environment that allows businesses to respond with speed when the demand for existing products suddenly changes or when new products must be introduced quickly into the marketplace is called

    a. methods improvement.
    b. flexible manufacturing.
    c. product layout.
    d. process layout.

12. Which of the following shows which product(s) will be produced, when production will occur, and what resources will be used in the coming months?

   a. a master production schedule
   b. a product layout
   c. a process layout
   d. detailed schedules

13. Purchasing large quantities of materials to fill a firm's needs for a long time is the practice of

   a. hand-to-mouth purchasing.
   b. lead timing.
   c. standardization.
   d. forward buying.

14. The additional earnings the company must pass up because of having funds tied up in inventory is called

   a. cost savings.
   b. forward buying.
   c. opportunity costs.
   d. the firm's break-even point.

15. Downtime for machines and workers while dies and molds are being changed are items included as

   a. materials inventory.
   b. setup costs.
   c. opportunity costs.
   d. process costs.

16. Ben and Jerry's Homemade, Inc., ice cream makers uses which of the following tools for production control to manage the entire ice cream production system?

   a. MRP II
   b. MRP
   c. PERT
   d. JIT

17. Which of the following production control tools is useful in planning, organizing, and controlling major projects that involve customized production and depends on coordination of production activities?

    a. JIT
    b. MRP
    c. Gantt Charts
    d. PERT

18. Using machines to do work previously done by people is the process of

    a. automation.
    b. production.
    c. mechanization.
    d. robotics.

19. The Japanese have pioneered flexible automation systems that allow machines to be adaptable to perform several functions. The flexible systems are also referred to as

    a. hard automation.
    b. soft automation.
    c. Gantt charts.
    d. robotics.

20. The manufacturing automation system that controls robots and the flow of materials and supplies in production as well as managing material requirements planning and JIT production systems is called

    a. CIM.
    b. CAD.
    c. CAM.
    d. DSS.

WRITING TO LEARN

1. What is utility? Describe the four basic types of utility. How may processes be classified? What are the responsibilities of the production manager?

2. What is the role of the production manager in production planning and scheduling? Why is production control and materials management important to the firm?

3. Is it important to have plenty of supplies on hand for production? What costs are involved in maintaining inventory? What tools are available to the manager for production control?

4. What are Gantt and **PERT** charts? How can these charts help managers control the overall production process? Can quality circles help in solving production problems?

5. Is there a difference between mechanization and automation? Will computers and robotics used in manufacturing help us increase productivity?

DISCUSSION OF THE CLOSING CASE

Although the current chapter deals with production, the concept of quality control can be applied to many business aspects other than production. As the Allied Automotive case illustrates, there are certainly costs to quality. A realist--or was it a cynic--once said that quality <u>control</u> can have two meanings. The first meaning is the generally-accepted meaning which refers to controlling the production process to such an extent that predetermined levels of quality will be maintained. In this traditional approach, the process must be stopped and corrected if it is determined that items resulting from that process are not measuring up to high quality requirements. The <u>second</u>, or darker, meaning of quality control is as follows. A firm must <u>control</u> the expenses and effort that will be directed toward the maintaining of quality. This notion carries with it the idea that a firm is not seeking perfection, is not seeking error-free production processes, is not seeking an absence of customer complaints. To pursue such lofty goals would mean terrific expenses that the firm may not be willing to assume. And such expenses must be <u>controlled</u>. A firm adhering to the latter definition of quality control will set a level of quality that it thinks it can afford, and will seek to maintain that level. Allied Automotive had a choice to make. By seeking to <u>control</u> quality expenses, the firm could probably not have made a deal with Toyota. Toyota wanted more of a quality commitment than that. By setting extremely high quality standards, however, Allied lost some control of quality expenses, but gained an amazing degree of control over what was coming out of its production processes. As of this writing, Allied Automotive would be most likely to say that the expenses and trouble have been worth it, for they have gained Toyota as a significant regular customer.

1.   What do you think of the cynic's idea that it is often quality <u>expense</u> that must be controlled?

2.   Do you feel that the Toyota quality standards were unrealistically high? Why or why not?

3.   Go back over the case and identify areas in which extra expenses were incurred by Allied in order to meet Toyota standards.

4.   How much of the correction process at Allied was accomplished by reorienting the employees' attitudes toward quality? Explain.

AN ADDITIONAL CASE

"Flowers by Fleming" is an expression that is known the world over. It is more than an expression; it is the name of one of the largest distributors of artificial floral designs--Flowers by Fleming (FBF). The innovation that put FBF over the top was its exquisitely-packaged "Floral Octette." The octette box consisted of eight plastic vases, each filled with a different floral arrangement. The idea behind the octette was to colorfully decorate your dining-room table with a vase of flowers that would be changed every week for eight weeks. Then, start the rotation all over again. Apartment dwellers from Paris to Baghdad found the "Floral Octette" a superb way to provide a creative touch to the dinner table. The octettes sold just as fast as Flowers by Fleming could manufacture them. By the time a first octette began to lose its novelty, customers came back to buy a totally- different set.

Keeping the world supplied with artificial flowers brought in attractive revenues--but it also incurred giant costs for the acquisition of raw materials. It was also discovered by the board of directors that flagrant and costly inefficiencies existed throughout the operation of the mammoth FBF plant in Walston, New Jersey. The way to correct matters, the board reasoned, was to replace their current CEO with David J. Riskin, a capable administrator who had gained a reputation as the "efficient physician." What this meant is that if your plant had an efficiency problem, ol' Dr. Riskin could provide the appropriate medicine.

"The first thing I'm going to do," Riskin told the board after his first week on the job, "is to rent out that huge warehouse I call 'Madison Square Garden' to an anxious tenant who is willing to pay an exhorbitant fee to move in his company."

"You're going to do WHAT?" board chairman Harry Fleming shouted. "That's where we keep our valuable inventory. That's the repository of all the raw materials we use to make products for the entire globe! My father bought that huge gym and by golly FBF is going to keep it in the business."

"Not if I'm the CEO." And David J. Riskin was serious. "You ladies and gentlemen have hired me to cut out the waste here at Flowers by Fleming, and that building symbolizes several types of waste. May I proceed?"

"Continue."

"First of all, we can certainly make use of the cash that will come from a monthly rental income on that facility. Second, we can eliminate virtually our entire inventory-control crew because there will be no inventory in that building anymore. Third, we can cut down on purchases and accounts payable that ensue when you keep a two-month supply of raw materials in a big barn like that warehouse." There was some gasping by board members. Finally, one got up the courage to say: "Now, just a minute here. Let me see, Mr. Riskin, if I can get this straight. You're planning to eliminate our inventory of vases and flowers. Swell! Then, please be kind enough to tell me how you are going to assemble the 'Floral Octettes' when you don't have any raw materials in house."

"Raw materials will arrive at our incoming loading dock as we need them. We start our production line at 8:00 A.M. each day, and raw materials to support one day's manufacturing will start arriving at 5:00 A.M. When the assembly crews arrive, their raw materials will be in place. By the end of each day, there will be no raw materials left on hand."

"What makes you think, Mr. Riskin," Chairman Fleming wanted to know, "that our suppliers will go along with your scheme?"

"I've already talked with several of them. One of our vase providers, for example, knows that 93 percent of his sales go to us. If he wants to keep our business, he will adapt to the new plan. Several of the flower suppliers have us as their sole customer. They'll want to cooperate fully."

"But you're setting up a pretty tight and precise schedule to be adhered to by a flower supplier all the way down in south Georgia. How are they going to have a truck at our dock every working day?"

"That Georgia supplier and I have already had extensive talks. We are making it very attractive for them to move their operation up to within twenty-five miles of our plant here in New Jersey. In fact, I have several suppliers who are willing--in due time-- to locate much closer to our plant. Ideally, every one of our suppliers should be just across the street. Of course, that's impossible."

"Although you're getting rid of a huge stand-by inventory on our premises, you may be forcing the suppliers to hold the large inventories instead. And suppose there is a breakdown in the system some morning. Will our production come to a halt?"

"To answer your first comment, these suppliers operate on a much smaller scale than do we, and there will be no big buildups of stock there. Second, for us there will be no breakdowns on any morning. To ensure that this will be the situation, I'm asking every supplier to prepare emergency plans that will enable their deliveries to always be here as needed. For those who balk, I may just have to pick another supplier. You see, under my scheme for FBF, the emergency plans fall on the suppliers and not on Flowers by Fleming."

The members of the board of directors were stunned. After their first few questions, they didn't quite know what to say. Chairman Fleming quietly summed up the collective reaction of the board: "This is so revolutionary that we don't have a whisper to offer in rebuttal."

"Revolutionary? You think this is revolutionary?" David Riskin asked. "My friends, the Japanese have been doing it this way for decades."

1.   Here's a very simple question. What have the Japanese been calling this innovation that Riskin is bringing to FBF?

2.   Is it realistic for Riskin to assume that suppliers will be as cooperative with him as he has indicated. Why or why not?

3.   Is Riskin wise to assume that emergencies will be taken care of by the suppliers--and not by FBF? Why or why not?

4.   If this type of inventory control becomes the new way for all American industry to operate, what does it say about having suppliers located geographically near the manufacturers they serve? Explain.

ANSWERS TO TRUE-FALSE QUESTIONS

1.	T	(p. 295)	6.	F	(p. 304)
2.	F	(p. 297)	7.	F	(p. 305)
3.	F	(p. 298)	8.	F	(p. 306)
4.	F	(p. 302)	9.	T	(p. 308)
5.	T	(p. 302)	10.	T	(p. 314)

ANSWERS TO MULTIPLE-CHOICE QUESTIONS

1.	D	(p. 295)	11.	B	(p. 304)
2.	C	(p. 295)	12.	A	(p. 306)
3.	B	(p. 296)	13.	D	(p. 307)
4.	A	(p. 297)	14.	C(p. 307)	
5.	D	(p. 297)	15.	B	(p. 308)
6.	C	(p. 298)	16.	A	(p. 308)
7.	B	(p. 302)	17.	D	(p. 309)
8.	A	(p. 303)	18.	C	(p. 312)
9.	D	(p. 304)	19.	B	(p. 312)
10.	C	(p. 304)	20.	A	(p. 313)

CHAPTER THIRTEEN

PRODUCING SERVICES

CHAPTER OVERVIEW

Service operations are business activities that provide services to their customers. In 1991, employment in service industries constituted 80 percent of the work force in the United States. As with the production of goods, production of services provides form, place, and time utility. It could be said that goods are produced and that services are performed. Services are looked upon as intangible, and services are typically customized. Services are characterized by a high degree of perishability. Since a space on an airline flight "perishes" when there is a "no show," airlines often overbook so that there will be no empty seats. Hotels and theaters face the same challenge of perishability. Services can be high-contact (restaurants, taxicabs, schools, medical clinics) or low-contact (banks, insurance, news syndicates, mail-order services). Service operations management can be divided into planning, scheduling, and control phases. Demand for and supply of services can be managed. Some service operations use pricing to shift demand to nonpeak periods--for example, cheap movie tickets for the early show. Supply of services can be managed by the use or non-use of part-time help. Just as in manufacturing a product, quality control is essential in the service industries. Publicized recognition of superior performance by an employee and monetary incentives are ways to keep service at a high level of quality.

LEARNING OBJECTIVES

1.   Identify the characteristics of services that make their production different from that of goods.

2.   Classify services according to the extent of customer contact and their similarity to manufacturing.

3.   Describe the major decisions in service operations planning and scheduling.

4.   Explain how managers can control the quantity and quality of services offered.

5.   Identify ways to overcome the special problems of service operations management.

DISCUSSION OF THE OPENING CASE

The United Parcel Service (UPS) case emphasizes the business phenomenon known as competition. First of all, let it be said that an entrepreneur does NOT always face competition.

You've read of a firm "finding its niche" in the market. This often means that an enterprise has found a service to provide that will not be duplicating a service already available. Sometimes such a niche is so distinct that it avoids competition altogether. However, if a firm in that niche is extremely successful, then you can bet that someone else will come along and try to operate in that same niche. Sometimes, a firm may elect not to compete in specific areas. For example, for many years, UPS chose not to compete in air transportation of packages. At some point, however, UPS officials decided that--in most aspects, at least-- their firm would compete directly against Federal Express. In the terminology of niche picking, it was decided that UPS would work in the very same niche that Federal Express had chosen; this would be direct head-to-head competition. Such a decision is a serious one that should not be made without prolonged consideration of the advantages and disadvantages entailed. In head-to-head competition, you must keep up with your rival or get off the playing field. Your rival may undertake extremely costly innovations in order to serve the public better. When this happens, you do not have the luxury of deciding whether or not you wish to engage in such an outlay of funds. You match the outlay of funds and continue to stay up with the rival, or you get out of the game. A middle course can often be to withdraw from a particular portion of the field of valor. Ask your teacher to tell you of the large American corporations that initially became heavily engaged in the manufacture of computers. These were giant firms with splendid reputations in appliances, electronics, etc. But at some point these firms concluded that continuing to compete in the computer field against the rising giant IBM would be a costly mistake. In essence, such firms were saying: "We're strong, we're competitive, but we're choosing NOT to compete in computers." So, for UPS the course is clear. You must stay up with Federal Express's every innovation and expansion of service or take your bat and ball and go home.

1. From what you can observe, how is United Parcel Service doing in its competition with Federal Express? Explain.

2. From what you may have gleaned from the case narrative and from watching television ads for UPS and Federal, are the two services clones of one another--and thus head-to-head competitors? Why or why not?

3. Read again what the case wrap-up says about United Parcel's corporate culture. Would you like to work for UPS? Why or why not?

4. Read the case wrap-up again. If you took a job with UPS, would you be tempted--just once--to fasten your seat belt with the right hand? Why or why not?

ANNOTATED KEY TERMS

Service Operations - Business activities that provide services to their customers.

High-Contact System - A service organization in which the customer must be a part of the system to receive the service.

Low-Contact System - A service organization in which the customer need not be part of the system to receive the service.

Pure Services - High-contact services in which the customer is part of the service production process. Pure services have no inventoriable products.

Quasimanufacturing - Low-contact services in which the customer need not be part of the service production process.

Mixed Services - Moderate-contact services in which the customer is involved in the service production process to a limited degree. Mixed services combine some characteristics of pure services with some characteristics of quasimanufacturing.

Service-Flow Analysis - A method of designing and improving services that involves labeling the flow of processes that make up the service and identifying potential problem areas.

Cross Training - Training employees to perform a variety of jobs.

Shared Capacity - An arrangement in which several individuals or companies share equipment, office space, or personnel.

Search Qualities - Qualities in a product that can be perceived prior to purchase by sight, hearing, or touch.

Experience Qualities - Qualities in a product that can be perceived after purchase by sight, hearing, or touch.

Credence Qualities - Qualities in a product that a purchaser believes to exist, but that are not subject to objective proof.

TRUE-FALSE QUESTIONS

1. Employment in service industries constituted almost thirty percent of the work force in the United States in 1991.

2. Employment in service industries has been much less stable than employment in goods industries.

3. All businesses are service operations to some extent.

4. Services are typically characterized by a low degree of perishability.

5. It is much harder to manage a high-contact system than it is to manage a low-contact system.

6. In low-contact systems, managers must plan capacity to meet peak demand.

7. In a low-contact service, work scheduling is based on desired completion dates or on the time of order arrival.

8. The executive suite concept is an example of cross training.

9. Most services have few search qualities.

10. Having customers as part of the process complicates the production of services.

MULTIPLE CHOICE QUESTIONS

1. Business activities that provide services to their customers are called

   a. production activities.
   b. manufacturing activities.
   c. line operations.
   d. service operations.

2. Stouffer's Hotels and Restaurants, Saks Fifth Avenue, and Fox Broadcasting Company are all

   a. manufacturing firms.
   b. domestic organizations.
   c. foreign owned.
   d. production oriented firms.

3. Goods are produced, while services are

   a. extracted.
   b. performed.
   c. uniform.
   d. manufactured.

4. All services have some degree of

   a. intangibility.
   b. production.
   c. low perishability.
   d. consistent quality.

5.   A public transit system is an example of a

        a. utility.
        b. mixed service.
        c. production operation.
        d. high-contact system.

6.   Gas and electric utilities, auto repair shops, and lawn care services are examples of a

        a. production operation.
        b. high-contact system.
        c. low-contact system.
        d. substitute technology.

7.   Hair styling or surgery are examples of

        a. quasimanufacturing.
        b. pure services.
        c. mixed services.
        d. low-contact systems.

8.   A main post office is a good example of

        a. quasimanufacturing.
        b. mixed services.
        c. pure services.
        d. a low-contact system.

9.   Deciding where to locate a service organization is especially important in

        a. mixed services.
        b. manufacturing organizations.
        c. low-contact services.
        d. high-contact services.

10.   Which of the following shows the flow of processes that make up the service and makes it
        easy to identify whether all the processes are necessary?

        a. facility layout
        b. overlapping layouts
        c. service flow analysis
        d. system design

11. McDonald's uses which of the following to provide maximum coverage during peak periods?

   a. quality control
   b. overlapping shifts
   c. frequent, unannounced recalls of employees
   d. cross training

12. Family night at the ballpark, matinee prices at movie theaters, and weekend long-distance telephone rates are examples of techniques for

   a. managing demand for services.
   b. confusing the customer.
   c. overlapping cost structures.
   d. controlling supply.

13. Training employees to perform a variety of jobs in a firm is called

   a. quality control.
   b. positive recognition.
   c. overlapping.
   d. cross training.

14. The executive suite concept is an example of

   a. cross training.
   b. quality control.
   c. shared capacity.
   d. tangibility.

15. When a product is a physical good, customers can see or touch its

   a. credence qualities.
   b. search qualities.
   c. experience qualities.
   d. custom qualities.

16. The value customers believe the service delivered is called

   a. credence quality.
   b. search quality.
   c. experience quality.
   d. custom quality. 17.Which of the following is not identified by the author of your textbook as a strategy for lowering the level of customer contact?

17. Which of the following is not identified by the author of your textbook as a strategy for lowering the level of customer contact?

   a. reservation
   b. payment
   c. consumption
   d. part-time help

18. Perishability of services means there is a potential for

   a. increasing demand.
   b. increasing supply.
   c. waste.
   d. reservation.

19. Which of the following is a high-contact service?

   a. repair shops
   b. schools
   c. mail-order services
   d. research labs

20. Which of the following is not a low-contact, quasimanufacturing service?

   a. medical clinics
   b. mail-order services
   c. news syndicates
   d. research labs

WRITING TO LEARN

1.   What are service operations? Has service sector employment grown over the past twenty-five years? How are service and manufacturing operations similar? How are they different?

2.   How are service operations classified? What are some examples of high, medium and low contact services?

3.   Discuss the capacity and location planning, scheduling, and control phases of service operations. Relate each phase to high and low contact services.

4.   Is it possible to control the quantity and quality of services? What techniques can be used to manage demand and control supply? How can training and motivating workers affect the success or failure of the business?

5. Discuss how intangibility, customization, perishability and the presence of customers within the production process create special problems for service operations managers. Provide some examples of how a service manager might reduce the level of customer contact.

DISCUSSION OF THE CLOSING CASE

When we read of Humana's attempt at "vertically integrated health care," we see an aggressive new approach that didn't quite work to perfection for the corporation. With such a result, there is a natural human tendency to write off the experiment as a failure. Here's an example of that "writing off." After observing many crashes of eccentric people in odd contraptions around the turn of the century, some people concluded that the idea of an object heavier than air being able to fly was a crazy notion. It would never work! Even when the Wright Brothers made their historic flight of a few seconds, skeptics said: "But what good is it going to do someone to stay in the air for a few seconds. You can't get to Saint Paul in that short a time." Such critics could not see that there would be improvements and refinements on what the Wright Brothers had done. Although Humana's grand scheme didn't come off completely as planned this time, the same tactic could work at another time in our nation's history. The funding of nursing home care went through such an experiment some time ago. The idea was that a well-to-do retired person would make a lump sum donation to a retirement-housing facility. The sum was to ensure that the housing facility would take care of the retired person until the latter's death. This meant that nursing home services, if they were needed, would be provided by the housing facility. The problem was that the lump sums asked for were too small to fund the responsibility that the housing facilities were taking on. Such plans, then, had to be greatly modified. Unfortunately, in some cases, these housing facilities had to file for bankruptcy. Such failure, tragic though it may be, does not necessarily signify that the idea was a poor one. This attempt to fund nursing home care in advance was a superb idea! With people living so much longer now than in generations past, we must find ways to cope with care of the elderly. But the implementation the first time around was flawed. It may work the next time. Likewise, wise health- provider planners will not write off the Humana vertical integration attempt as a failure. Instead, they will see it as a possible way of the future--if implemented well. Goodness knows, the field of health care is in need of some new approaches to a problem that seems to be growing more complex with the passing of each year.

1. Despite the difficulties it ran into, do you feel there will be a need for vertically integrated health care such as that specifically envisioned by Humana? Why or why not?

2. Comment upon the consequences of Humana taking a "cavalier attitude" toward area doctors.

3. Do you feel that doctors sometimes take a "cavalier attitude" toward their patients? Why or why not?

4. If you were directing Humana at the time of the vertical-integration attempt, where are some places you would have coordinated matters before jumping off with the new approach?

AN ADDITIONAL CASE

Achilles Airlines, "Passageway of the Gods," operates several direct flights between Paris and Athens. Rather than taking pride in listing all the world capitals that it serves, Achilles specializes in just one run--Paris to Athens, and back. To cover this run adequately, there are twenty-four flights per day--one every hour. We had wanted to furnish specifics on the type of aircraft used by Achilles, but their public relations officer at Athens told us that there have been some recalls on these planes, and the airline does not want to publicize mechanical problems that Achilles and other carriers have been experiencing with their aircraft. The officer was willing to tell us that the planes carry an average passenger list of 300 persons.

With so many flights along the one route, there are seldom booking problems. Since Achilles has just the one run, it never transfers baggage and thus the problem of Achilles being blamed for lost baggage is avoided. With just the one route in operation, Achilles tries to keep its rate structure simple. For example, it even toyed with the idea of making the entire plane one class-- no tourist, no first-class, no business class, etc. But that was eventually deemed to be a little too creative. However, a little adjustment in fares has been utilized by Achilles. As you might guess, requests for Achilles flights on Friday afternoon and early evening are engulfing. Greek business people want to head home after a week of business affairs in Paris. The same goes for French in Athens. A similar phenomenon develops on Monday mornings--as business people head for a foreign capital. To relieve this bottleneck a little, the airline offers special discounts to those people who will avoid the Friday and Monday rushes. In addition, if you're willing to travel between midnight and 5:00 A.M., you receive still another discount.

Air fares on Achilles will reflect just how pressing is the competition furnished by other airlines along this same route. As a result, there may be frequent changes in the rates. However, the following figures will provide some idea of what it costs to fly the "Passageway of the Gods." Keep in mind that these figures may be absolutely out of tune with rates existing at this very moment. If you call Achilles and seek to book a Paris- Athens flight, do not expect the following rates to prevail. The standard tourist round-trip rate that is in force during the business rush hours is $400. For those willing to avoid the rush period, the fare is $275. If you select a flight that operates between midnight and 5 A.M., the fare is $200.

Alcibiades Nachridonides, CEO of Achilles, has from the very beginning tried to establish an organization in which every employee feels himself or herself an important factor in the success of the firm. Although Alcibiades has a clearly- delineated organizational chart that is familiar to all employees, he has always preached innovation of each employee at each level of command.

"I can't be in all places at the same time," he has often been quoted as saying. "So, I want each of you to be a little Alcibiades. Whatever you're doing, wherever you are, do what you think Alcibiades would do. And always do it for the good of the company. Will your supervisor block this kind of initiative? Of course not, and I'll tell you why! I've assembled around me supervisors who are motivated and who want people under them who are motivated and ready to try things a new and better way."

In this atmosphere of individual initiative, there will be employees of the firm who may step forward a little too far. Alcibiades must be careful in allowing such a person to be reprimanded, for such a criticism could turn down the flame of initiative--throughout the entire airline. For this reason, the matter of Didier Lafont was particularly fascinating to your case writers.

Didier Lafont works at the ticket counter of Achilles Airlines at De Gaulle Airport in Paris. Since he is a 20-year-old full-time student at l'Universite de Paris, Didier works from 10:00 P.M. to 6:00 A.M. At such hours, he is pretty much on his own. In July, Didier was written up by his supervisor (who is present for only about half of Didier's shift) for "giving away seats on flights from Paris to Athens." The report of the supervisor went on to say that in so doing, Didier "had severely hampered the inflow of revenues for Achilles Airlines."

By one of those quirks of organizational life, the matter could not be settled at the ticket-counter level. Three layers of management touched the case, each taking a dim view of Didier's actions. The affair reached the desk of Alcibiades Nachridonides himself. When he had thoroughly investigated the case, Alcibiades called in the three supervisors and explained what had happened.

"Didier Lafont observed that Flight 977, scheduled to leave Paris at 3:00 A.M. on July 25, had 100 empty seats. In a rather quiet terminal at that hour, Didier noticed a group of Swedish college students sleeping all around the lounge area. With a little inquiry, he learned that they were on a whirlwind tour of the world--traveling 'wherever the wind blows.' Ideally, they told him, they would catch a special British jet flight for $200 to Chicago at dawn. Didier told them they could all catch a round- trip flight to Athens for FIFTY DOLLARS. One hundred Swedish students jumped at this special bargain price and made the 3:00 A.M. flight to Athens. That, I take it, is what you supervisors have been calling 'giving away' airline tickets. Do my findings harmonize with your findings?"

"Yessir."

"Well, I'm giving Didier a promotion! When he saw that he could put 100 students on a flight with 100 empty seats, he moved into action. Since the flight had fixed costs, it would cost the same to send that plane to Athens with or without those 100 students. You supervisors are right. The fare for one of those seats should have been $200. But those students didn't have that kind of money for this particular trip. By selling tickets at a reduced rate, he brought us revenues of $5,000--money we would never have made if those students hadn't taken that flight. Didier understood the concept of.... Well, I needn't bother you folks with that, you know the nature of services."

1. What is that concept that Didier understood? Here's a hint: Didier knew that those 100 seats would be of no value to the firm once the plane took off at 3:00 A.M.

2. Should Didier's action cause Achilles officials to rethink the rates for middle-of-the-night flights? Why or why not?

3. Comment upon this advertisement to appear in college newspapers all across Europe. "College students: Going to Athens? There's no cheaper way than the 3:00 A.M. special flight from Paris at special low rates for students. Call your travel agent for details or dial direct--Achilles Airlines. You won't believe how cheaply we can take you to Athens and back."

4. Has Didier hit upon an idea that might make it possible for Achilles to pack _every_ flight it operates between Paris and Athens? How would you set up a "never-an-empty-seat" campaign?

ANSWERS TO TRUE-FALSE QUESTIONS

1.	F	(p. 323)	6.	F	(p. 329)	
2.	F	(p. 324)	7.	T	(p. 333)	
3.	T	(p. 324)	8.	F	(p. 336)	
4.	F	(p. 326)	9.	T	(p. 338)	
5.	T	(p. 328)	10.	T	(p. 340)	

ANSWERS TO MULTIPLE-CHOICE QUESTIONS

1.	D	(p. 323)	11.	B	(p. 334)
2.	C	(p. 324)	12.	A	(p. 335)
3.	B	(p. 325)	13.	D	(p. 336)
4.	A	(p. 325)	14.	C	(p. 336)
5.	D	(p. 327)	15.	B	(p. 338)
6.	C	(p. 327)	16.	A	(p. 338)
7.	B	(p. 328)	17.	D	(p. 339)
8.	A	(p. 328)	18.	C	(p. 339)
9.	D	(p. 329)	19.	B	(p. 328)
10.	C	(p. 331)	20.	A	(p. 328)

CHAPTER FOURTEEN

MANAGING INFORMATION WITH COMPUTERS

CHAPTER OVERVIEW

Data are raw facts and figures. Information is based on data, but it is a meaningful, useful interpretation of data. A management information system (MIS) is an organized method of transforming data into information that can be used for decision making. MIS needs will vary with the managerial level. Four features that make a computer useful in business are: speed of processing; accuracy of processing; ability to store programs; and ability to make comparisons. Every computer system has five parts: hardware; software; people; control; and data. Most applications programs fall into one of four categories: word processing; spreadsheets; database management; and graphics. Four basic categories of computer systems are: microcomputers; minicomputers; mainframes; and supercomputers. System architecture can be classified as centralized, decentralized, or distributed. A computer network is a group of interconnected computer systems at different locations that are able to exchange information. The modern history of computers can be broken down into five "generations," with the latest of these being characterized by artificial intelligence, expert systems, office automation, and manufacturing information systems. The computer has proven itself to be extremely useful to small businesses.

LEARNING OBJECTIVES

1. Discuss why a business needs to manage information and how computers have revolutionized information management.

2. Identify the five components of a computer system and four major types of business applications programs.

3. Categorize computer systems by size and structure.

4. Trace the history of computers.

5. Discuss trends in business information management.

DISCUSSION OF THE OPENING CASE

No doubt about it, there is plenty in the Compaq case to interest a computer buff. But among the several messages that it conveys is one that seems to run counter to many success stories. In such stories, we see a business idea put into action on a most modest scale by an entrepreneur who dreams first of having a profitable small business. If the entrepreneur has yearnings to command a vast industrial empire, we usually don't hear about those yearnings in the early stages of the account. We are apt to pick up the idea that all businesses must start out small. Look, for example, at the McDonald Brothers of Southern California. They started with a hamburger stand, so the legend goes, and were completely happy with a most successful small business operation. Their one or two burger stands would still be operating as individual entities to this very day if Ray Kroc hadn't dropped by their place. It was Kroc who changed the McDonald's concept from a local phenomenon into a mammoth international franchise success. The approach of the McDonald Brothers was different from that of Rod Canion, William Murto, and Jim Harris of Compaq. We are told that, right from the very beginning, the three thought of their firm as one that would very quickly have national impact. Beyond just thinking that way, the three made plans for that broad scope. A best example of this is the accounting system that was looked upon by some as "overkill at the start." Yes, it would be overkill for a small computer equipment store, but not for a national marketer of a new computer concept. The Hewlitt Packard 3000 minicomputer, far too ambitious for a small local store, was just right for the new far-horizons Compaq corporation. But the key, perhaps, to the success of Compaq is a key that can make the difference with a small business as well. The three founders--Canion, Murto, Harris--were extremely astute in surveying the computer landscape and locating a niche for their new firm. The whole tale of Compaq is crammed with instances of the firm detecting exactly what they were going to do in this lucrative--but highly competitive--market. There may have been, and still may be, major mistakes by Canion, Murto, and Harris, but as a rule, they are brilliant operators.

1.   Show several contrasts between the McDonald Brothers of Southern California and Canion-Murto-Harris.

2.   Provide some examples of how Canion-Murto-Harris took advantage of current conditions in the computer industry.

3.   What do you suppose Canion-Murto-Harris would say to an offer by IBM to acquire Compaq? Explain

4.   What are some of the possible pitfalls of planning and financing on a large scale the way Compaq did?

ANNOTATED KEY TERMS

Data - Raw facts and figures.

Information - A meaningful, useful interpretation of data.

Management Information System (MIS) - A system designed to transform raw data into information that can be used for decision making.

Garbage In Garbage Out (GIGO) - If a computer is given the wrong data to process, it is likely to give back incorrect information.

Computer System - An electronic method of turning data into information. Its five components are hardware, software, people, control, and data.

Hardware - The physical components of a computer system.

Input Device - A device through which data is entered into the computer system.

Central Processing Unit (CPU) - The part of the computer system in which data processing takes place.

Bit - A way of representing data in a computer as one of two digits (0 or 1); abbreviation for binary digit.

Byte - A series of eight bits that, together, represent a single character in a computer.

Primary Storage - The part of the computer's CPU that houses the computer's memory of those programs it needs in order to operate.

Control Unit - The part of the computer's CPU that locates instructions, transfers data to the arithmetic logic unit for processing, and transmits results to an output device.

Program - A sequence of instructions to a computer.

Arithmetic Logic Unit (ALU) - The part of the computer's CPU that performs logical and mathematical operations.

Output Device - The part of a computer system that presents results to users, either visually on a screen or in printed form.

Secondary Storage - Any medium that can be used to store data and information outside the computer's primary storage facility.

Hard Disks - Rigid metal disks that are permanently enclosed in the computer; used for storing data and information.

Floppy Disk - Portable disks that can be easily inserted into and removed from the computer; used for storing data and information.

Software - Programs that instruct the computer in what to do.

System Program - A program that tells a computer what resources to use and how to use them.

Language Program - A program that allows users to give the computer their own instructions.

Application Program - A program that processes data according to the special needs of the user.

Database - A centralized, organized collection of related data.

Batch Processing - A method of transforming data into information in which data is collected over a period of time and then processed as a group or batch.

Real-Time Processing - A method of transforming data into information in which data is entered and processed as soon as it is collected.

Word Processing - Application programs that allow computers to store, edit, and print letters and numbers.

Electronic Spreadsheet - Application programs that allow the user to enter data and determine the effect of changes in one category (e.g., materials costs) on other categories (e.g., expenses and profits).

Database Management - Applications programs that keep track of all relevant data in a business.

Modem - A computer-to-computer link via telephone wires.

Computer Graphics - Applications programs that convert numeric and character data into pictorial information such as graphs and pie charts.

Microcomputer - The smallest, slowest, least expensive form of computer available today.

Minicomputer - A computer whose capacity, speed, and cost fall between those of microcomputers and mainframes.

Mainframe - A computer whose capacity, speed, and cost fall between those of minicomputers and supercomputers.

Supercomputer - The largest, fastest, most expensive form of computer available today.

System Architecture - The way in which a computer system's data entry, data processing, database, data output, and computer staff are located.

Centralized System - A form of computer system architecture in which all processing is done in one location, using a centralized staff of systems analysts and programmers with a centralized database.

Decentralized System - A form of computer system architecture in which processing is done in many locations, using separate databases and computer staffs.

Computer Network - A group of interconnected computer systems at different locations that are able to exchange information with one another.

Local Area Network (LAN) - A network of computers and workstations, usually within a company, that are linked together by a cable.

Wide Area Network - A network of computers and workstations located far from each other and linked together by telephone wires.

Debugging - Removing problems from a program so that it can be carried out smoothly.

Transistor - A tiny electronic device that controls the flow of electric current without the need for a vacuum tube; used by the second generation of computers.

Integrated Circuit - A group of transistors and other electric components integrated onto a silicon chip; used by the third generation of computers.

Microprocessor Chip - A single silicon chip, the size of a paper clip, that contains the computer's central processing unit; used by the fourth generation of computers.

Large Scale Integration (LSI), Very Large Scale Integration (VLSI) - The inclusion of many circuits with different functions on a single chip; used by many fourth-generation computers.

Artificial Intelligence - The construction and programming of computers to imitate human thought processes.

Expert System - A form of artificial intelligence that attempts to imitate the behavior of human experts in a particular field.

Electronic Mailbox - A computer system that can electronically transmit letters, reports, and other information between computers.

Fax Machine - A machine that can transmit copies of documents and graphics over telephone lines.

TRUE-FALSE QUESTIONS

1. Information is less condensed and summarized as it moves up through the management hierarchy.

2. Computers do not have the ability to make comparisons.

3. Information is available for use only after it has been transferred into primary storage, never while it is in secondary storage.

4. A production manager who receives a weekly report on inventory is a programmer of the computer system.

5. Computers convert data into information.

6. Floppy disks can retrieve and process data faster than hard disks.

7. Centralized systems are often less efficient and less responsive to the needs of users at remote locations than are decentralized systems.

8. Debugging refers to removing problems from a program so that it can be carried out smoothly.

9. So far, no one is quite sure what the third generation of computers will be like.

10. A major business application for the future of artificial intelligence is in robotics.

MULTIPLE CHOICE QUESTIONS

1. Raw facts and figures are

   a. information.
   b. word processing software.
   c. management information systems.
   d. data.

2. Which of the following is designed to transform data into information that can be used for decision making?

   a. decision support systems
   b. word processing software
   c. management information systems
   d. system programs

3. Which of the following is not mentioned by the authors of your textbook as a feature that makes computers useful in business?

   a. speed of processing
   b. GIGO
   c. ability to store programs
   d. ability to make comparisons

4. The physical components of a computer system are referred to as

   a. hardware.
   b. software.
   c. programs.
   d. decision support systems.

5. Punched cards, a magnetic tape, a mouse, and a keyboard are examples of

   a. software.
   b. decision support systems.
   c. the central processing unit.
   d. input devices.

6. Logical functions and calculations are performed in the

   a. hard drive.
   b. software.
   c. arithmetic logic unit.
   d. input devices.

7. Rigid metal disks that are permanently enclosed in the computer are called

   a. floppy disks.
   b. hard disks.
   c. software.
   d. programs.

8. Programs that tell the computer what resources to use and how to use them are called

   a. system programs.
   b. application programs.
   c. word processing programs.
   d. secondary storage programs.

9. Lotus 1-2-3 and WordPerfect are examples of

   a. hardware.
   b. system programs.
   c. analysis hardware.
   d. application programs.

10. Personnel who write the instructions that tell the computer what to do are

    a. operations personnel.
    b. end-users.
    c. programmers.
    d. systems analysts.

11. A method of transforming data into information in which data is collected over a period of time and then processed as a group is called

    a. word processing.
    b. batch processing.
    c. real-time processing.
    d. systems programming.

12. Programs that keep track of and manipulate all relevant data in a business are called

    a. database management programs.
    b. spreadsheet programs.
    c. wordprocessing programs.
    d. decision support services.

13. Lexis deals solely with legal materials and is an example of a

    a. spreadsheet program.
    b. wordprocessing program.
    c. graphics program.
    d. secondary database.

14. The largest, fastest, and most expensive form of computer available today is the

    a. microcomputer.
    b. minicomputer.
    c. supercomputer.
    d. mainframe computer.

15. Teller machines at all branches of a bank that need to have the same information, would generally have a system architecture described as a

    a. computer network.
    b. centralized system.
    c. decentralized system.
    d. LAN.

16. A group of interconnected computer systems at different locations that are able to exchange information with one another is called a

   a. computer network.
   b. centralized system.
   c. microcomputer.
   d. management information system.

17. The British mathematician who is often called the "Father of Computers" is

   a. Herman Hollerith.
   b. Howard Aiken.
   c. Steven Jobs.
   d. Charles Babbage.

18. A small electronic device that controls the flow of electric current without the need for a vacuum, whose application marked the start of the second generation of computers is the

   a. microprocessor chip.
   b. integrated circuit.
   c. transistor.
   d. LSI circuit.

19. The construction and programming of computers to imitate human thought processes is called

   a. debugging.
   b. artificial intelligence.
   c. generation.
   d. CAD.

20. A system that can electronically transmit letters, reports, and other information between computers is a(n)

   a. electronic mailbox.
   b. fax machine.
   c. expert system.
   d. CAM machine.

WRITING TO LEARN

1.   What is the difference between data and information? Do different levels of management have different information needs? What features do computers provide to business that make them useful?

2.   Describe the elements of a computer system. What people are involved in the construction and use of a computer system? Discuss the four categories of computer applications for business.

3.   How are computer systems categorized? Discuss the three types of system architectures covered in your textbook.

4. Discuss the history of computer systems. What is the difference between the third and fourth generation of computers?

5. What will the fifth generation of computers be like? How can artificial intelligence be used in business? What is an expert system. Describe today's attempts to automate the office.

DISCUSSION OF THE CLOSING CASE

This case contains a lesson that has been heard before--many times--but which still deserves repeating. It is a lesson that we think of as being aimed at older people, but many young entrepreneurs show their need for the teaching. The lesson is: Things do not stay the same, they are in a constant state of change. Many a business has faltered because it assumed that the current situation would remain intact forever. History is filled with entities that once prospered, but then either lost their luster or completely faded away: canal traffic, the Pony Express, the telegram, the stagecoach, minor-league baseball, silent movies, network radio, vaudeville, the rumble seat, drive-in movies, passenger-train travel. Change can be exciting but it can also be painful. That latter quality sometimes forces us to hope that matters will remain static for awhile. There is an irony in this lesson being taught to us yet another time with the computer industry being used as the example. The irony is that it has been the computer industry that has been the agent of change for numerous other industries. Take, for example, a small aspect of the publishing business. It wasn't too many years ago that the words you would be reading in a study guide, such as this one you now hold in your hands, would have originated on a portable typewriter--not even electric--wielded by some tired, old professor in a dusty basement office of an ancient classroom building somewhere in the vast Midwest. That professor may well have started the writing process by sketching out thoughts on a yellow pad with a stubby Number 2 pencil. TODAY, to produce these words, a sharp, young faculty member sits at a word processor in a bright and sunny office with a big picture window looking out on a verdant campus--making use of floppies, hard drive, hard copies, backup diskettes, perhaps even modems. It has been the computer that made the difference. It has been the computer industry that has shown authoring professors, as one limited example, that they had to get rid of that old portable typwriter and be a part of the modern word-processing world. Now, the supreme irony is that the computer industry is experiencing first-hand that nothing is stable and that their own industry is entering new phases. The secret to survival is to adapt to altered states of the market. The computer industry is no exception.

1.   The case seems to hint that so many computers have been sold that the world is saturated. Do you agree? Why or why not?

2.   Do you agree that the number of computer companies worldwide will be reduced drastically by the year 2000? Why or why not?

3.   What kind of prediction would you make concerning the fate of IBM between now and the year 2000? Will Big Blue gobble up smaller competitors?

4.   Based on what you already know of Compaq, do you feel that Compaq will be one of the surviving firms between now and the year 2000? Why or why not?

AN ADDITIONAL CASE

(If this were the year 1960, a case that attempted to sell students on the marvels of the computer would certainly be in order. However, in the mid-1990s, just about every college freshman understands and uses computers, and thoroughly believes they are highly-capable tools. Making believers of students is not the challenge. Many students in business courses will graduate from college and move gradually into managerial positions. It is in these leadership spots that these graduates will still be faced with convincing <u>others</u> of the wonders of the computer. The industry spotlighted in the following case has largely made its peace with computerization, although there still remain exceptions, just as there will remain pockets of resistance to the computer up until the world has lost its spin.)

Michael Scott was a successful political writer for several newspapers in Chicago. He came by the skill naturally because he had been raised in a journalistic family. Michael's father and uncle operated <u>The Mansfield Star-Bulletin</u>, a respectable and highly-profitable Southern newspaper with a circulation of some 89,000. In the middle of 1993, Michael Scott received the distressing news that his uncle, the surviving member of the old ownership team, had passed away. It was at the funeral that an attorney revealed for the first time that Michael Scott was the sole heir to <u>The Mansfield Star-Bulletin</u>. For the first time, Michael learned that not only was his uncle the only owner of the paper, but the chief operating officer as well. His death left a gaping hole in the organization. Michael Scott felt honor-bound to fill that hole.

Moving from the journalistic world of Chicago to what was happening with the <u>Star-Bulletin</u> turned out to be a major shock for Michael. He knew the Dixie newspaper was solid, stable, and profitable and operated basically free from viable competition. But the paper was years behind Chicago! Perhaps the thing that bothered Michael the most was the antiquated way that the reporters and columnists put together their stories. Although the main editorial offices resembled a set for a 1930s movie about a newspaper, that wasn't a problem. A good newspaper office needs a "quaint touch." No, the major drawback was how the writers put words on paper!

In one corner of what journalists call the "city room," Mary McCarthy, the religion editor, was using an early-model word processor, and she was very happy with the results. Everyone else used a typewriter, and not all of the machines were electric. Michael just could not tolerate this. So, he held a meeting of all editorial employees and explained that word processors were being ordered and would arrive shortly. Not only did he explain how a good word processor can help in the development and editing of a story, but the press room would be set up so that some last-minute stories could be networked directly to the presses, after a quick check for proofing (both human and electronic). When a reporter handed over a diskette to an editor, the latter would be able to quickly alter the piece and then send it on to the composition people virtually ready for the press room.

Fortunately, many of the editorial employees applauded the announcement of the word processors being on order, with comments equivalent to: "It's about time." This gave Michael the impression that it was his uncle who had stood in the way of the computers before. But, much to Michael's surprise, several of the staff were clearly negative. Typical of this group would be Hal Turner. "When I signed on here in 1954," Hal said, "I had just come back from the Korean War. That was a heyday of the American newspaper. I was given a brand-new portable typewriter and it has served me well. I keep it in good repair, and it has never caused me to miss a deadline--never! The kind of police reporting that I do does not call for some fancy gimmickry with those little diskettes being passed around like sandwiches." Several others of Hal's era said "amen" to his arguments.

"Neverthless," Michael responded, "the word processors will arrive soon, and I'll expect you to use them--for the good of the paper."

Then, Sam Parker stood up to say his piece. Sam was 71 years of age and had served as the sports editor of the Star-Bulletin for some thirty years. Old Sam had been in that spot when Michael Scott was just a kid. Michael knew a word from old Sam, elder statesman of the staff, could bolster any resistance to the word processors. Although Michael respected old Sam, he hated to hear his words.

"Here's how I feel about the word processors coming to the Star- Bulletin. This is the way the industry is moving--has already moved--and there is no way that we can live in the Dark Ages any longer. Yesterday is nothing. It's today and tomorrow that really count. We can't afford to cling to those relics of a bygone era. As for me, I can't wait for my new word processor to arrive. It'll take me a time to learn to use it, but I know I'll be better off keeping up with what this business is doing TODAY-- not yesterday! I can't wait to throw away my old clunker of a typewriter. Thank God you've come, Michael, to rescue us from the clutches of an era that has long since passed."

Michael was stunned, but delighted.

Although Sam Parker waded into learning word processing and praised the change, three of his younger sports staff had great difficulty adapting. He encouraged them and helped them at every stage. Two writers of editorials, Joe Hunt and Esther Tyler, had shiny new word processors sitting on their desks but they still produced copy with typewriters. Michael Scott told one of the proofreaders: "Some night, I'm going to come steal the typewriters from those two guys, and they'll be forced to convert."

Fortunately, that wasn't necessary. The "incident of the lost editorial" won over Hunt and Tyler. By a freak occurrence, a copy boy LOST an editorial that Esther Tyler had labored over for a full afternoon. Michael Scott told her: "If you'd done that on your word processor, you'd have several kinds of backup." Next morning, Esther took the cover off of her word processor.

1.   Do you feel that the lost editorial was indeed a "freak occurrence," or perhaps a contrived ploy? Explain your answer.

2.   Comment upon the attitude of Sam Parker, the elder sports editor. What is the likelihood of finding a 71-year-old with Parker's approach to the innovation?

3. What are some more drastic measures that Michael Scott could have taken to "sell" his word processor approach to the more resistant members of the staff?

4. Report on a business similar to <u>The Star-Bulletin</u> that experienced some difficulty in switching to word processors.

ANSWERS TO TRUE-FALSE QUESTIONS

1.	F	(p. 350)	6.	F	(p. 361)
2.	F	(p. 352)	7.	T	(p. 363)
3.	T	(p. 354)	8.	T	(p. 366)
4.	F	(p. 355)	9.	F	(p. 367)
5.	T	(p. 357)	10.	T	(p. 368)

ANSWERS TO MULTIPLE-CHOICE QUESTIONS

1.	D	(p. 349)	11.	B	(p. 357)
2.	C	(p. 350)	12.	A	(p. 359)
3.	B	(p. 351)	13.	D	(p. 359)
4.	A	(p. 352)	14.	C	(p. 361)
5.	D	(p. 352)	15.	B	(p. 363)
6.	C	(p. 352)	16.	A	(p. 365)
7.	B	(p. 353)	17.	D	(p. 366)
8.	A	(p. 354)	18.	C	(p. 366)
9.	D	(p. 354)	19.	B	(p. 368)
10.	C	(p. 354)	20.	A	(p. 368)

CHAPTER FIFTEEN

UNDERSTANDING ACCOUNTING ISSUES

CHAPTER OVERVIEW

Accounting is a comprehensive information system for collecting, analyzing, and communicating financial information. Bookkeeping, just one phase of accounting, is the recording of accounting transactions. Certified public accountants (CPAs) derive their name from the fact that they are members of firms who offer accounting services to the public. Virtually all CPA firms provide three types of services: audit services, tax services, and management services. Private accountants are salaried employees of a specific company and perform for that firm a variety of services. A third category is a non-certified public accountant. A journal is a chronological record of financial transactions. Ledgers are summations of journal entries. The accounting equation is: Assets = Liabilities + Owners' Equity. An asset is anything of value owned by the firm. A liability is a debt the firm owes to others. Owners equity is the amount of money a firm's owners would receive if they sold all the firm's assets and paid off its liabilities. Double-entry bookkeeping requires that all transactions be recorded in two ways. A balance sheet presents the firm's assets, liabilities, and owners' equity. The income statement contains descriptions of a firm's revenues and expenses and it results in a figure on the firm's profit or loss. By using statistics and ratios, we can analyze and compare financial statements from different firms. Accounting functions are easier with the help of the computer.

LEARNING OBJECTIVES

1.   Identify the role of accountants and distinguish between the kinds of work done by public and private accountants.

2.   Explain why journals and double-entry accounting ledgers are useful tools for financial analysis.

3.   Describe the three basic financial statements and how they reflect the financial condition and activities of a business.

4.   Explain how computing key financial ratios can help in analyzing a business's financial strength.

5.   Discuss the importance of budgets in internal planning and control.

6.   Describe some ways that companies use computers to handle accounting functions.

204

DISCUSSION OF THE OPENING CASE

Sei dir selber treu
und daraus folgt, so wie die Nacht dem Tag,
du kannst nicht falsch sein gegen irgendwen. (1)

That, in German translation, is what Polonius said to his son Laertes in a scene from Shakespeare's Hamlet: "This above all, to thine own self be true, and it must follow, as the day the night, thou canst not then be false to any man." It is not the purpose of this case commentary to make any judgments concerning the handling of the Lincoln Savings audits by several members of the Big Six accounting firms. Instead, it is worth our time to consider how we might have conducted ourselves had we been the auditors of that ill-fated S and L. This opening case is not so much an accounting exercise as it is one in business ethics. A strong sense of personal integrity can often provide answers to serious questions that business people must sometimes ask themselves. Many times, the straight answer to such a question is NOT the route to greater profit. Sometimes, being true to your own high ethical standards can lead to severe financial losses. The case narrative hints that a motivation for an auditor to "go easy" on a client might be to remain in the good graces of the client, and thus keep the fees coming. The case narrative also hints that such may not be the best course of action in the long run. Did you also notice that one of the accounting firms has indicated that the auditing firm from which they took over did not adequately warn them of some of the pitfalls in the Lincoln Savings fiasco? If such allegation is true, does the second firm have the right to seek multi-million- dollar damages from the first accounting firm? Then, there is the matter of the "Keating Five"--highly-respected United States Senators who allegedly engaged in conduct of a questionable nature. If, indeed, the final judgments indicate that the auditors as well as the Senators acted improperly, then their sins are all the more abominable because in both cases, the perpetrators will have broken a trust placed in them. Perhaps, they should have read Hamlet.

(1) Carey, Elizabeth. "Was soll ich tun?" Herold der Christlichen Wissenschaft, February, 1979. Reprinted in Was soll ich tun?. Boston: The Christian Science Publishing Society, 1979, pages 9-13.

1. Based on what you have read of the Lincoln Savings case, do you see evidence that any of the accounting firms acted improperly? Explain.

2. From an ethical standpoint, which of the alleged misdeeds are the more objectionable-- those of the auditors or those of the Senators?

3. You are a CPA with a major accounting firm, and you are auditing the books of a large corporation. How would you answer the following statement from an executive of that company? "To have a favorable net profit to show the stockholders, we are using a little 'creative accounting.' If you can't go along with us on this one, then we may have to get another auditor."

4.   Comment upon Arthur Young's quitting as auditors of American Continental (parent of Lincoln Savings) over a difference of opinion over a $55 million "gain."

ANNOTATED KEY TERMS

Accounting - A comprehensive information system for collecting, analyzing, and communicating financial information.

Bookkeeping - The recording of accounting transactions.

Accounting System - An organized means by which accounting information about a company's activities is identified, measured, recorded, and maintained so that it can be used in accounting statements and management reports.

Controller - The person in charge of all of a firm's accounting activities; the firm's chief accounting officer.

Certified Public Accountant (CPA) - An accountant licensed by the state, who offers his or her services to the public.

Audit - A systematic examination of a company's accounting system to determine whether the company's financial reports fairly present its operations.

Generally Accepted Accounting Principles (GAAP) - The generally accepted rules and methods used by accountants in preparing financial reports.

Management Advisory Services - Specialized services offered by accountants to help managers resolve a variety of business problems.

Private Accountants - Accountants who are hired by businesses as salaried employees and who are responsible for carrying out the firm's day-to-day accounting activities.

Certified Management Accountant (CMA) - An accountant who specializes in management accounting, has met certain educational and professional standards, and has passed the examination given by the Institute of Management Accounting.

Journal - A chronological record of a firm's financial transactions along with a brief description of each transaction. Ledgers - A record of all the transactions entered in a firm's journal by category. Ledgers allow managers to keep track of the balance in each category (cash, sales, purchases, etc.).

Fiscal Year - The 12-month period used by a firm for annual financial reporting purposes.

Asset - Anything of economic value owned by a firm or individual.

Liability - A debt owed by a firm or an individual.

Owners' Equity - The amount of money a firm's owners would receive if they sold all the company's assets and paid off all its liabilities.

Double-Entry System - A bookkeeping system that requires all transactions to be recorded in two ways, with one entry showing how the transaction affects assets and the other entry showing how the transaction affects liabilities and owners' equity.

Debit - In bookkeeping, an increase in assets or a decrease in liabilities and owners' equity; always entered in the left column of a journal or ledger.

Credit - In bookkeeping, a decrease in assets or an increase in liabilities and owners' equity; always entered in the right column of a journal or ledger.

Financial Statements - Any of several types of reports regarding a company's financial status; used by managers to make informed decisions.

Balance Sheet - A financial statement that summarizes a firm's financial position by listing its assets, liabilities, and owners' equity.

Current Assets - Assets that can or will be converted into cash in the following year.

Liquidity - The ease with which an asset can be converted into cash.

Marketable Securities - Assets, such as government securities and money market certificates,that can be converted to cash quickly, if necessary.

Accounts Receivable - Amounts due from customers who have purchased goods on credit.

Merchandise Inventory - The cost of merchandise that has been acquired for sale to customers and is still on hand.

LIFO (Last-In-First-Out) Method - A method of valuing inventories that assumes that inventories received most recently (last in) are sold first.

FIFO (First-In-First-Out) Method - A method of valuing inventories that assumes that older inventories (first in) are sold first.

Prepaid Expenses - Expenses for coming periods that are paid before those periods; examples include supplies on hand and prepaid rent.

Fixed Assets - Assets that have long-term use or value, such as land, buildings, and equipment.

Depreciation - The process of distributing the cost of a major asset over the life of the asset.

Intangible Assets - Non-physical assets such as patents, trademarks, and copyrights that have economic value, but whose precise value is difficult to calculate.

Current Liabilities - Debts that must be repaid within the year.

Accounts Payable - Unpaid bills to suppliers. Wages and taxes that must be paid in the coming year.

Long-Term Liabilities - Debts that are not due until more than one year hence.

Paid-In Capital - Additional money, over and above the proceeds from the sale of stock, paid directly into the firm by its owners.

Retained Earnings - A company's net profits less its dividend payments to stockholders; the amount retained by the company for use by the company.

Income Statement (Profit-and-Loss Statement) - A financial statement that lists a firm's annual revenues and expenses and whose "bottom line" shows the firm's annual profit or loss.

Revenues - The funds that flow into a business from selling its products or services.

Cost of Goods Sold - The total cost of obtaining the materials used to make the products sold by a firm during the year.

Gross Profit (Gross Margin) - A firm's revenues (net sales) minus its cost of goods sold.

Operating Income - A firm's gross profit minus its operating expenses.

Operating Expenses - The costs--other than the cost of goods sold--incurred by a firm in producing its product or service. Often broken down into selling expenses and general/administrative expenses.

Net Income (Net Profit or Net Earnings) - A firm's gross profit minus its operating expenses and income taxes.

Statement of Cash Flows (Statement of Changes in Financial Position) - A financial statement that describes the sources and uses of a firm's cash during the year.

Liquidity Ratios - Measures of a firm's ability to pay its immediate debts.

Current Ratio - A firm's current assets divided by its current liabilities. Used to determine a firm's credit worthiness.

Working Capital - The difference between a firm's current assets and its current liabilities.

Quick Ratio (Acid-Test Ratio) - A company's quick assets divided by its current liabilities. Used to determine a firm's ability to meet expected demands for cash.

Quick Assets - Cash plus assets one step removed from cash (marketable securities and accounts receivable).

Debt Ratios - Measures of a firm's ability to meet its long-term debts.

Debt-to-Owners'-Equity Ratio - A firm's total debt divided by total owners' equity. Used to determine the extent to which a firm is financed through borrowing.

Leverage - The process of using borrowed funds to make purchases.

Profitability Ratios - Measures of a firm's overall financial performance in terms of profits.

Return on Sales (Net Profit Margin) - A firm's net income divided by its total sales. Used to determine the percentage of a firm's income that is profit.

Return on Investment (Return on Equity) - A firm's net income divided by total owners' equity. Used to determine how much net income the business earns for each dollar invested by the firm's owners.

Earnings Per Share - A firm's net income divided by the total number of common shares outstanding. Used to determine how large a dividend a firm can pay its shareholders.

Activity Ratios - Measures of how efficiently a firm uses its resources.

Inventory Turnover Ratio - A firm's total cost of goods sold divided by its average inventory. Used to determine the average number of times inventory is sold and restocked during the year.
Budget - A detailed statement of a firm's estimated receipts and expenditures for a period of time in the future, usually one year.

TRUE-FALSE QUESTIONS

1. Bookkeeping is much more comprehensive than accounting because bookkeeping involves more than just recording of information.

2. The larger CPA firms earn about 60 percent to 70 percent of their revenue from audit services.

3. CPAs are always independent of the firms they audit.

4. Accounts in a journal contain only minimal descriptions of transactions.

5.   If a company's assets exceed its liabilities, then the owners' equity is negative.

6.   The accounting equation must always balance.

7.   The method used in calculating inventory need not be disclosed in a firm's financial statements.

8.   The higher a firm's liquidity ratios, the higher the risks involved for investors.

9.   Quick assets include land, plant and equipment.

10.   Companies with debt-to-equity ratios above 1 are probably relying too much on debt.

MULTIPLE CHOICE QUESTIONS

1.   A comprehensive information system for collecting, analyzing, and communicating financial information is

   a. bookkeeping.
   b. controlling.
   c. data processing.
   d. accounting.

2.   The head of the accounting system and the person who manages all of the firm's accounting activities is the

   a. bookkeeper.
   b. CPA.
   c. controller.
   d. production manager.

3.   When an accountant examines a company's accounting system to determine whether the company's financial reports fairly present its operations, the process is called a(n)

   a. journal entry.
   b. audit.
   c. investigation.
   d. ratio analysis.

4. A chronological record of financial transactions along with a brief description of the transaction is found in a

   a. journal.
   b. ledger.
   c. ratio.
   d. financial statement.

5. Land, buildings, equipment, and inventory are

   a. liabilities.
   b. marketable securities.
   c. components of owners' equity.
   d. assets.

6. An increase in an asset and a decrease in a liabilities account or owners' equity is a(n)

   a. current asset.
   b. long-term debt item.
   c. debit.
   d. credit.

7. Cash and marketable securities are

   a. long-term liabilities.
   b. current assets.
   c. long-term assets.
   d. components of owners' equity.

8. Patents, trademarks, and copyrights are examples of

   a. intangible assets.
   b. liabilities.
   c. owners' equity items.
   d. current assets.

9. Which of the following assumes that the older inventories are sold first, and the newer inventories are held for later use?

   a. GAAP
   b. CMA
   c. LIFO
   d. FIFO

10.   Accounts payable is an example of a(n)

   a. current asset.
   b. long-term asset.
   c. current liability.
   d. long-term liability.

11.   A company's net profits less dividend payments to stockholders are its

   a. current assets.
   b. retained earnings.
   c. owners' equity.
   d. liabilities.

12.   The funds that flow into a business from selling products or providing services are called

   a. revenues.
   b. assets.
   c. owners' equity.
   d. gross margin.

13.   Subtracting operating expenses and income taxes from gross margin yields

   a. assets.
   b. liabilities.
   c. gross margin.
   d. net income.

14.   The statement that describes a company's cash receipts and cash payments for the year is the

   a. revenue statement.
   b. balance sheet.
   c. statement of cash flows.
   d. income statement.

15.   Management's salaries, insurance expenses, office supplies, and maintenance costs are

   a. assets.
   b. general and administrative expenses.
   c. selling expenses.
   d. operating income.

16. Return on investment is a

   a. profitability ratio.
   b. liquidity ratio.
   c. debt ratio.
   d. activity ratio.

17. The ratio that describes the extent to which a firm is financed through borrowings is the

   a. quick ratio.
   b. return on investment ratio.
   c. price-earnings ratio.
   d. debt-to-owners'-equity ratio.

18. The ratio that indicates the percentage of income that is profit to the company is the

   a. current ratio.
   b. price-earnings ratio.
   c. net profit margin.
   d. market-to-book ratio.

19. The ratio that measures the average number of times inventory is sold and restocked during the year is the

   a. quick ratio.
   b. inventory turnover ratio.
   c. price-earnings ratio.
   d. current ratio.

20. A detailed statement of estimated receipts and expenditures for a period of time in the future, usually one year, is called a(n)

   a. budget.
   b. audit.
   c. balance sheet.
   d. income statement.

WRITING TO LEARN

1. What is accounting? Describe the different types of accounting specialists covered in the chapter. What services do they provide?

2. Describe the record-keeping process for a firm's financial transactions using journals and ledgers. What is the accounting equation, and how does it affect double-entry accounting?

3. Discuss the balance sheet, income statement, and statement of cash flows reports. What accounts are found in each report?

4. How can financial statements be used by investors or managers to make decisions? Discuss the major classifications of ratios and what each indicates.

5. What is a budget? How do managers use budgets?

DISCUSSION OF THE CLOSING CASE

The Mitchell/Titus story is certainly one of a firm growing ever and ever larger and more significant in its profession. But we see here something far more important and something whose application spreads beyond the borders of mere growth. In the saga of Bert N. Mitchell, we see not merely the keys to the success of an African-American, but rather the keys to the success of any person in a business venture. Those keys seem to be: obtain a good solid education, and then learn everything you can on any job you take. When Bert Mitchell was working for Lucas, Tucker, and Company, we can imagine that he went far beyond the normal requirements of the job and absorbed all the knowledge available about the accounting profession. It would be our guess that he sought out particularly-challenging clients, for that is where you really learn the profession. This approach of learning every nook and cranny of accounting procedures is where competence comes from. It's almost as if you take on as an adversary the whole accounting process and say: "I can whip it. There won't be an accounting procedure that I have not mastered." It takes extra effort. It's like training to run a marathon (26.2 miles). To be able to enjoy that delightfully delirious emotional high that comes when you cross the finish line after several hours of running, there are many days of uninspiring drudgery to prepare the body for such a grueling feat. We wish we could tell you that there is an easy way to get ready for a marathon; but there is not! The secret is to put in those running miles day after day, week after week--whether in boiling sun, blizzard cold, flat surfaces or hills. That is, more than likely, how Bert N. Mitchell got where he is today-- being willing, even eager, to put in many hours of self-initiated training. We are NOT talking "workaholic" here. A successful entrepreneur such as Bert N. Mitchell knows the value of getting away from it all from time to time. He knows that time away can help to restore that energy needed to carry on the crusade yet another day. One can easily imagine the inspiration Bert can be to those young people fortunate enough to work under him at Mitchell/Titus and Company.

1.   How important in the Bert Mitchell story has been the role of "the right move at the right time"?

2.   Regardless of how you answered Number 1 above, compare the importance of that "right move" with Mitchell's own personal drive to succeed. Which is more important? Explain.

3.   How much motivation was there, do you feel, for Mitchell/Titus to be "able to deliver, shoulder to shoulder, toe to toe, with our majority firm partners"?

4.   What do you feel might be the attitude of Bert Mitchell concerning the hiring of non-blacks for his firm?

AN ADDITIONAL CASE

For a corporation with a large body of stockholders, the annual report is a most important document. Should the firm be a member of the Fortune 500, that annual report is must reading for stock brokers, security analysts, portfolio managers, pension fund administrators, and anyone charged with keeping up with the market value of various securities. That is why determining the specific handling of the contents of an annual report includes a series of momentous decisions. The best possible "spin" must be put on any and all events in the life of the company for the year in question. As an example, the statement of the chairman of the board (often composed by a technical writer at headquarters) will normally begin with something like: "I am happy to inform you...." Yes, even if it was a catastrophic year for the firm, the chairman can say: "I am happy to inform you that a loss once projected to be at $50 million turned out to be only of the magnitude of $27 million." Technical writers can play around with words for the annual report, and accountants will play around with figures. That's what was happening at Storm Industries.

Sally Adamson, technical writer, knew that her entire annual salary--a very respectable figure, by the way--would all be earned by the way she was going to handle the annual report. Storm Industries, with revenues for the year of $11,795,000, was able to grind out a figure for EBT (earnings before taxes) of MINUS $2,975,000. The bad year had come about as the result of a head-to-head struggle pitting Storm Industries (maker of innovative plastic sportswear) against the leader in the field. Apparently, the "leader" had won. It had been hoped and expected that changes wrought by the Federal government in the industry would make the environment much more friendly for Storm. That did not develop. Here's what we mean by making the environment more friendly.

The leader in the plastic sportswear field had held a commanding portion of market share for years. Then, along came the upstart Storm Industries. To defend itself against Storm, the industry leader engaged in some relationships that tended to deny market entrance to Storm. For example, the industry leader began to discriminate against retail stores that carried Storm products. The basic plastic suppliers, it turned out, had all been signed to lucrative contracts with the industry leader, making it virtually impossible for Storm Industries to purchase the needed raw materials. The monopolistic tendencies of the industry leader were so manifest that Storm Industries cited anti-trust legislation in contacting Federal agencies, imploring the latter to do something about the practices of the industry leader.

The case against the industry leader went to Federal court, and in 1985, a district court in Richmond, Virginia awarded Storm Industries damages of $40,000,000. Upon appeal, the award dropped to $21,000,000. Before the case could go to The United States Supreme Court, attorneys for the industry leader settled the matter out of court, agreeing to pay Storm Industries the paltry sum of $4,000,000 but also agreeing (as a binding part of the settlement) to dissolve all restricting arrangements with suppliers and retailers. That was in late 1989. Here in the middle of the 1990s, the check for $4,000,000 finally arrived at Storm.

At any rate, the full story of the Storm Industries year is NOT the kind of news that stockholders like to hear. Sally's job was to make the facts as pleasant as possible so that when she wrote the board chairman's paragraphs, he could begin with his usual, "I am happy to inform you...."

To gather more material before sitting down to type up the chairman's statement, Sally met with Irmgard J. Thallmand of the accounting department. Irmgard would be called a "private accountant" since she was in the full-time employment of Storm Industries.

"Why so glum Sally," Irmgard cheerily chirped, "when we've had such a great year?"

"Great year? Not so, happy clown, for we're in the hole by $2,975,000. And I'm the poor fool who has to make it sound nice."

"Wrong, oh composer of peaceful paragraphs. We made a profit of $1,025,000! That's our best year by far in a long time."

"What income statement are you reading from? Let me take a look."

In response, Irmgard Thallmand handed over a revised profit and loss statement. Here's a quick summary of what Sally saw:

Revenues	$15,795,000
Expenses	14,770,000
Earnings before taxes	$1,025,000

Sally saw instantly that the out-of-court settlement of $4,000,000 with the industry leader had been included as "revenues," and she questioned this interpretation of what happened.

"If it takes $4,000,000 to help us chalk up a profit this year, what will we do next year when we won't have that $4,000,000 to save us? It isn't fair to mislead our stockholders this way. Here's the way it should be presented, using parentheses around the earnings figure to represent a NEGATIVE value."

Revenues	$11,795,000
Expenses	14,770,000
Earnings before taxes (EBT)	($2,975,000)
Extraordinary gain	4,000,000
EBT plus extraordinary gain	$1,025,000

"When you talked to our auditor about this," Sally asked of Irmgard, "what did he say?"

"I haven't talked with him about it yet."

1.   What will the auditor say about the way that Irmgard Thallmand has drawn up the income statement? Explain.

2. Do you feel that Irmgard's version is indeed misleading the stockholders?

3. What is your opinion about a footnote explaining how the $4,000,000 was included in revenues? If such a footnote were developed, should it avoid great specificity? Why or why not?

4. Which of the two versions would Storm Industries want a stockbroker to see? Explain.

ANSWERS TO TRUE-FALSE QUESTIONS

1.	F	(p. 377)	6.	T	(p. 383)
2.	T	(p. 378)	7.	F	(p. 386)
3.	T	(p. 380)	8.	F	(p. 389)
4.	F	(p. 381)	9.	F	(p. 391)
5.	F	(p. 383)	10.	T	(p. 391)

ANSWERS TO MULTIPLE-CHOICE QUESTIONS

1.	D	(p. 377)	11.	B	(p. 387)
2.	C	(p. 377)	12.	A	(p. 387)
3.	B	(p. 378)	13.	D	(p. 388)
4.	A	(p. 381)	14.	C	(p. 388)
5.	D	(p. 383)	15.	B	(p. 388)
6.	C	(p. 384)	16.	A	(p. 392)
7.	B	(p. 385)	17.	D	(p. 391)
8.	A	(p. 386)	18.	C	(p. 392)
9.	D	(p. 386)	19.	B	(p. 393)
10.	C	(p. 387)	20.	A	(p. 394)

CHAPTER SIXTEEN

UNDERSTANDING MARKETING PROCESSES AND CONSUMER BEHAVIOR

CHAPTER OVERVIEW

Marketing is the process of planning and executing the conception, pricing, promotion, and distribution of ideas, goods, and services to create exchanges that satisfy individual and organizational objectives. The marketing mix consists of product, pricing, promotion, and place. Production creates form utility, but marketing creates time, place, and possession utility. Target markets are groups of people with similar wants and needs. Market segmentation is dividing a market into categories of customer types. Markets may be segmented by geographic, demographic, psychographic, and product-use variables. Market research is the study of what buyers need and how best to meet those needs. The study of consumer behavior focuses on the decision process by which customers come to purchase and consume a product. Four major influences upon consumer behavior are: psychological; personal; social; and cultural. The consumer buying process consists of: problem recognition; information seeking; evaluation of alternatives; the purchase decision; and post-decision evaluations. Rational motives involve a logical evaluation of product attributes--cost, quality, and usefulness. Emotional motives--fear, sociability, imitation of others, and aesthetics--lead to irrational decisions. International marketing involves the use of marketing strategy to support global, rather than just domestic, business operations.

LEARNING OBJECTIVES

1.   Define marketing and explain its functions.

2.   Discuss how and why market segmentation is used for target marketing.

3.   Describe the role of market research in marketing.

4.   Describe the factors that influence the consumer buying process.

5.   Explain how international and cultural differences affect marketing strategies.

6.   Identify potential problems and strategies in the marketing activities of small businesses.

220

DISCUSSION OF THE OPENING CASE

When an advertiser uses national television on a regular basis, that advertiser pictures the typical household into which the advertising message is being sent. Today, so we are told, there are "scientific" and "demographic" techniques to reveal what that typical household looks like. In earlier days, perhaps, the view of the typical household was developed with less of the precision methods of today. In the heyday of radio (1930s, 1940s), with Procter and Gamble advertising heavily, the typical household in the daytime was pictured pretty much as follows. Husband was off to his job and wife was home. After getting the kids off to school, she would do the dishes, clean the house, do the laundry (in washtubs or perhaps an automatic washing machine), listen to a few "soap operas" and then have a leisurely bite of lunch. After the kids came home from school, she would give them a small snack (cookies and milk, of course) and send them merrily out to play. While the kids were outside, Mother would take her bath and be fresh and perky for the time of supper preparation. In fact, there was a soap commercial in that heyday which advised: "Toward the end of the day, take your beauty bath so you'll be fresh and clean when friend husband comes home." When supper was on the table, hubby would pull into the driveway, and the housewife would greet him at the door with a big kiss. Procter and Gamble--and all the other advertisers--aimed their <u>daytime</u> messages at this housewife you have just met. Millions upon millions of such housewives responded to the messages by purchasing, with <u>mucho gusto</u>, Procter and Gamble products. When televison came along in the early 1950s, daytime advertisers pictured that same idyllic household. But the case tells us that the home we have just presented to you does not exist on the broad scale that it once did. For the career woman with children in a day-care facility, those Procter and Gamble messages were not being received in the home, and the case points out that P&G was losing touch with its potential customers. What P&G had to do was recreate its picture of the typical daytime American home and then beam messages to that population. Obtaining a more accurate picture of your target market is an aspect of marketing that must not be overlooked.

1.   Do you feel that the "typical household" pictured above ever existed in reality? Why or why not?

2.   Why didn't Procter and Gamble--in those early days--beam more commercials toward <u>men's</u> programs?

3.   In that "heyday of radio" picture of the typical American household, what did "friend husband" usually do after supper? Did his post-supper activities give any hint as to how P&G should aim its advertising?

4.   Think of a "soap opera" you have watched on television, one that you don't particularly like. Describe the kind of audience the program's producers, and its advertisers must be envisioning as watching the show.

ANNOTATED KEY TERMS

Marketing - The process of planning and executing the conception, pricing, promotion, and distribution of ideas, goods, and services to create exchanges that satisfy individual and organizational objectives.

Consumer Goods - Products purchased by a consumer for personal use.

Industrial Goods - Products used by companies to produce other products.

Marketing Mix - The combination of product, pricing, promotion, and distribution strategies used to market a product.

Product - A good, service, or idea that attempts to fill consumers' wants.

Product Differentiation - The creation of a product or product image that differs enough from existing products to attract consumers.

Pricing - The part of the marketing mix concerned with selecting the appropriate price for a product.

Promotion - The part of the marketing mix concerned with selecting the appropriate techniques to sell a product to consumers.

Advertising - Any form of paid, nonpersonal communication used by an identified sponsor to persuade or inform certain audiences about a good, service, or idea.

Personal Selling - A promotional technique that uses person-to- person communication to sell products.

Sales Promotion - A promotional technique involving one-time direct inducements (such as coupons, trading stamps, and package inserts) to consumers to purchase a product.

Public Relations - All promotional activities directed at building good relations with various sectors of the population.

Publicity - Communication to the public (usually through the mass media) about a product or firm. The firm has no control over the content of the message.

Distribution - The part of the marketing mix concerned with getting products from the producer to the consumer.

Exchange - Any transaction in which two or more parties trade things of value.

Target Market - A group of people with similar wants and needs that can be expected to show interest in the same product(s).

Market Segmentation - The process of dividing a market into categories of customer types.

Psychographics - The mental traits--such as opinions, attitudes, and motivations--of a target market.

Market Research - The study of what buyers need and how businesses can best meet those needs.

Secondary Data - Data readily available as a result of previous research.

Primary Data - Data developed through new research.

Observation - A market research technique that involves simply watching what is happening.

Survey - A market research technique that uses a questionnaire that is either mailed to individuals or used as the basis of telephone or personal interviews.

Focus Group - A market research technique in which a group of about 6 to 15 individuals are gathered, presented with an issue, and asked to discuss the issue in depth.

Experimentation - A market research technique that attempts to compare the responses of the same or similar individuals under different circumstances.

Consumer Behavior - The various facets of the decision process by which customers come to purchase and consume a product.

Rational Motives - Those reasons for purchasing a product that are based on a logical evaluation of product attributes (such as cost, quality, and usefulness).

Emotional Motives - Those reasons for purchasing a product that are based on non-objective factors.

Purchase Anxiety - A consumer's feeling that a recent purchase decision was wrong. Also called buyer's remorse.

International Marketing - The use of marketing strategy to support global, rather than just domestic, business operations.

TRUE-FALSE QUESTIONS

1.   Marketing can be applied to ideas.

2. For a marketing strategy to be successful, it must take into account only one of the four P's--pricing.

3. High prices will generally lead to a larger volume of sales.

4. Automobiles, appliances, and stero equipment are often promoted through the use of premiums.

5. Payment for a good or service does not always involve money.

6. By definition, the members of a market segment must share some common traits or behaviors that will affect their purchasing decisions.

7. Demographics have little affect on how a firm markets its product.

8. Market segments differ in how they respond to the four components of the marketing mix.

9. Market segmentation can never be perfect.

10. Standard U.S. promotional devices always succeed in other countries.

MULTIPLE CHOICE QUESTIONS

1. Cologne, cold medicine, and cars are examples of

   a. retail goods.
   b. service goods.
   c. industrial goods.
   d. consumer goods.

2. Which of the following is not one of the four P's of marketing?

   a. product
   b. price
   c. production
   d. promotion

3. A good, service, or idea that attempts to satisfy consumers' wants is a

   a. marketing mix.
   b. product.
   c. barter item.
   d. marketing function.

4. Advertising, personal selling, sales promotions, and public relations are forms of

   a. promotion.
   b. price.
   c. production.
   d. distribution.

5. Trading stamps, coupons, and package inserts are all

   a. distribution elements.
   b. pricing components of the marketing mix.
   c. forms of advertising.
   d. sales promotions.

6. Sponsorship of softball teams, special olympics, and public television programming are examples of

   a. distribution.
   b. marketing functions.
   c. public relations efforts.
   d. advertising.

7. Any transaction in which two or more parties trade things of value is a(n)

   a. function of marketing.
   b. exchange.
   c. barter transaction.
   d. product decision.

8. Groups of people with similar wants and needs make up a(n)

   a. target market.
   b. standardized product.
   c. product mix.
   d. exclusive environment.

9. Dividing a market into categories of customer types is called

   a. target marketing.
   b. promotional segmentation.
   c. unilateral marketing.
   d. market segmentation.

10. Individual characteristics and traits such as age, income, gender, ethnic background, and marital status are called

a. geographics.
b. psychographics.
c. demographics.
d. production characteristics.

11. Traits such as motives, attitudes, activities, interests,   and opinions are called

a. geographics.
b. psychographics.
c. demographics.
d. product use variables.

12. The study of what buyers need and how best to meet those needs is called

a. market research.
b. market segmentation.
c. market psychographics.
d. the marketing mix.

13. The first step in the research process is

a. collecting data.
b. selecting a research method.
c. writing a report.
d. to study the current situation.

14. Information developed through new research by the firm or its agents is

a. stale data.
b. secondary data.
c. primary data.
d. database information.

15. Which of the following is not mentioned by the authors of your textbook as a basic method used by market researchers?

a. observation
b. direction
c. survey
d. experimentation

16. The heart of any survey is the

    a. questionnaire.
    b. focus group.
    c. researcher.
    d. experiment.

17. The study of the process by which customers come to purchase and consume a product or service is referred to as

    a. a focus group.
    b. experimentation.
    c. a survey.
    d. consumer behavior.

18. Which of the following was not mentioned by the authors of your textbook as a major influence on consumer behavior?

    a. psychological influencers
    b. personal influencers
    c. the marketing mix
    d. social influencers

19. Lifestyle, personality, economic status, and life cycle state are components of which of the following influencers?

    a. psychological influencers
    b. personal influencers
    c. social influencers
    d. cultural influencers

20. In the purchase decision, cost, quality, and usefulness are

    a. rational motives.
    b. emotional motives.
    c. irrational motives.
    d. behavioral motives.

WRITING TO LEARN

1. What is the definition of marketing? Discuss the components of the marketing mix. What are the functions of marketing?

2. How are markets segmented? Are there requirements for market segmentation? Why is it important for the manager to clearly define and identify a target market?

3. Is market research important to a company? Discuss the market research process. What are the four basic methods used by market researchers to conduct market research?

4. Why is understanding consumer behavior important to the firm? What influences consumer behavior? Describe the consumer buying process.

5. Do foreign customers differ from domestic buyers? How does marketing products internationally differ from marketing products domestically?

DISCUSSION OF THE CLOSING CASE

The narrative tells us that J.B. Pratt did some market research that indicated "consumers are even willing to pay slightly more for environment-friendly products." Yes, that's what the studies showed. Unfortunately, the studies also showed that such consumers are not yet to be found in large numbers. Here is where J.B. Pratt faced a dilemma that had, perhaps, ethical dimensions. Pratt believed in establishing an "environmentally conscious" store. Yet, the response, he knew, would not be overwhelming. The question became: Should I forge ahead with something I believe in, or should I shelve this idea and go with something with a greater profit potential? Pratt chose the former course. How can we help to make his Enviromarket more successful? Let's brainstorm that a little. From a promotion standpoint, we must help Enviromarket to locate those people who will be enthusiastic about Pratt's concept. Let's rephrase that: We must locate great numbers of people who will be enthusiastic about Pratt's concept. This brings us to the idea of market segmentation. Once we have defined that market segment, then we can seek to reach it by means of appropriate effective promotion. A demographic angle may be the way to construct that segment. Of people who tend to be environmentally-conscious, what can we say about their: age, education, family life cycle, family size, income, nationality, race, religion, and sex? Let's say, for example, that such people are: in their early thirties, have bachelor's degrees, have usually two young children, moderate to high income, are Anglo-Saxon, and Protestant. Some further relevant questions to be asked are as follows. Which periodicals in the Oklahoma City area are they reading? Which radio stations are they listening to? Which television shows do they watch most often? (Notice that you can't ask which TV stations do they watch because such a station almost always appeals to too broad a market segment.) When these latter questions have been answered, it is time to swing into action with an aggressive, carefully pin-pointed (segmented) promotional campaign--if there are funds!

1. The segment of the market that is seeking high-quality boxing gloves can be rather carefully defined. Unfortunately for a boxing-glove manufacturer, the segment is small in any one geographic area. How does the environmentally-conscious segment compare with the boxing-glove segment?

2. In our case discussion we have tried to describe an environmentally-conscious segment. Could it be that such persons are so sprinkled throughout the population that they defy segmentation? Explain.

3. If our segment is indeed as described in the discussion above, what types of print and electronic media would you use to reach them?

4. What are some other ways to reach our segment above and beyond the print and electronic media?

AN ADDITIONAL CASE

Minerva Kravitz opened a video store she called The Golden Era, a new concept in video rentals because it handled only the <u>black- and-white</u> masterpieces of the so-called Golden Age of Hollywood. At first, she had difficulty locating enough of such fare to stock her shelves; many of the "golden oldies" were not out on video. A few long-standing inside contacts in Hollywood, however, resulted in a flood of the nostalgia material for Minerva's store. You see, Minerva's screen name was Betty Hayworth, and her brief career in the films peaked in the 1941 feature, "Foreign Legion Affair." Her total time on screen in that thriller was 37 minutes and 12 seconds, including a short exchange with Humphrey Bogart, who was playing Captain LaFleur.

The Golden Era was situated in a strip mall in a fashionable distant suburb of Phoenix. Really, Minerva felt, the distance from the center of the big city didn't make any difference, because those people who wanted great black-and-white film fare would be willing to journey to Minerva's Golden Era. So, she set about building up an overflowing inventory of films. The facility was fully stocked, and all that was needed now was a regular clientele.

Of course, a catchy neon sign was not quite enough to draw crowds into her shop. Being a great believer in radio, Minerva sought out the Phoenix station with the best overall ratings. Together with one of the account executives there, she worked out a heavy schedule of spot announcements. In addition, every three hours, Golden Era would sponsor the weather on the station. During the first weekend of her contract with the station, a disc jockey did a remote from The Golden Era, and this gathered a fairly decent crowd--and generated a healthy level of rentals.

Yes, there was a flurry of interest in The Golden Era. But Minerva realized that a flurry now and then would not make ends meet on the new venture. Something had to be done to keep a steady flow of loyal customers. Minerva sought the advice of Professor Stephan Zsork, marketing specialist with one of the community colleges in the area. From past experience, Minerva knew that Dr. Zsork would take a lot of her time and ask a lot of questions and move very slowly. In the end, however, he'd arrive at some excellent suggestions. So, on March 12, 1992, Zsork came to The Golden Era.

Dr. Zsork complimented Minerva on her choice of a product. He further indicated that she was certainly making use of market segmentation by dealing in a product that would appeal, hopefully, to older citizens who remember the great days when Hollywood was king.

"A problem you always encounter in market segmentation," Zsork offered, "is that of how big the segment should be. For example, there are several people in the world who love the sound of the Baroque double-flute. If you could cater to their tastes, you'd have an extremely loyal clienetele. But the clientele would be so small that you couldn't keep in business just serving them. Now the question with your concept for The Golden Era is: Have we made the clientele group too small?"

"Why, of course not! I believe in the depths of my heart that this is a superb product with an immense following out there somewhere."

"And I'm inclined to agree with you. Now, in getting ready for this meeting, I did a little checking on that radio station you're using for your advertising. I heard your commercials--and they're real good. But why did you pick that particular radio station?"

"They have the best overall ratings in the whole Phoenix area, that's why. I knew I'd reach more listeners that way."

"Do you ever listen to that station," the professor wanted to know.

"Not really."

"Well, I've been listening to them lately and I can tell you the kind of music they play. Here are some of the things I heard. Paul Young was singing 'What Becomes of the Brokenhearted.' Elton John and George Michael were teamed up on 'Don't Let the Sun Go Down on Me.' And then there was that terribly sad song, 'Tears in Heaven' by Eric Clapton. Rod Stewart was doing 'Your Song,' Michael Bolton and Kenny G had 'Missing You Now,' while Amy Grant was climbing to the top of the charts still another time with 'Good for Me.' Also coming up fast was 'Masterpiece' sung by Atlantic Star. And for a backward glance, they were playing last summer's biggest hit-- 'Everything I Do, I Do It for You' by Bryan Adams."

"Enough already with the songs! I don't know any of those. That's all that rock stuff."

"That's my point, Minerva. You don't know those songs, and the people who love those songs don't know your movies. In short, your radio commercials are being heard by the wrong market segment. You're wasting your money with that station."

"What'll I do?"

"I recommend another specific radio station. Here's what I heard this other station playing. 'Temptation' by Perry Como, 'Careless Hands' by the Swing-and-Sway orchestra of Sammy Kaye, 'Boo-Hoo,' by Guy Lombardo and his Royal Canadians, 'Sentimental Journey' by Les Brown and his Band of Renown (with a vocal by Doris Day), 'Opus Number One' by Tommy Dorsey (the Sentimental Gentleman of Swing), and 'Moonlight Cocktail' by Glenn Miller's orchestra. Jan Garber, Idol of the Airlanes, was playing 'Carolina Moon,' and Bing Crosby was singing 'Just One More Chance.'"

"Now that, my dear Professor Zsork, is my kind of music!"

1. It seems rather obvious. Nevertheless, what is Minerva Kravitz going to do with her radio advertising? Explain.

2. Regardless of what the professor said, do you feel that Minerva has cut for herself too small a market segment? Keep in mind that a great many retired persons live in the greater Phoenix area.

3. If the professor's revealing of the nostalgia station is a new shining light in marketing strategy for Minerva, what are some additional things she might do to establish contacts with her market segment?

4. In light of this case, evaluate the impact of the following possible line from a recent news story: "Research has shown that 90 percent of America's VCRs are to be found in homes in which the head of household is 40 years of age or below. VCRs are not greatly in use by retired persons."

ANSWERS TO TRUE-FALSE QUESTIONS

1.	T	(p. 413)	6.	T	(p. 420)
2.	F	(p. 417)	7.	F	(p. 420)
3.	F	(p. 416)	8.	T	(p. 422)
4.	F	(p. 416)	9.	T	(p. 424)
5.	T	(p. 417)	10.	F	(p. 432)

ANSWERS TO MULTIPLE-CHOICE QUESTIONS

1.	D	(p. 413)	11.	B	(p. 422)
2.	C	(p. 415)	12.	A	(p. 424)
3.	B	(p. 415)	13.	D	(p. 424)
4.	A	(p. 416)	14.	C	(p. 424)
5.	D	(p. 416)	15.	B	(p. 425)
6.	C	(p. 416)	16.	A	(p. 425)
7.	B	(p. 417)	17.	D	(p. 427)
8.	A	(p. 419)	18.	C	(p. 427)
9.	D	(p. 419)	19.	B	(p. 427)
10.	C	(p. 420)	20.	A	(p. 429)

CHAPTER SEVENTEEN

DEVELOPING AND PRICING PRODUCTS

CHAPTER OVERVIEW

Product features are tangible qualities that the company "builds into" products. There are buyers of consumer products and buyers of industrial products. Consumer products are classified as convenience goods, shopping goods, or specialty goods. Industrial products are classified as expense items or capital items. The group of products a company has available for sale is that company's product mix. The stages in the product development process are: ideas; screening; concept testing; business analysis; prototype development; testing and test marketing; and commercialization. The product life cycle is a natural process that consists of the stages of introduction, growth, maturity, and decline. The growth-share matrix classifies products as stars, cash cows, question marks, or dogs. Some kinds of brand names are national brands, licensed brands, private brands, and generic products. A trademark is the exclusive legal right--granted by the U.S. government--to use a brand name. Packaging is the physical container in which a product is sold, including the label. The two major pricing objectives are profit-maximizing and market-share. Three basic tools for price determination are: economic supply-demand comparison; cost-oriented pricing; and break-even analysis. Two strategies for pricing new products are skimming and penetration pricing. Some pricing tactics are price lining, psychological pricing, and discounting.

LEARNING OBJECTIVES

1. Describe what a product is and distinguish between consumer and industrial products.

2. Trace the steps in new product development and the stages of the product life cycle.

3. Explain the importance of brand names, packaging and labeling.

4. Identify the various business objectives that govern pricing decisions and the tools used in making these decisions.

5. Discuss pricing strategies and tactics for existing and new products.

DISCUSSION OF THE OPENING CASE

We all realize that companies dealing in scientific innovations--and 3M certainly fits this category--must encourage discovery, invention, and creativity. Knowing that our great scientific breakthroughs first appeared utterly silly to original scoffers, 3M executives have adopted a tolerant attitude that does not allow laughing at someone's off-the-wall idea. In one sense, 3M is taking advantage of a large mass of brain power at its disposal. Now, the company could easily say: "Charlie Adams is in charge of new ideas. Charlie is the only member of the staff who can propose new products. The rest of you just stay at your assigned tasks." Instead, 3M seems to be saying: "We want virtually <u>everyone</u> in the organization to be thinking about new approaches we might take. We want a lot of keen minds actively innovating. And we shall have respect for those persons who make an effort to innovate--regardless of the outcome of that innovation. We'd rather see you do something that turns out wrong than to do nothing!" Apparently, this method of drawing out new product ideas is working wonderfully well for 3M. The question that comes up as we read of 3M's creative atmosphere is: "Why can't more companies operate thusly. Why do so many companies go to great efforts to discourage new ideas and innovation?" Think of places where you have worked. Did you ever make a suggestion? Was it adopted immediately by the management? Chances are that what you recommended was largely ignored. How do we know that for sure? Because that is just the way most business firms operate! The first miracle at 3M is how they have been able to establish such an atmosphere that is so tolerant of trying out new things. The second miracle is how they have been able to avoid bringing in executives who would quash such an atmosphere. Chances are the firm you locate with following college will not make tape, Post-It Notes, or slipper- shaped scouring pads. But the firm you join can always make use of new ways of doing things--so long as those "new ways" are more in tune with the new social and business environments than the old ways. At some point in recent history, some employee of a large department store in downtown Miami must have said: "In the near future, we're going to need sales personnel who speak Spanish!"

1.   Just for fun, let's assume that "Charlie Adams" is the single person in charge of new ideas at 3M. This being the case, sketch briefly the fate of 3M.

2.   When that department store employee made the remark quoted at the end of the narrative above, what, more than likely, was the response of the manager hearing the remark? Explain.

3.   How might 3M go about ensuring that the quality of new ideas and products proposed remains high? Could such "quality control" moves stifle creativity?

4.   Tolerant of new ideas, is 3M's management different from that of a large hotel? Why or why not?

ANNOTATED KEY TERMS

<u>Convenience</u> <u>Goods</u> <u>and</u> <u>Services</u> - Relatively inexpensive consumer goods and services that are purchased and consumed rapidly and regularly.

<u>Shopping</u> <u>Goods</u> <u>and</u> <u>Services</u> - Moderately expensive consumer goods and services that are purchased infrequently.

Speciality Goods and Services - Expensive consumer goods and services that are purchased rarely.

Expense Items - Relatively inexpensive industrial goods and services that are purchased and consumed rapidly and regularly.

Capital Items - Relatively expensive, long-lasting industrial goods and services that are purchased infrequently.

Product Mix - The group of products a company has available for sale.

Product Line - A group of similar products intended for a similar group of buyers who will use them in similar ways.

Prototype - A preliminary version of a new product, used in test marketing and as a way of identifying production problems.

Test Marketing - The introduction of a new product into a limited market to gauge its reception by consumers.

Product Life Cycle (PLC) - The profit-producing life of a product.

Concurrent Design - An approach to production that combines concept testing, prototype development, and product testing with production planning at a single location.

Growth-Share Matrix - A tool for classifying businesses or products into four categories according to their current market share and their market growth potential: stars (high market growth, high market share); cash cows (low market growth, high market share); question marks (high market growth, low market share); and dogs (low market growth, low market share).

Brand Names - The specific names of products associated with a manufacturer, wholesaler, or retailer that serve to distinguish those products from similar products of the competitors.

National Brands - Brand name products that are produced by, distributed by, and carry the name of the manufacturer.

Licensed Brands - Brands that carry the name of a nationally recognized company or personality, not the manufacturer.

Private Brands - Products carrying a name associated with a retailer or wholesaler, not the manufacturer.

Generic Products - Products with no brand names that are packaged and marketed as low-cost alternatives to branded products.

Brand Loyalty - Customers' recognition of, preference for, and insistence on purchasing a product with a particular brand name.

Trademark - The exclusive legal right to use a brand name.

Packaging - The physical container in which a product is sold.

Label - The part of a product's packaging that identifies the product's name, manufacturer, and contents.

Markup - The amount added to the cost of an item to earn a profit for the business.

Variable Costs - Those costs that change with the number of goods or services produced or sold.

Fixed Costs - Those costs that are unaffected by the number of goods or services produced or sold.

Break-even Analysis - An assessment of how many units of a product must be sold before the company begins to earn a profit.

Break-even Point - The number of units of a product that must be sold to just cover both fixed and variable costs.

Price Leader - A dominant firm that establishes the selling price of a product. The other firms in the same industry then adopt the same price for their product.

Price-skimming Strategy - Pricing a new product at a very high price to cover costs and generate profits.

Penetration-Pricing Strategy - Pricing a new product at a very low price to establish the product on the market.

Price Lining - The practice of offering all items in certain categories at a limited number of prices.

Psychological Pricing - Pricing that takes advantage of the fact that consumers are not always rational when making purchases.

Odd-even Psychological Pricing - A form of psychological pricing in which prices are not stated in even dollar amounts.

Threshold Pricing - A form of psychological pricing in which prices are set at what appears to be the maximum price consumers will pay for an item.

Discount - Any reduction in price offered by sellers to consumers as an incentive to purchase a product.

Cash Discount - A form of discount in which customers who pay with cash (rather than credit) receive a lower price.

Seasonal Discount - A form of discount in which lower prices are offered to customers for making a purchase at a time of year when sales are traditionally slow.

Trade Discount - A form of discount in which the companies involved in a product's distribution pay lower prices.

Quantity Discount - A form of discount in which customers buying large amounts of a product pay lower prices.

TRUE-FALSE QUESTIONS

1. Customers buy products because they like what the products can do for them.

2. Marketing a good or service to consumers is the same as marketing the good or service to a company.

3. Consumers will go from store to store, often traveling many miles and spending a great deal of money and time to get the sought-after convenience good.

4. Product development begins with concept testing.

5. According to the authors of your textbook, it takes five new product ideas to generate one product that reaches the commercialization stage.

6. Concurrent design combines several stages of the product development process with production planning at a single location.

7. A company loaded with cash cows has a great present, but a very questionable future.

8. The costs of developing a positive image for a national brand are low.

9. Usually, only specialty products have much potential for developing brand insistence in a large group of consumers.

10. Companies pricing above the market play on customers' beliefs that higher price means higher quality.

MULTIPLE CHOICE QUESTIONS

1. Tangible qualities that a company "builds" into products are product
   a. costs.
   b. classifications.
   c. accessories.
   d. features.

2. Milk and newspapers are examples of

   a. shopping goods.
   b. speciality goods.
   c. convenience goods.
   d. capital goods.

3. Stereos and tires are examples of

   a. convenience goods.
   b. shopping goods.
   c. speciality goods.
   d. industrial goods.

4. Materials and services that are consumed within a year by firms producing other goods or supplying other services are

   a. expense items.
   b. capital items.
   c. installations.
   d. convenience goods.

5. Water towers, baking ovens, offices, and factories are called

   a. convenience goods.
   b. expense items.
   c. shopping goods.
   d. installations.

6. Which of the following steps in new product development gives a company its first information on how consumers will respond to a product under real market conditions?

   a. concept testing
   b. screening
   c. test marketing
   d. commercialization

7.   The concept that holds that products have a limited profit-producing life is called

      a. commercialization.
      b. the product life cycle.
      c. new product development.
      d. concept testing.

8.   During this stage of the PLC, the product begins to show a profit.

      a. the growth stage
      b. the introduction stage
      c. the maturity stage
      d. the decline stage

9.   The product earns its highest profit level in the

      a. decline stage.
      b. introduction stage.
      c. growth stage.
      d. maturity stage.

10.   Products are classified according to market share and growth potential on the

      a. product life cycle.
      b. new product development cycle.
      c. growth-share matrix.
      d. break-even analysis.

11.   During the growth stage of the PLC, products most closely resemble

      a. dogs.
      b. stars.
      c. cash cows.
      d. question marks.

12.   Products in the decline stage of the PLC are

      a. dogs.
      b. stars.
      c. cash cows.
      d. question marks.

13. Noxzema, Prudential, and Minute Maid are examples of

    a. generic products.
    b. cash cows.
    c. trademarks.
    d. brand names.

14. Craftsman tools and Kenmore appliances are examples of

    a. national brands.
    b. licensed brands.
    c. private brands.
    d. generic brands.

15. Customers' recognition of, preference for, and insistence on buying a product with a certain brand name is referred to as

    a. a trademark.
    b. brand loyalty.
    c. packaging.
    d. a convenience good.

16. Which of the following is granted for 20 years and may be renewed indefinitely?

    a. trademarks
    b. brands
    c. copyrights
    d. labels

17. The part of a product's packaging that identifies the product's name and contents and sometimes its benefits is called a

    a. trademark.
    b. brand.
    c. code.
    d. label.

18. The amount added to the cost of an item in order to earn a profit for the retailer or wholesaler is referred to as the

    a. amount of fixed costs.
    b. breakeven point.
    c. markup.
    d. amount of variable costs.

19. The number of units that must be sold at a given price before the company covers all its variable and fixed costs is the

    a. markup.
    b. breakeven point.
    c. market matrix.
    d. contribution margin.

20. A form of discount in which companies involved in a product's distribution pay lower prices is a

    a. trade discount.
    b. seasonal discount.
    c. marginal discount.
    d. price lining discount.

WRITING TO LEARN

1. What is a product? What makes a product successful? How are consumer and industrial goods classified? What is the product mix?

2. Describe the stages of new product development. Discuss the concept of the product life cycle. What are the stages in the product life cycle? What is the relationship between the product life cycle and the growth-share matrix?

3. Is it important for a product to have a brand name? Discuss the different types of brand names. What is a trademark? Is packaging and labeling a product important to the consumer?

4. How does a company determine the price of its product? Discuss the tools used by managers to help determine the price of a product.

5. What pricing strategies are used for new and existing products? Discuss price lining, psychological pricing, and discounting from the firm's perspective.

DISCUSSION OF THE CLOSING CASE

The Club Med case is intriguing because it touches several aspects of marketing. It is easy to spot that Club Med is NOT in the earliest stage of its product life cycle. It is somewhere in the stage in which a firm attempts to do something to extend the life cycle. Sometimes this entails making minor changes in the product. At other times, a change in perception of the product is enough. Consider the television commercials for Kellogg's Corn Flakes. The firm is trying to alter the public's perception of its plain old corn flakes. With almost all other cereals having a gimmick--bright colors, high nutrition, frosting, prizes included, extra coupons--Corn Flakes is the newest concept, a no- gimmick cereal! Is Club Med making major alterations in its product, or is it strongly attempting to alter the public's perception of Club Med? The pleasure cruise lines that serve the Caribbean are in somewhat the same position. And various lines handle the challenge in different ways. One line's commercials show persons in their twenties enjoying the many amenities of the ship. Another cruise line uses a musical theme based on the tune "Ain't We Got Fun?" This song was popular in the 1930s. Does that tell you anything about the market segment the cruise line is trying to reach? Perhaps, it makes sense that this latter cruise line wants older Americans to perceive their line as a comfortable place for senior citizens. To muddy the waters a bit, let's say that Club Med wants to cater to wealthy senior citizens [and we must rush in here to aver that "wealthy" and "senior citizens" are not necessarily synonymous terms]. Would ads and commercials depicting family groups with happy children be appropriate? Maybe not, because some senior citizens don't enjoy having rambunctious kids running all over the resort. Well then, would Club Med want to attract senior citizens by showing in their TV commercials lots of old people limping around with canes? That may not be a good ploy either, because old people forced to limp around with canes may not respond favorably to such commercials. Their reaction might be: "I don't want to hang around with all those old people!" So, altering a product or altering a perception of it takes plenty of careful planning and strategy.

1.   Pick a side. Is Club Med trying to significantly alter its product, or is it attempting to alter the public's perception of the product?

2.   If you operated a resort similar to Club Med, and you wanted to attract senior citizens (aged 60 and up) who were indeed wealthy, what kind of TV commercials would you devise?

3.   The case has hinted that Club Med may be competing against the pleasure cruise lines. In TV commercials, which aspects of its facilities should Club Med emphasize to best eliminate the rivalry of the cruise lines?

4.   If Club Med is indeed now shifting to an "older audience," will this shift prevent them from shifting back to young, active single persons at some point in the future? Why or why not?

AN ADDITIONAL CASE

Holly Lamb was an experienced exhibitor in the motion picture industry. "Exhibitor" is movie lingo for a person who operates a theater and shows motion pictures to the local clientele. She had been very successful in some of the suburbs of Salt Lake City. The condition of her aging mother caused her to move to Stanton, an ordinary city of some 150,000 residents in the upper Midwest. Stanton, Holly felt, was ready for a new approach to moviegoing. Here was a big-city exhibitor standing by to make waves in complacent Stanton.

Holly had great advantages working in her favor. First, she had longstanding contacts with the major film distributors. This didn't necessarily mean that she could book the top films for her Stanton theater complex while local competitors took the scraps left over. But it did mean that she could compete on an even basis for the top Hollywood releases that would be coming to Stanton. Second, Holly was astute enough to know that using Salt Lake City tactics in Stanton would be a mistake. And so, she carefully studied the Stanton market before opening the Stanton Six--her sterling new motion picture complex. "I'm going to bring creative pricing into the motion picture industry," Holly told her mother. "Of the six features I'll be showing at any one time, each may have a different admission price. For example, Maw, when I get a top Hollywood thriller that has captured the public's imagination even before it gets to town, I'll charge whatever the traffic will bear--really sock it to 'em. If the public just has to see such a winner, I can charge $6.00 or $7.00 a head. On the other hand, for what I call the 'bummers' I can let people in for $1.00. I can't afford to show a film for less than $1.73--that's what I call my average cost to let a person in the theater. But I can go below the $1.73 so long as someone else in the complex is paying way above $1.73 to see a film. In addition to that, my calculations have determined that if I can take in an average admission of $1.73 per head, I will need to fill 373 of my 793 seats on any given evening to hit the break-even point for that date."

"My daughter the business whiz! Tell me, how will you know what to charge for which film? Do you ever go at cost and offer a movie for $1.73?"

"Very good questions, Mommy. That shows you're listening. Let me take your second question first. I would never let the public know how magic that $1.73 is for me. I usually go for whole dollar figures--$1,00, $3.00, $6.00, etc. The only exception is when the theater down the street is charging $2.00 for a film. I offer a movie of equal quality for $1.95--beating the competition. Now, on that first question about how much to charge for a film. In The Stanton News-Gazette, there is a movie reviewer whose column appears the very day that a film opens. Now, I've been in contact with her and she's willing to let me know how she's going to rate a film. She went along with this advance-notice system when I promised that I would never in any way attempt to influence what she had to write about a film. If the reviewer praises a film and gives it a 10 on her 10-point scale, I shall charge $6.00 for admission to that film. If, on the other hand, she calls a film a complete waste of time and rates it at a 2 or 3, I'll charge $1.00 for that one."

"What will you do when the reviewer writes that every new picture in town is a 'bummer' and you can't put a premium price on any movie?"

"In that case, the crowds and I shall determine which of the films is a 'winner.' If I notice--and I keep very careful statistics on this--that the film in Salon One has packed them in the first night, then the next day I treat it as a winner and raise the admission fee. I call such a move 'Operation Rescue' in which I step in and rescue my revenues. But that kind of quick adapting to new situations happens all the time anyway."

"How do you mean?"

"Well, let's say that the reviewer picks the film in Salon Three to be a perfect 10! I charge $6.00 and get only a skimpy crowd in Salon Three. Meanwhile, I notice that the 3-rating film in Salon Five is causing an overflow. Next night, I reduce the $6.00 movie in Salon Three to $1.00 and raise the 3-rating film in Salon Five to $6.00. Even the reviewer and I can both be fooled. There is never a guarantee that what the reviewer thinks is good will be an opinion shared by these Stanton folks."

"Give me an example."

"Well, a month ago, I had a romantic film playing called 'He Met Her in Seattle.' The reviewer gave the film a 1--the lowest possible rating. In her review, the columnist had this set of sentences: 'To make this film a complete misappropriation of studio funds, it has a tractor-pull scene that lasts for a full eleven minutes. Imagine that much time out of your evening devoted to a tractor pull. You might as well sit on your back porch and watch the grass grow. Don't waste your time and money on this flick.'"

"That's a pretty damaging remark, Holly."

"Exactly what I thought, Maw. The hard part was that her acid comments came on a weekend when all my other shows were 'bummers.' However, that mention of the tractor pull brought an overflow crowd to see 'He Met Her in Seattle.' Before the second showing--and I already noticed the mob forming outside--I raised that film's admission price to $6.00. Would you believe that we packed people into 'He Met Her in Seattle' for three weeks straight--all because of that tractor-pull sequence?"

"Amazing."

"Well, I better go now, Maw. I'm pretty concerned about a big blizzard that's going to hit town in a day or so. Foul weather plays hob with show business, you know."

1. If you were Holly Lamb, what pricing moves would you make in the next few days to ensure that you still had patrons coming to your theater despite the big blizzard that is hitting Stanton?

2. Show where Holly Lamb has brought economic supply-demand comparisons into her pricing decisions. How about use of the break-even point?

3.   Show where Holly Lamb has made use of discounting and psychological pricing.

4.   Did you find Holly Lamb's pricing to have a cost-oriented aspect? Explain. Was there
        use of price-lining?

ANSWERS TO TRUE-FALSE QUESTIONS

1.	T	(p. 441)	6.	T	(p. 447)
2.	F	(p. 441)	7.	T	(p. 450)
3.	F	(p. 442)	8.	F	(p. 451)
4.	F	(p. 446)	9.	T	(p. 451)
5.	F	(p. 446)	10.	T	(p. 459)

ANSWERS TO MULTIPLE-CHOICE QUESTIONS

1.	D	(p. 441)	11.	B	(p. 450)
2.	C	(p. 441)	12.	A	(p. 450)
3.	B	(p. 441)	13.	D	(p. 450)
4.	A	(p. 444)	14.	C	(p. 451)
5.	D	(p. 444)	15.	B	(p. 451)
6.	C	(p. 446)	16.	A	(p. 452)
7.	B	(p. 448)	17.	D	(p. 453)
8.	A	(p. 448)	18.	C	(p. 457)
9.	D	(p. 449)	19.	B	(p. 459)
10.	C	(p. 449)	20.	A	(p. 461)

CHAPTER EIGHTEEN

PROMOTING GOODS AND SERVICES

CHAPTER OVERVIEW

Promotion is any technique designed to sell a product. Marketers also use promotion to communicate information, position products, and control sales volume. A company with a push strategy will aggressively push its product through wholesalers and retailers. In a pull strategy, the appeal is directly to the consumers. The promotional mix is the best combination of advertising, personal selling, sales promotions, and publicity. Some forms of advertising are informative, persuasive, comparative, and reminder. The advertising media include television, radio, newspapers, direct mail, magazines, and billboards. Newspapers are the most widely used advertising medium. Some types of advertising are brand, advocacy, institutional, retail, cooperative, trade, and industrial. Personal selling provides a personal link between buyer and seller. Carrying out sales and research goals via the telephone is called telemarketing. Personal selling can be classified as retail and industrial. Personal selling tasks are order processing, creative selling, and missionary selling. The personal selling task consists of: prospecting/qualifying; approaching; presenting and demonstrating; handling objections; closing; and following up. Some types of sales promotions are coupons, point-of-purchase displays, samples-stamps-premiums, trade shows, and contests- sweepstakes. Publicity is free. The type of advertising and the type of personal selling chosen by a small business will depend on the market the firm is trying to reach.

LEARNING OBJECTIVES

1. Identify the objectives of promotion and the considerations involved in selecting a promotional mix.

2. Describe advertising strategies and advertising media.

3. Outline the tasks associated with personal selling and list the steps in the personal selling process.

4. Discuss the types of sales promotions and explain how publicity is used for promotion.

5. Explain how small businesses use promotion.

DISCUSSION OF THE OPENING CASE

When a business textbook discusses the three basic forms of business ownership, it is pointed out that the death of a sole proprietor means the end of the business entity. It is also indicated that the death of a member of a partnership means the dissolution of that particular partnership arrangement. It is usually stated that the death of a founder of a corporation does not mean the end of the corporation; the corporate entity has an almost everlasting quality about it. However, it seems that the death of Estee Lauder could possibly have a detrimental effect on the corporation of the same name. Current executives of the firm, including Estee's son Leonard, are aware of the impact of such an eventuality--and have plans developed for implementation when such a time comes. One way to avoid this particular aspect of the succession problem is to have in place as a personal representative of the corporation an individual who is "immortal." This is what General Mills did many years ago in giving birth to Betty Crocker. Has Betty Crocker aged? Not at all; in fact much the opposite. As the years have gone by, Betty Crocker's face, dress, and hairdo have kept up with the times. The depiction of the Betty Crocker of today looks even younger than the original. In her early days, she seemed more real, for not only did we see a drawing of her on General Mills products, but we <u>heard</u> her speaking on the radio! Surely, we thought, there must be a real Betty Crocker. This image representing General Mills will never die--unless General Mills so ordains. But why have such a personal image anyway? What does a corporation gain by use of such a "persona." The idea is that consumers like to deal with individuals. When James Cash Penney was still living, people liked the idea of going into a store owned by a man they knew--if only at a very great distance. It was known that J.C. Penney was a terribly honest man who wanted to treat all his customers in a fair manner. Surely, each of his employees would follow this example. If they failed to do so, we could write a letter of complaint to old J.C. himself! In this age of computerized communication, consumers still like to get on the phone line a <u>person</u> who can work out problems for them. Yes, having a person closely identified with a corporation has advantages--so long as we can keep the person alive.

1. What do you think of the idea of gradually slipping <u>Evelyn</u> Lauder into the role of personifying Estee Lauder, Inc.?

2. Is the American buying public too sophisticated today to identify with a character such as Betty Crocker, Mrs. Paul, or Aunt Jemima? Why or why not?

3. Comment upon this remark: "At least, we'll never read in the tabloids anything bad that Betty Crocker has done to tarnish her own image."

4. Give advantages of running a corporation with a generic name such as National Merchandise, Limited and with no individual (real or fictional) personifying the corporation.

ANNOTATED KEY TERMS

Promotion - The part of the marketing mix concerned with selecting the right techniques to sell a product to consumers.

Product Positioning - The establishment of an easily identifiable product image in the minds of consumers.

Push Strategy - A promotional strategy in which a company aggressively pushes its product through wholesalers and retailers, who then persuade customers to buy it.

Pull Strategy - A promotional strategy in which a company appeals directly to consumers, who demand the product from retailers, who demand the product from wholesalers.

Promotional Mix - The combination of promotional tools used to sell a product.

Advertising - Any form of paid, nonpersonal communication used by an identified sponsor to persuade or inform certain audiences about a good, service, or idea.

Informative Advertising - An advertising strategy that is aimed at developing an awareness of the company and its product among potential buyers.

Persuasive Advertising - An advertising strategy that is aimed at influencing consumers to buy a company's products, not the products of its rivals.

Comparative Advertising - An advertising strategy in which two or more similar products are compared directly.

Reminder Advertising - An advertising strategy aimed at keeping the product's name on the consumer's mind.

Advertising Medium - The specific communication device that is used to carry a firm's advertising message to potential consumers.

Direct Mail - Advertisements mailed directly to consumers' homes or places of business.

Media Mix - The combination of media that a company uses to advertise its products.

Brand Advertising - Advertising that promotes a specific brand.

Advocacy Advertising - Advertising that promotes a particular candidate or cause.

Institutional Advertising - Advertising that promotes a firm's long-term image.

Retail Advertising - Advertising done by retailers to reach end-users of consumer products.

Cooperative Advertising - Advertising whose cost is shared by a manufacturer and a retailer or wholesaler.

Trade Advertising - Advertising used to allow a firm to communicate with the companies that distribute its products.

Industrial Advertising - Advertising used in industrial markets to reach purchasing agents and managers buying raw materials or components.

National Advertising Review Board - The advertising industry's self-regulation board; investigates complaints against national advertisers.

Personal Selling - Selling in which a salesperson communicates one-to-one with potential customers.

Telemarketing - The use of the telephone to carry out many marketing activities, including sales and research.

Retail Selling - Selling products to consumers for their own use or for household use.

Industrial Selling - Selling products to other businesses, either for manufacturing other products or for resale.

Order Processing - In personal selling, the process of receiving an order and following through on the handling and delivery of that order.

Creative Selling - In personal selling, the use of techniques designed to persuade a customer to buy a product when the benefits of that product are not readily apparent or when the item is very expensive.

Missionary Selling - In personal selling, the promotion of a particular company.

Prospecting - In personal selling, the process of identifying potential customers.

Qualifying - In personal selling, the process of determining whether or not prospects have the authority and the ability to pay for a product.

Closing - In personal selling, the process in which the salesperson asks the prospective customer to buy the product.

Coupon - A sales promotion technique featuring a certificate that entitles the bearer to a stated savings off a product's regular price.

Point-of-Purchase (POP) Display - A sales promotion technique in which a product display is located in a retail store in such a way as to stimulate sales.

Premium - A sales promotion technique in which some item is offered free or at a bargain price in return for buying a specified product.

Trade Show - A sales promotion technique in which the various members of an industry rent booths to display and demonstrate their products to consumers who have a special interest in the products or who are ready to buy.

Publicity - Communication to the public (usually through the mass media) about a product or firm. The firm has no control over the content of the message.

Public Relations - All promotional activities directed at building good relations with various sectors of the population.

TRUE-FALSE QUESTIONS

1. The ultimate objective of any type of promotion is to increase sales.

2. A promotional mix that is good for one company is good for another.

3. Consumers ignore the bulk of the advertisements they see and/or hear.

4. Advertising strategies most often depend on which stage of the product life cycle the product is in.

5. Television is the most widely used advertising medium.

6. Personal selling is the least expensive form of promotion per contact.

7. Telemarketing can be used to handle any stage of the personal selling process.

8. Most industrial products involve missionary selling.

9. Marketers often have little control over publicity.

10. The type of advertising chosen by a small business depends on the market the firm is trying to reach.

MULTIPLE CHOICE QUESTIONS

1. The establishment of an easily identifiable image of a product in the minds of consumers is called

   a. a push strategy.
   b. a pull strategy.
   c. communication of information.
   d. product positioning.

2. Which of the following is not among the four types of promotional tools noted by the authors of your textbook?

   a. advertising
   b. personal selling
   c. the product matrix
   d. sales promotions

3. Personal selling is critical during which stage of the buyer decision process?

   a. the first stage
   b. the third stage
   c. the second stage
   d. the fourth stage

4. Informative advertising is most important during which stage of the product life cycle?

   a. the introduction stage
   b. the growth stage
   c. the maturity stage
   d. the decline stage

5. Television accounts for about what percent of all advertising expenditures?

   a. 80 percent
   b. 12 percent
   c. 76 percent
   d. 22 percent

6. Advertising that promotes Kodak 126 film and Nike Air Jordan shoes is

   a. institutional advertising.
   b. informative advertising.
   c. brand advertising.
   d. advocacy advertising.

7. Advertising by manufacturers designed to reach potential wholesalers and retailers is called

    a. brand advertising.
    b. trade advertising.
    c. industrial advertising.
    d. cooperative advertising.

8. The use of the telephone to carry out many of the activities involved in marketing a company's products is called

    a. telemarketing.
    b. retail selling.
    c. industrial selling.
    d. promotion.

9. Selling products to other businesses, either for manufacturing other products or for resale is called

    a. telemarketing.
    b. retail selling.
    c. missionary selling.
    d. industrial selling.

10. In personal sales, the indirect promotion of a product by offering technical assistance and/or promoting the company's image is referred to as

    a. order processing.
    b. creative selling.
    c. missionary selling.
    d. prospecting.

11. In personal sales, the process of identifying potential customers is called

    a. qualifying.
    b. prospecting.
    c. closing.
    d. creative selling.

12.	The part of the personal selling process in which the customer is asked to buy the product is known as the

	a.	close.
	b.	prospecting.
	c.	approaching.
	d.	qualifying.

13.	A sales-promotion method that features a certificate that entitles the bearer to a stated savings off a product's regular price is a

	a.	free sample.
	b.	trade show.
	c.	point-of-purchase display.
	d.	coupon.

14.	Pens, pencils, calendars, and coffee mugs that are given away to consumers in return for buying a specified product are

	a.	coupons.
	b.	free samples.
	c.	premiums.
	d.	sweepstakes.

15.	Company influenced publicity is called

	a.	a sales promotion.
	b.	public relations.
	c.	promotion.
	d.	personal selling.

16.	Any technique designed to sell a product to a customer is

	a.	promotion.
	b.	production.
	c.	personal selling.
	d.	product positioning.

17.	A promotional strategy in which a company appeals directly to customers, who demand the product from retailers, who demand the product from wholesalers, is called a

	a.	marketing strategy.
	b.	production strategy.
	c.	push strategy.
	d.	pull strategy.

18. The type of advertising that usually emphasizes the quality of the firm's products or services and is used to influence consumers to buy the company's products, not those of its rivals is

    a. informative advertising.
    b. comparative advertising.
    c. persuasive advertising.
    d. reminder advertising.

19. Television, radio, newspapers, direct mail, magazines, and billboards are

    a. life cycle components.
    b. advertising media.
    c. personal selling devices.
    d. direct selling techniques.

20. The most widely used advertising medium is

    a. newspapers.
    b. television.
    c. radio.
    d. magazines.

WRITING TO LEARN

1. Describe a company's promotional objectives. What promotional strategies might a company use to achieve its objectives? Why is the selection of the right tools for the promotional mix important?

2. Is there a relationship between advertising strategies and the product life cycle? Discuss the different forms of advertising medium. Is advertising dependent upon the company's target market?

3. Why is personal selling important? What tasks are associated with personal selling? Describe the personal selling process.

4.   Discuss the forms of sales promotion. What is the difference between publicity and public relations for a firm?

5.   What promotional practices are used in small business? Does small business use sales promotions and publicity?

DISCUSSION OF THE CLOSING CASE

The story of the Fox network illustrates several business concepts. First, there was the matter of the lag between expenditure of funds for operational purposes and the receiving of funds through advertising revenues. Until a network is firmly established, major advertisers may be hesitant to give the new medium a try. How many new networks can hang on long enough to wait until enthusiastic advertisers begin flocking to the network with fees in hand? How long is long enough? There might have been, in the beginning, moments when Fox executives thought that the new venture was not going to make it financially. The existing market structure of major networks (ABC, CBS, NBC) was a pretty good approximation of the traditional oligopoly--sometimes referred to as a "plural monopoly." A characteristic of an oligopoly is that its barriers to entry are hard to crack. But Fox has been capable of accomplishing this nearly impossible feat. A possible secret would be to provide provocative programming that would capture the imagination of an important segment of the overall American market. But there is a caution to be observed in airing "provocative" material. Could the programming be so "provocative" as to offend certain advertisers and their customers? [Keep in mind that some cable channels do not have advertisers to worry about.] Having such steamy fare watched by millions while advertisers stand idly by, afraid to identify with such programming, would not lead to financial success. Fox wisely established an equilibrium between scintillating programming and advertiser satisfaction. Another wise move, perhaps, was to invest in only a short slate of programs in the beginning--a testing of the waters, if you will. It cannot be denied that the powers behind Fox were able to develop some superb programs. Relevant to this chapter is the matter of publicity--the free brand of promotion. A spectacular example of word-of-mouth publicity springs from "The Simpsons." No sooner had it hit the air than school kids, columnists, school teachers, and comedians, to name a few, were repeating lines from the popular cartoon show. It seemed that everyone was talking about Bart Simpson. Soon, his likeness began appearing everywhere. Although Bart's being everywhere occurred through carefully-compensated franchise and licensing arrangements, each appearance was at the same time a bit of publicity for the show-- driving the ratings meter still higher, and making Fox an ever-strengthening competitor in the network oligopoly.

1. Chances are you have seen some Fox programming. Does it differ from programming on ABC, CBS, and NBC? If so, how?

2. Do you feel that Fox has been hurt by not offering nightly news shows? Why or why not?

3. In addition to specific mentions of it in the narrative above, give examples of promotion for Fox that you have experienced.

4. Well, now, if there was room for Fox, a fourth traditional network, is there room, do you feel, for a fifth such network? Why or why not? If so, what approach should it use?

AN ADDITIONAL CASE

Ever since he got the idea in a visit to Chicago, Eric Slerman had wanted to start a monthly magazine in Portland. He would call it <u>Portland Alive</u>. He knew it would be a great success because it was something that Portland needed. Along with the suburbs of Evanston, Albany, Plummer, and Pine Vista, the greater Portland area had a population of close to 222,000 people. The enthusiasm of Eric Slerman was matched by the pessimism of his closest friends. "Eric," they would say, "this is a guaranteed way to lose every cent you put into the magazine. Please don't ask us to put up funds for your disposal."

Eric proceeded nevertheless. A banker at Seminole National was impressed enough with the idea--and with Eric's personal solvency--to advance a major loan. The banker may not fully have understood that Eric was investing much of his own money to accompany the bank's funds. Consequently, if the magazine was a complete failure, then Eric's respectable solvency would be somewhat compromised and repayment of the bank loan could be problematical.

Eric felt that there was little to be gained by trying to promote a magazine that did not exist yet. As a result, he determined that the first issue would be printed and available on newsstands before the great promotion campaign began. He assembled a small editorial staff, began negotiating with a printer, and started putting together what would be Volume I, Number 1 of <u>Portland Alive</u>, scheduled to come out in early November. Eric's idea was that people would be so impressed by the new publication that they would want to order one-year subscriptions as Christmas gifts for their friends and relatives.

That first issue was not grabbed up very quickly at the newsstands of greater Portland. At least, Eric reassured himself, the magazine was a reality, and now he had something he could promote. Although only 237 of the November issue were purchased, Eric planned on selling over 5,000 in December.

Now that there were actual physical copies of the magazine available, Eric set up a staff to procure advertising from the local merchants. Making prospective advertisers less than enthusiastic was the fact that only 237 Portlanders bothered to buy a copy of <u>Portland Alive</u>. Buying an ad that would be viewed by only 237 people would be a poor investment. It thus became clear that by some means or other, the circulation figures on the publication had to be significantly upgraded. While a portion of the magazine's employees would be out trying to sell ads, another portion would be making efforts to rapidly increase the readership.

First, Eric purchased space in the Portland daily newspaper, <u>The Chronicle</u>, alerting readers that a new era for the city was beginning with the appearance of Eric's magazine. In several Sunday issues, <u>The Chronicle</u> sold Eric a full page. Each of these contained a coupon for subscribing to <u>Portland Alive</u>. Happily, quite a few of these coupons (accompanied by checks) began to make their way into the magazine's circulation office.

Eric's circulation manager was able to recruit numerous youth organizations to go from door to door selling subscriptions. For every one-year subscription sold, the youth organization retained a dollar. The warm-hearted people of Portland found it hard to turn down a pink-cheeked grammar school student with bright eyes. This venture brought good results for both Portland Alive and the youth organizations. [These Portland youth organizations have asked that their names not be given; some local chapters violated national regulations by working in concert with a commercial venture such as the magazine.]

Eric Slerman was fairly well-known in the greater Portland area and he made use of his local ties. Three local television talk shows had Eric as a guest, allowing Eric to explain fully just what he was going to do with Portland Alive. Of course, each interview concluded with the host saying: "And, by the way, if you would like to take out a one-year subscription, send a check for $40.00 to Box 77, Portland South Station." One of the talk shows, "Annie's Angles" on Channel 33, devoted its entire half hour to Eric explaining, with ample visualization, all the joys to be gained by subscribing to Portland Alive.

Being a hometown boy making good, Eric was interviewed twice by The Chronicle and once by The Portland Business Weekly Newsletter. Just as was the case with the TV interviews, these articles stirred up interest that resulted in quite a few new subscriptions.

By Thanksgiving Day, Eric's promotional efforts were in high gear. The traditional high school football game on that holiday would be an important event for Portland Alive. As people filed in to see the Portland Pioneers play the Ralston Red Raiders, Eric and his staff gave each patron a free copy of the magazine. Each copy contained--of course--a subscription application. In addition, the printed program for the Pioneers-Red Raiders game contained a full page declaring the wonders of the new magazine. Quite a few of the subscription blanks distributed at this game made their way back to the circulation office of Portland Alive.

Weather for the Thanksgiving game was less than ideal, and Eric had several thousand copies of his first issue still on hand. By a special arrangement with the grocery chain Granny's Grubb (with 11 stores in greater Portland), the circulation staff set up point-of-purchase (POP) displays in each store. At each POP display, there was a pile of the magazines and a banner reading: "Next month, these will cost you $4.00 each; TODAY they are FREE. Take all you want!" They were gobbled up quickly, and far more subscription blanks found their way to the ciculation office than expected.

Prospective advertisers were gradually taking notice of Eric's efforts, and this resulted in several large new accounts. Volume I, Number 2 was destined to be far more successful than its forerunner. But Eric knew there was still plenty of promotion-- on a continuing basis--to be performed before his brainchild would be fully alive and well.

1.   What do you think of Eric's idea that there was little to be gained by promoting a magazine that did not yet exist? Explain.

2.   Comment upon Eric's plan to have people buy one-year subscriptions to Portland Alive as Christmas gifts, considering that the first-ever issue appeared in November. How

could this have been better handled? 3. Would Eric have been wise to give away all the copies of Volume I, Number 1? Why or why not? If he did that, which kind of promotion would this be?

4. Go back over Eric's saga and point out instances of advertising, sales promotions, publicity, and personal selling.

ANSWERS TO TRUE-FALSE QUESTIONS

1.	T	(p. 469)	6.	F	(p. 482)
2.	F	(p. 472)	7.	T	(p. 482)
3.	T	(p. 473)	8.	F	(p. 483)
4.	T	(p. 473)	9.	T	(p. 487)
5.	F	(p. 475)	10.	T	(p. 487)

ANSWERS TO MULTIPLE-CHOICE QUESTIONS

1.	D	(p. 470)	11.	B	(p. 484)
2.	C	(p. 471)	12.	A	(p. 484)
3.	B	(p. 473)	13.	D	(p. 486)
4.	A	(p. 474)	14.	C	(p. 486)
5.	D	(p. 475)	15.	B	(p. 487)
6.	C	(p. 479)	16.	A	(p. 468)
7.	B	(p. 479)	17.	D	(p. 470)
8.	A	(p. 482)	18.	C	(p. 474)
9.	D	(p. 482)	19.	B	(p. 475)
10.	C	(p. 482)	20.	A	(p. 475)

CHAPTER NINETEEN

DISTRIBUTING GOODS AND SERVICES

CHAPTER OVERVIEW

Individuals and firms other than producers who help distribute a product are known as intermediaries, once called "middlemen." They fall in the two broad categories of wholesalers and retailers. A distribution channel is the path that a product follows from producer to end-user. A channel can be as simple as leading from producer to consumer without any intermediaries or as complex as to contain numerous intermediaries. Intensive distribution entails distributing a product through as many channels as possible. In exclusive distribution, a manufacturer grants to very few intermediaries the exclusive right to distribute. Selective distribution falls between intensive and exclusive. Wholesalers are divided into two categories: merchant wholesalers and agents/brokers. Some types of retailers are department stores, speciality stores, bargain stores, convenience stores, supermarkets, and hypermarkets. Some non-store kinds of retailing are mail order, direct selling, and video marketing. A warehouse can be private (used by the firm owning the warehouse) or public (in which space is leased to other firms for their storage uses). Transportation methods used by manufacturers and intermediaries are trucks, planes, railroads, water carriers, and pipelines. Companies specializing in transportation can be common carriers, freight forwarders, contract carriers, or private carriers. Containerization makes intermodal transportation more efficient.

LEARNING OBJECTIVES

1. Outline and discuss the channels of distribution and distribution strategies.

2. Explain the differences between merchant wholesalers and agents/brokers.

3. Identify the different types of retail stores and explain the wheel of retailing theory.

4. Describe the three major activities in the physical distribution process.

5. Compare the five basic forms of transportation and identify the types of firms that provide such transportation.

DISCUSSION OF THE OPENING CASE

The Liz Claiborne story reminds one of your study guide authors of a visit he made with a group of students to the executive offices of perhaps America's premier manufacturer of men's dress shirts. The surroundings were not at all pretentious. The two executives who briefed our student group on the shirt industry were <u>not</u> wearing the typical New York executive "uniform"--gray suit, white button-down shirt, subdued red necktie, black wing- tip shoes. Instead, the two white-haired gentlemen greeted our group wearing just a shirt and tie. Having previously visited several prestigious firms, and having been served lunch in the executive dining room of one of the nation's largest banks, the students expected more of the executives' quarters of the shirt manufacturer. On the evening after the visit with the shirt executives, the professor leading the student group explained that we had met with two men each of whom deserved the title "genius." They were not necessarily experts at designing new shirts for men, nor were they adept at playing the slick advertising game. What made each a genius was a broad and deep understanding of how to distribute a product properly. This kind of knowledge comes only from being a part of a massive distribution effort over a long period of time. When the Liz Claiborne story refers to "marketing specialist Jerry Chazen," we can assume that here is a man who knows garment industry distribution well enough to help the firm chart a proper course. Note that Liz Claiborne and her husband "put up their life savings" to launch the firm. It would have been utter folly to make such a commitment without someone on board who knew how to get the product to retail stores and then into the hands of the consumers. We can further assume that the effective manner of dealing with retailers--specifically the "buyers"--is a reflection of what Jerry Chazen knows about distributing. Also worthy of our attention is the fact that Liz Claiborne set out to satisfy the wants and needs of America's <u>working</u> women. Demographers will tell us that had such a goal been established in the 1930s, Liz Claiborne would have been playing to a much smaller audience. So, the Claiborne organization is totally in tune with the times. Chances are excellent that the firm will remain in harmony with new trends as they develop in society.

1.   Do you feel that the Liz Claiborne organization is a little too tough on buyers from retail establishments? Why or why not?

2.   Which do you think is the most important key to the success of Liz Clairborne? Explain.

3.   Why did Liz Claiborne's 1987 line have so little success?

4.   Do you feel that more conversations with buyers from retail stores could have helped Liz Claiborne to avoid the problems with the 1987 line? Why or why not?

ANNOTATED KEY TERMS

<u>Distribution Mix</u> - The combination of distribution channels used by a firm in getting its product to the end users.

<u>Intermediary</u> - An individual or firm, other than producers and their employees, that helps to distribute a product.

<u>Wholesalers</u> - Intermediaries who sell products to other businesses, who in turn resell them to the final consumer.

<u>Retailers</u> - Intermediaries who sell products directly to consumers.

<u>Distribution Channel</u> - The path a product follows from the producer to the end user.

<u>Direct Channel</u> - A distribution channel in which the product travels from the producer to the consumer with no intermediaries.

<u>Sales Agents/Brokers</u> - Intermediaries who represent a manufacturer and sell to wholesalers. Brokers usually represent many companies and are independent of any one producer.

<u>Industrial Distribution</u> - The network of distribution channel members involved in the flow of manufactured goods to industrial customers.

<u>Sales Office</u> - An office maintained by a manufacturer as a contact point with its customers.

<u>Intensive Distribution</u> - A distribution strategy in which a product is distributed through as many channels as possible.

<u>Exclusive Distribution</u> - A distribution strategy in which a manufacturer grants the exclusive right to distribute or sell a product to a limited number of wholesalers or retailers in a given geographic area.

<u>Selective Distribution</u> - A distribution strategy in which a company uses only wholesalers and retailers who will give special attention to the product.

<u>Channel Conflict</u> - Conflict that arises when the members of a distribution channel disagree over the roles they should play or the rewards they should receive for their services.

<u>Channel Captain</u> - The channel member that is most powerful in determining the roles and rewards of the other channel members.

<u>Vertical Marketing System (VMS)</u> - A union of several separate businesses to form a unified distribution channel.

<u>Merchant Wholesaler</u> - An independent wholesaler that buys and takes legal possession of the goods produced by a variety of manufacturers, then resells these goods to other businesses.

<u>Full-Service Merchant Wholesaler</u> - A merchant wholesaler that provides credit, marketing, and merchandising services in addition to the traditional buying-and-selling services of wholesalers.

<u>Rack Jobber</u> - A full-function merchant wholesaler that sets up and maintains display racks in retail stores.

<u>Limited-Function Merchant Wholesaler</u> - A merchant wholesaler that provides only a few wholesaling services.

<u>Drop Shipper</u> - A limited-function merchant wholesaler that receives orders from the customer, negotiates with producers to supply the goods, takes title to the products, and arranges for their shipment to the customer.

<u>Department Stores</u> - Large retail stores characterized by their organization into specialized departments.

<u>Specialty Stores</u> - Small retail stores that carry one line of related products.

<u>Bargain Stores</u> - Retail stores that offer special deals to customers.

<u>Variety Stores</u> - Bargain stores that sell a wide range of merchandise at low prices and that seldom carry high-priced items.

<u>Discount Houses</u> - Bargain stores that offer goods at substantial price reduction in order to generate a large sales volume.

<u>Off-Price Stores</u> - Bargain stores that buy the excess inventories of well-recognized, high-quality manufacturers and sell these products at discounted prices.

<u>Catalog Showroom</u> - Bargain stores in which customers place orders for an item they have seen in a catalog and pick up that item from an on-premises warehouse.

<u>Factory Outlets</u> - Bargain stores that are owned by manufacturers whose products they sell.

<u>Warehouse Club (Wholesale Club)</u> - Bargain stores that offer large discounts on brand-name merchandise to people who have paid an annual fee for membership in the club.

<u>Convenience Stores</u> - Retail stores that offer easy accessibility, extended hours, and fast service.

<u>Supermarkets</u> - Large retail stores that offer a variety of food and food-related items divided into specialized departments.

<u>Hypermarkets</u> - Very large retail stores that carry a wide variety of unrelated products.

<u>Scrambled Merchandising</u> - The retail practice of carrying any product that is expected to sell well, whether or not it fits into the store's original product offering.

<u>Mail Order</u> - A form of nonstore retailing in which customers place orders for merchandise shown in catalogs and receive their orders through the mail.

<u>Direct Selling</u> - Door-to-door sales.

<u>Video Marketing</u> - Selling to consumers via standard and cable television.

Wheel of Retailing - A theory of the evolution of retail stores that holds that low-price, low-services stores gradually add services and raise prices until they lose price-sensitive customers. New firms then enter the market to fill the gap for low-price stores.

Physical Distribution - Those activities needed to move a product efficiently from the manufacturer to the ultimate consumer.

Order-Processing - That part of a product's distribution that involves filling orders as they are received.

Order-Cycle Time - The total time elapsed between the placement of an order and the time that order is received.

Warehousing - That part of a product's distribution that is concerned with the storage of goods.

Private Warehouses - Warehouses that are owned by and provide storage for just one company.

Public Warehouses - Warehouses that are independently owned and operated and that store the goods of many firms.

Storage Warehouses - Warehouses that provide storage for extended periods of time.

Distribution Centers - Warehouses used to provide short-term storage of goods for which demand is constant and high.

Inventory Control - The part of warehouse operations that keeps track of what is on hand and ensures that an adequate supply of a product is in stock at all times.

Bar Coding - A method of inventory control in which bar code labels are attached to inventory items. Hand-held scanners read the bar codes and transmit the inventory data directly to a computer.

Materials Handling - The transportation, arrangement, and orderly retrieval of goods in inventory.

Unitization - A materials-handling strategy in which goods are transported and stored in containers of a uniform size, weight, or shape.

Automated Storage and Retrieval System (AS/RS) - A materials- handling system that uses computer-guided vehicles to move, store, and retrieve inventory and to keep track of inventory as it enters and leaves the warehouse.

Intermodal Transportation - The combined use of several different modes of transportation.

Containerization - A method of transportation in which goods are sealed in a container at their source and not opened until they reach their final destination.

Transportation Infrastructure - A nation's system of roads, bridges, highways, waterways, pipelines, railroad tracks, and airline routes that permits products to be transported from one point to another.

Common Carriers - Truck lines and railroads that transport goods for anyone wishing to make a shipment.

Freight Forwarders - A common carrier that leases bulk space from other carriers, then resells that space to firms making smaller shipments.

Contract Carriers - Independent transporters who usually own the vehicle that transports the products.

Private Carriers - Manufacturers and retailers that maintain their own transportation systems.

TRUE-FALSE QUESTIONS

1.   All channels must begin with a manufacturer and end with a consumer or an industrial user.

2.   Unlike consumer products, industrial products traditionally are distributed through channels 1 or 2.

3.   In channel 6, the use of a wholesaler between a manufacturer and an industrial user accounts for a large percentage of distribution.

4.   Intensive distribution is normally used for high-cost, consumer goods such as Rolex watches.

5.   All merchant wholesalers take title to merchandise.

6.   Rack jobbers most commonly handle nonfood items.

7.   Over one-half of the nation's retailers account for less than 10 percent of all retail sales.

8.   There are two basic types of warehouses: private and foreign.

9.   The cost of physically moving a product is the lowest cost faced by many manufacturers.

10. Water transportation is the least expensive of all the transportation modes available.

MULTIPLE CHOICE QUESTIONS

1. Individuals and firms other than producers and their employees who help to distribute a product are known as

   a. marketers.
   b. the sales force.
   c. price determiners.
   d. intermediaries.

2. Which of the following intermediaries sells products to other businesses, who in turn resell them to the final consumer?

   a. retailers
   b. producers
   c. wholesalers
   d. manufacturers

3. Avon, Fuller Brush, Tupperware and many encyclopedia distributors use which of the following channels?

   a. channel 6
   b. channel 1
   c. channel 4
   d. channel 3

4. The path a product follows from the producer to the end user is called the

   a. distribution channel.
   b. retail channel.
   c. channel conflict.
   d. merchant wholesale channel.

5. Sales agents or brokers are found in the most complex distribution channel, which is

   a. channel 1.
   b. channel 2.
   c. channel 6.
   d. channel 4.

6. Steel, transistors, and conveyers are distributed through

   a. channel 6.
   b. channel 1.
   c. channel 5.
   d. channel 2.

7. The network of channel members involved in the flow of manufactured goods to industrial customers is called

   a. the wheel of retailing.
   b. industrial distribution.
   c. intensive distribution.
   d. selective distribution.

8. A distribution strategy in which a product's distribution is limited to only one wholesaler or retailer in a given geographic area is called

   a. exclusive distribution.
   b. intensive distribution.
   c. selective distribution.
   d. channel conflict.

9. The channel member that is most powerful in determining the roles and rewards of the other channel members is the

   a. channel conflict.
   b. channel cell.
   c. channel marketing system.
   d. channel captain.

10. All stages in the channel are under single ownership in a

    a. administered VMS.
    b. contractual VMS.
    c. corporate VMS.
    d. distributed VMS.

11. Macy's, Marshall Field's, and Dayton-Hudson are examples of

    a. specialty stores.
    b. department stores.
    c. bargain stores.
    d. convenience stores.

12.   Safeway, A&P, and Kroger are examples of

       a. supermarkets.
       b. hypermarkets.
       c. bargain stores.
       d. convenience stores.

13.   The retail practice of carrying any product expected to sell well, regardless of whether it
       fits into the store's original product offering is called

       a. nonstore retailing.
       b. a catalog showroom.
       c. the wheel of retailing.
       d. scrambled merchandising.

14.   According to the authors of your textbook, possibly the oldest form of retailing is

       a. video marketing.
       b. nonstore retailing.
       c. direct selling.
       d. warehousing.

15.   The theory of the evolution of retail stores in which low- price, low-service stores gradually
       add services and raise prices until they lose price-sensitive customer, and new firms enter
       the market to fill the gap is called

       a. warehousing.
       b. the wheel of retailing.
       c. distribution.
       d. the marketing mix.

16.   Activities needed to move a product from the manufacturer to the ultimate consumer are
       referred to as

       a. physical distribution.
       b. marketing.
       c. order processing.
       d. rack jobbing.

17. The total amount of time from order placement to the customer's actually receiving the order is called

   a. distribution time.
   b. manufacturing time.
   c. EOQ.
   d. order-cycle time.

18. Producers of seasonal items, such as agricultural crops, use which of the following types of warehouses for extended periods of time?

   a. distribution centers
   b. hypermarkets
   c. storage warehouses
   d. private warehouses

19. The part of warehouse operations that keeps track of what is on hand and plans to assure adequate supplies of products in stock at all times is

   a. order-cycle time.
   b. inventory control.
   c. warehousing.
   d. materials handling.

20. Common carriers that lease bulk space from other carriers and resell that space to firms making small shipments is called a

   a. freight forwarder.
   b. contract carrier.
   c. private carrier.
   d. intermodal carrier.

WRITING TO LEARN

1. What are some of the factors that enter into the distribution mix decision? Discuss the six primary distribution channels.

2. Is there an appropriate distribution strategy for each firm? When does a channel conflict occur?

3. What role does the wholesale intermediary play in distribution? Describe the different types of wholesale intermediaries and the services they provide.

4. Distinguish between the various types of retail outlets. What goods and services are offered through nonstore retailing?

5. What does physical distribution of a product involve? Describe the theory of the wheel of retailing. What are the basic types of warehouses? List the advantages and disadvantages of the modes of transportation mentioned in your textbook.

DISCUSSION OF THE CLOSING CASE

Although the textbook names truck lines and railroads as the two best examples of "common carrier," the Evergreen fleet of ships would be classed as a common carrier--a transportation firm that offers space to any client desiring transportation service. Such a carrier--like any other business--must have a special eye to the future of its industry and must, as well, depend on the good graces of The Fates. When, in 1982, Chang Yung-fa ordered 24 new container ships, "industry insiders questioned his sanity." Evidently, Chang saw in the recession of that era not the end of the world, but instead a shiny, golden opportunity. Did he indeed see an opportunity, or was he taking a supreme risk, and gambling on the future of his entire operation? Surely, the purchase of 24 new ships meant the shouldering of heavy debts by Evergreen. [If the ships were purchased by cash on hand, such an arrangement is even more foolish.] This assumption of heavy debt is often the first stepping stone in the direction of bankruptcy. Had Evergreen filed for bankruptcy, a feature writer for some national business periodical would have opened his or her story on Evergreen in this way: "Saddled with debts approaching a billion dollars while watching its operational revenues falling in our current recession, the Evergreen Group had no alternative but to file for Chapter 11 bankruptcy. Whether the firm is capable of reorganizing and restoring itself to a solid and stable basis is uncertain at this time. When asked at a press conference how Evergreen fell into its current abyss, founder Chang Yung-fa replied that perhaps the straw that broke the camel's back was the purchase of 24 container ships at a cost of $30 million each." However, the bold move by Chang did _not_ lead to bankruptcy. Much to the contrary, adding those 24 ships allowed Evergreen to expand its service, move toward greater efficiency, garner new customers, and leave much of the competition behind. The transportation industry is one of those industries requiring very expensive fixed assets--such as container ships. The industry also requires a balance between bold moves and cautious moves. At this writing Chang Yung-fa seems to have a keen sense of timing about his industry.

1.   What kinds of new opportunities await Chang Yung-fa's Evergreen Group in mainland China in the next few years?

2.   Should getting the 24 container ships at a "bargain price" be the only consideration of Chang in making such a major purchase decision? Why or why not?

3.   How much longer can Chang count on "low wage rates for Taiwanese sailors"? Explain.

4.   Has Chang been just plain lucky with his Evergreen Group, or does he indeed have a crystal ball telling him what will be happening in the transportation industry in the years to come?

AN ADDITIONAL CASE

When the old canning facility closed down in Albany (population 43,000), both the community's morale and its economic stability took a heavy hit. For nearly a half century, Mason Fruit Products had operated the cannery and employed 500 persons. Mason was involved in canning peaches, pears, and apricots, and distributed the same through much of the Pacific Northwest. In recent years, the big-name national fruit canners (due to the economics term "economies of scale") were able to so effectively cut their prices that Mason just could not compete. What this meant in practical terms was that thousands of Mason cans would just sit on a grocer's shelves gathering dust--because their prices were too high when compared with those of the national fruit packers.

The mayor of Albany and several members of the Chamber of Commerce tried to find someone who could bring the old plant to life again. Although they were not successful in locating another manufacturer who could make use of canning equipment, the Albany representatives found Clevon Tash who would use the old cannery building and put fifty people to work immediately. If Tash's product went over with a bang, many more workers would be needed a little bit later.

Clevon Tash would be preparing what he called "peach-pecan shortcakes," a delicacy for the frozen food section of your grocery. Coming in a clear plastic container, a shortcake would consist of a small sugar biscuit, topped by a lucious peach, a generous serving of whipped cream, and a sprinkling of large pecan bits. Fortunately, some of the old canning equipment could be utilized by the Tash operation. For a product that hadn't even been on the market yet, Clevon Tash was counting on success right from the start.

And that is exactly what came to him!

By one of those flukes that even the marketing experts cannot explain, people in the Pacific Northwest found the peach-pecan shortcakes were a perfect way to top off a special meal. Even grocers who were skeptical about the attracting power of such a product were now openly euphoric about the sales in the first month alone. For the moment, Tash's plant was able to keep up with the demand--just barely. There were signs, however, that the Tash organization would not be able to maintain the pace dictated by its own success. The main problem was the distribution system, or more accurately, the absence of a distribution system.

Once the shortcakes came off the assembly line and were packed into two refrigerated trucks that belonged to Tash, the two drivers headed out on their respective routes. The distribution area for the shortcakes was a large circle centered in Albany with a radius of fifty miles. On a quick day, a driver could make up to thirty stops at grocery stores. But that was really pushing it, when you consider that the stores were widely separated. The two drivers complained constantly that thirty stops a day (unloading, settling financial matters with each grocer, taking orders for the next trip, talking to grocery stores that had not yet agreed to stock the shortcakes, etc.) were too many. Hardly paying any attention to the drivers, Clevon Tash planned to "solve" the problem by adding two more trucks and then bring plant personnel up to 110 workers.

The business was booming so beautifully that now all four of the drivers were complaining about being overworked. Even Clevon's brother, Clive, joined the chorus of complaint.

"Clevon," Clive began, "you're at a crossroads in your shortcake career. Either you want to manufacture shortcakes or you want to get into the trucking business."

Clevon was more than just a little defensive: "What are you talking about?"

"Our business has been so good, and our product is well known enough now that we are ready to deliver our shortcakes to a wholesaler and let the wholesaler worry about getting the product into its many nooks and crannies."

"I won't hear of that. I won't have some middleman--excuse me, I mean intermediary--getting in my marketing channel and raising the retail price of my shortcakes."

"Clevon, surely you've heard the old saying: 'You can eliminate the intermediary, but you can't eliminate his or her <u>function</u>.' By being a trucking company in addition to making shortcakes, you are performing the function of a middleman. And, by the way, these retail grocers to whom you deliver are all themselves intermediaries. So, you aren't cutting out the middle man even now."

Clevon was listening now: "What would you suggest, Brother?"

"You and I can get in touch with several merchant wholesalers, let them know what great success we've had with the shortcakes, and try to sell them large lots of the cakes. They'll take it from there. Then, you and I can concentrate on producing more and more shortcakes."

Happy to say, Clevon took the advice of Clive. The brothers granted exclusive distribution rights to four merchant wholesalers--each serving a different geographical area. The worker population at the Tash plant rose to 213, and peach-pecan shortcakes were rolling fast off the assembly line.

To check on distribution, Clive spent one Saturday afternoon driving from store to store in small towns near Albany. When he entered a store, he went right to the frozen food section to see how his shortcakes were being displayed. What he saw displeased him greatly. The stock of his shortcakes was always low. This meant that each week numerous customers would find the store was out of Tash's shortcakes. In addition, the cakes were situated in the shadows of other frozen products. Clearly, the wholesalers and retailers were not doing right by the Tash product.

1.   If you were Clevon Tash, how would you alter the marketing channel to correct this saddening situation he has just experienced?

2.   In addition to altering the marketing channel as in Number 1 above, what are some things Clevon can do to make both merchant wholesaler and retailer more attentive to the sales fate of the shortcakes?

3.   Respond to this comment one could make to Clevon Tash: "What difference should it make to you how the shortcakes are displayed by the merchant wholesaler and retailer? After all, the wholesaler has already paid you, hasn't he?"

4. In the previous chapter, you read about "missionary selling." Could a missionary salesperson help Clevon in this hour of need? Why or why not?

ANSWERS TO TRUE-FALSE QUESTIONS

1.	T	(p. 497)	6.	T	(p. 503)
2.	F	(p. 499)	7.	T	(p. 504)
3.	F	(p. 501)	8.	F	(p. 511)
4.	F	(p. 501)	9.	F	(p. 512)
5.	T	(p. 503)	10.	T	(p. 514)

ANSWERS TO MULTIPLE-CHOICE QUESTIONS

1.	D	(p. 497)	11.	B	(p. 505)
2.	C	(p. 497)	12.	A	(p. 507)
3.	B	(p. 498)	13.	D	(p. 507)
4.	A	(p. 497)	14.	C	(p. 509)
5.	D	(p. 498)	15.	B	(p. 509)
6.	C	(p. 499)	16.	A	(p. 510)
7.	B	(p. 499)	17.	D	(p. 511)
8.	A	(p. 501)	18.	C	(p. 511)
9.	D	(p. 502)	19.	B	(p. 512)
10.	C	(p. 503)	20.	A	(p. 515)

CHAPTER TWENTY

UNDERSTANDING MONEY AND BANKING

CHAPTER OVERVIEW

An object can serve as money if it is portable, divisible, durable, and stable. Money serves as a medium of exchange, a store of value, and as a unit of account. The M1 money supply consists of currency, demand deposits, and other "checkable" deposits. Time deposits require prior notice to make a withdrawal and cannot be transferred to others by means of a check. Commercial banks accept deposits and use these deposits to make loans and thus to earn profits. Credit cards are extremely profitable to the issuing companies. Although originally created to provide financing for homes, the savings and loan institutions have ventured into other investments. At mutual savings banks, depositors are considered as owners. A credit union is an institution that accepts deposits only from its members, and a pension fund is essentially a pool of funds managed to provide retirement income for its members. Every national bank is subject to regulation by the Comptroller of the Currency. Over 98 percent of commercial banks are members of the Federal Deposit Insurance Corporation. The Federal Reserve System, with its twelve districts, plays several roles--serving as the government's bank, serving as the banker's bank, overseeing the banking community, and controlling the money supply. Its tools for the latter function are reserve requirements, the discount rate, and open-market operations.

LEARNING OBJECTIVES

1. Define money and identify the different forms of money in the nation's money supply.

2. Discuss the different kinds of financial institutions that comprise the U.S. financial system and the services they offer.

3. Explain how banks create money and by whom they are regulated.

4. Describe the Federal Reserve System's functions and the tools it uses to control the money supply.

5. Discuss five ways in which the financial market is changing.

DISCUSSION OF THE OPENING CASE

Concerning the recent failures of so many savings and loan associations, commentary will flow in torrents for years and years to come. It is impossible to pinpoint one cause of the debacle; the picture is exceedingly complex. Nevertheless, we shall attempt here to emphasize just two contributing factors. First, your case presentation has wisely used the term "greed." Greed in the investment world translates into willingness to take on great risks in order to realize great profits! Making a loan means there will be income in the form of interest payments. The bigger the loan, the bigger the interest payments. It would make sense for an S&L loan officer to go through the following mental process. "If I REFUSE the loan, the S&L will pass up a great chance at additional revenue. If I APPROVE the loan, we will make additional revenue. Also, if I approve a loan that other institutions have found too risky, then the S&L can charge a much higher interest rate--and our net income will be improved. I'll do it!" In this manner, many loan officers lent funds to ventures that encountered severe financial difficulties and the borrowers involved had to default. To second-guess S&L loan officers, we could say that had all of them been ultraconservative in making loans, then the S&L tragedy would not have developed. In other words, more of these loan officers, we say with our perfect hindsight, should have learned to say: "I'm terribly sorry, but we do not feel that your project is a safe investment for our institution." Had that statement been used more frequently, there would be some very small S&L's in our country, but many more of them would have been solvent. Second, it has been voiced here and there that S&L loan officers tended to play free and easy with depositors' money because the depositors' money was insured by Uncle Sam's Federal Savings and Loan Insurance Corporation (FSLIC). In other words, the U.S. agency is taking much of the risk. This inspired a false sense of security that enabled S&L loan officers, so the opinion goes, to be less careful with the doling out of funds. Here's an analogy. If your insurance man tells you that the homeowner's policy does not cover your bicycle, then you lock it up inside your dwelling carefully every night. If, on the other hand, the insurance man rules that the bike is indeed covered, then you feel more free to lay your bike out in the front yard at the end of a day. Perhaps that was the attitude S&L officers took, knowing there was some backing by the FSLIC.

1. What are some other reasons you can identify for the S&L failures?

2. Have you heard of the role of the "Keating Five" in the S&L saga? If so, comment on the appropriateness of the five.

3. For the future, what are some ways that the FSLIC or a similar agency can better assure that S&L loans are being provided on a more careful and conservative basis?

4. React to this statement: "Regardless of the financial fall of many S&L's, their wild granting of money for shaky investments provided a tremendous upsurge in the American economy. These S&L's are to be applauded for that!"

ANNOTATED KEY TERMS

Money - Any object that is portable, divisible, durable, and stable and that serves as a medium of exchange, a store of value, and a unit of account.

M-1- A measure of the money supply that includes only the most liquid (spendable) forms of money: currency, demand deposits, and other checkable deposits.

Currency - Paper money and metal coins issued by the government.

Check - An order instructing a bank to pay a given sum to a specified person or firm.

Demand Deposits - Funds deposited in bank accounts that may be withdrawn at any time without notice.

M-2 - A measure of the money supply that includes all the components of M-1, plus the forms of money that cannot be spent directly, but are easily converted into spendable form: time deposits, money-market mutual funds, and savings deposits.

Time Deposits - Funds deposited in banks that cannot be withdrawn without notice and against which checks cannot be written.

Money-Market Mutual Funds - A form of investment in which a nonbank institution pools the assets of many investors to buy a collection of short-term, low-risk financial securities. Ownership of and profits or losses from the sale of these securities are shared among the investors in the fund.

Money-Market Deposit Accounts - A form of investment in which a bank or other depository institution pools the assets of depositors to buy a collection of short-term, low-risk financial securities. Ownership of and profits or losses from the sale of these securities are shared among the depositors in the account.

Commercial Bank - A federally-chartered or state-chartered company that accepts deposits and uses them to make loans and thus to earn profits.

State Bank - A commercial bank that is chartered by an individual state, but not by the federal government.

National Bank - A commercial bank that is chartered by the federal government and thus is a part of the Federal Reserve System.

Prime Rate - The interest rate available to a bank's best (most creditworthy) customers.

Savings and Loan Association (S&Ls) - A company that accepts deposits and makes loans primarily for home mortgages.

282

<u>Mutual Savings Bank</u> - A bank whose depositors are also its owners and therefore share in any of its profits.

<u>Credit Union</u> - An institution that accepts deposits only from and makes loans only to its members. Usually, employment at a particular company is necessary to gain membership into the credit union.

<u>Pension Fund</u> - A pool of funds managed to provide retirement income for its members.

<u>Insurance Companies</u> - Companies that collect a large pool of funds from the premiums they charge for their insurance coverage and then invest these funds in stocks, real estate, and other assets.

<u>Finance Companies</u> - Companies that specialize in making loans to businesses and consumers.

<u>Securities Investment Dealers (Brokers)</u> - Companies that buy and sell stocks and bonds on stock exchanges for investors.

<u>Investment Bankers</u> - Financial intermediaries that match buyers and sellers of newly issued securities.

<u>Individual Retirement Account (IRA)</u> - Tax-deferred pension funds that wage-earners and their spouses can set up to supplement any other retirement funds they might have.

<u>Keogh Plan</u> - Tax-deferred pension plans for self-employed people.

<u>Trust Services</u> - Services in which a commercial bank manages an individual's investments, payments, or estate in return for a fee.

<u>Letter of Credit</u> - A written promise by a bank, issued on behalf of a buyer, to pay a designated firm a certain amount of money if specified conditions are met.

<u>Banker's Acceptance</u> - A written promise by a bank, issued on behalf of a buyer, to pay a designated firm a certain amount by a particular date.

<u>Automatic Teller Machine (ATM)</u> - Electronic machines that allow customers to withdraw money, make deposits, check balances, and transfer funds between their accounts 24 hours a day, seven days a week.

<u>Electronic Funds Transfer (EFT)</u> - The communication of financial information or the transfer of funds over wire, cable, or microwave.

<u>Federal Deposit Insurance Corporation (FDIC)</u> - The federal agency that guarantees the safety of all deposits up to $100,000 in the banks it insures. Depositors who lose their money in bank failures are reimbursed through the FDIC's Bank Insurance Fund (BIF).

Office of Thrift Supervision (OTS) - The federal agency that regulates the state-chartered and federal thrift institutions belonging to the Savings Association Insurance Fund, which insures savings and loan associations and mutual savings banks.

Resolution Trust Corporation (RTC) - The government agency set up to resolve all troubled thrift cases from January 1989 to August 1992. Under the FDIC's supervision, the RTC manages thrifts that are placed in receivership, approves mergers between failed thrifts and healthy institutions, liquidates other troubled thrifts, and disposes of assets obtained by the government from failed companies.

Federal Reserve System (The Fed) - The central bank of the United States; it acts as the government's bank and the bankers' bank, and controls the nation's money supply.

Float - The total amount of checks that have been written, but not yet cleared through the Federal Reserve.

Monetary Policy - The policies instituted by the Federal Reserve System to manage the nation's money supply and interest rates.

Reserve Requirement - The percentage of its deposits that a bank must hold in cash or on deposit with a Federal Reserve Bank.

Excess Reserves - Any reserves held by a bank in excess of its reserve requirement.

Discount Rate - The interest rate at which member banks can borrow money from their Federal Reserve district bank.

Open-Market Operations - The Fed's sales and purchases of securities in the open market.

Selective Credit Controls - The Fed's authority to set margin requirements for consumer purchases of stocks and to set credit rules for certain other types of consumer purchases.

Debit Card - A plastic card that allows an individual to transfer money from one account to another.

Point-of-Sale-Terminal (POS) - An electronic device in use in some stores that allows customers to pay for their purchases with debit cards.

Financial Supermarket - A nonbank firm that offers a broad array of financial services.

TRUE-FALSE QUESTIONS

1.   When the money supply is high, the value of money increases.

2. Demand deposits are counted in M-1.

3. Credit cards are not money.

4. S&Ls primarily lend money for common stock investments.

5. Every national bank is subject to regulation by the Comptroller of the Currency.

6. Over 98 percent of all commercial banks are members of the FDIC and pay a fee for membership.

7. Changes in the reserve requirement are frequently used by the Fed to control the money supply.

8. Reserve requirements are not identical for all banks.

9. The margin requirement stipulates the amount of credit the banker can extend to the broker.

10. The Fed's Board of Governors consists of fourteen members appointed by the Congress.

MULTIPLE CHOICE QUESTIONS

1. An object that serves as a medium of exchange, a store of value, a unit of account and is portable, divisible, durable, and stable is

    a. currency.
    b. coin.
    c. barterable.
    d. money.

2. Which of the following is not a characteristic of money?

    a. portability
    b. durability
    c. a demand deposit
    d. stability

3.	The most common measure of the money supply that counts only the most liquid forms of money is

a.	M-2
b.	M-1
c.	M-3
d.	L

4.	Checking accounts are also called

a.	demand deposits.
b.	currency.
c.	time deposits.
d.	money market funds.

5.	Which of the following are operated by investment companies who form a pool of assets from many investors and, in turn, buys a collection of short-term, low risk financial securities?

a.	commercial banks
b.	investment bankers
c.	the Fed
d.	money market mutual funds

6.	A special interest-bearing checking account that can only be held by individuals and nonprofit organizations in savings banks and savings and loan associations is the

a.	time deposit.
b.	CD.
c.	NOW account.
d.	money market mutual fund.

7.	Nationally or state-chartered companies that accept deposits and use them to make loans and thus to earn profits are

a.	money market mutual funds.
b.	commercial banks.
c.	pension funds.
d.	finance companies.

8. All nationally chartered banks must belong to the

   a. Fed.
   b. state bank association.
   c. SEC.
   d. CUNA association.

9. The oldest form of savings institution in the United States is the

   a. commercial bank.
   b. savings and loan association.
   c. credit union.
   d. mutual savings bank.

10. An institution that accepts deposits only from its members is a

    a. commercial bank.
    b. mutual savings bank.
    c. credit union.
    d. pension fund.

11. A pool of funds managed to provide retirement income for its members is a

    a. commercial bank.
    b. pension fund.
    c. savings and loan association.
    d. credit union.

12. The lowest interest rate available to the bank's most creditworthy commercial customers is called the

    a. prime rate.
    b. mortgage rate.
    c. variable rate.
    d. margin rate.

13. Companies that do not take in deposits but who specialize in loans to businesses and consumers at rates higher than those demanded by banks are called

    a. savings and loans.
    b. mutual savings banks.
    c. financial supermarkets.
    d. finance companies

14. Firms that buy and sell stocks and bonds on the New York Stock Exchange and other exchanges for investors are called

    a. investment bankers.
    b. commercial banks.
    c. securities investment dealers.
    d. finance companies.

15. Savings plans established by self-employed people for the purpose of saving for retirement are

    a. IRAs.
    b. Keogh Plans.
    c. money market mutual funds.
    d. financing plans.

16. ATMs are the most popular form of

    a. electronic funds transfer.
    b. saving.
    c. brokerage services.
    d. money market accounts.

17. The nation's central bank is the

    a. U.S. Treasury.
    b. First City National.
    c. SEC.
    d. Fed.

18. The management of the nation's money supply and interest rates is referred to as

    a. interest rate parity.
    b. fiscal policy.
    c. monetary policy.
    d. Congressional action.

19. The organization established to resolve all troubled thrift cases that occurred from January 1989 to August 1992 was the

    a. Office of Thrift Supervision.
    b. Resolution Trust Corporation.
    c. Comptroller of the Currency.
    d. Federal Deposit Insurance Corporation.

20. Sales and purchases of U.S. Treasury notes and bonds and other government securities by the Fed in the market in order to control the money supply is called

   a. open-market operations.
   b. adjusting the discount rate.
   c. setting a bank's reserve requirements.
   d. using selective credit controls.

WRITING TO LEARN

1. What are the characteristics and functions of money? How is the money supply measured?

2. Discuss the U.S. commercial banking system. What roles do pension funds, insurance companies, and finance companies have in the banking system?

3. What role does the Federal Reserve System have in our financial system? What is the structure of the Fed?

4.   What tools does the Fed have at its disposal to control the money supply? How do these tools work?

5.   How has the U.S. money and banking system changed since 1980? What role has technology played in banking?

DISCUSSION OF THE CLOSING CASE

Please don't allow yourself to be impressed by the fact that 8 million Universal cards were issued in 1990. P.T. Barnum is supposed to have said that "a sucker is born every minute." Following the Barnum Theorem, one could extrapolate that selling 8 million of anything in promotion-dizzy America is no great feat, and should not be taken as a token of any trend. You can produce cans of strawberry-flavored salmon and, with a potent media blitz, you can probably sell 8 million cans rather quickly. Take the phenomenon of the in-car telephone. Whether you need one or not, it looks cool to be sitting at a busy intersection while talking on the phone. Following this craze, here's a superb new idea. [We relinquish our claims to full patent rights to it.] Manufacture dummy telephones for use in cars. You can't make a call on one, BUT in busy traffic you will give the appearance of the upwardly-mobile professional whose busy day demands a phone held to the right ear while motoring! What does all of this have to do with AT&T's Universal card? Simply this. It is too early to tell for sure whether the card is an idea whose time has come. It may be the wave of the future and may totally revolutionize the credit-card industry. Ten years from now, business historians may say that it was AT&T that brought about absolutely the most significant change in short- term consumer financing. On the other hand, ten years from now, business historians may say that the Universal card was an ill- conceived mistake that proves that phone companies should stay in their own industry. The Universal card may be ranked with the Edsel, the three-wheeled truck, and refrigerators for eskimos as the most outstanding business follies of our age. We shall just have to wait and see. A change in the consumer financing landscape can well determine what will become of the Universal card. As these lines are being written, several of the large credit-card companies are offering more favorable conditions to their customers. Should a ripple of such "user-friendly" innovations become a tidal wave, the uniqueness of the Universal card may fade. At the moment, however, the AT&T sally looks good.

1.   Are more favorable conditions that are being offered by existing credit card companies a direct result of the appearance of the Universal card? Why or why not?

2.   How does the Universal card, as described in this case, compare with similar credit cards you now possess?

3.   Of the characteristics of the Universal card, which one impresses you as being the most favorable? Explain.

4.   Evaluate this statement: "Most credit card companies tell you of their great exclusive features, but when you read the fine print, you see they're all alike."

AN ADDITIONAL CASE

Harvey Felch has just been named as a loan officer at Third National Farmers-Merchants Bank and Trust Company in Walshton. He has been an assistant in the loan department for several years, and has been working on an MBA at Livermore Tech. The senior loan officer and vice-president, Sondra Kelling, walks over to Harvey's desk and makes a rather official announcement.

"Mr. Harvey Felch, loan officer, may I present Jason Filbern, founder and sole owner of Filbern Cans. Mr. Filbern's factory manufactures large metal double-stress containers for shipping crackers in bulk. His Filbern containers will eventually go all over the country. He's come to Third National Farmers-Merchants Bank and Trust Company to secure some additional funds for needed expansion. Mr. Filbern, Mr. Felch."

Handshaking and the usual pleasantries were exchanged by Filbern and Felch. Although Harvey Felch had never met Mr. Filbern in person, he felt that he knew him well. That is because Sondra had instructed Harvey to carefully go over a packet of financial statements on both Filbern and his business. Mr. Filbern, then, proceeded to explain why he needed around $500,000.

"You see, if our orders continue to progress at the current rate, by year's end we will be incapable of servicing the demand. We need to add several processing machines plus some storage space, and we feel that half a million will do the trick."

Harvey had done his homework for this case, and his astute remarks showed this preparation. "Due to a substantial element of risk in this venture...."

"What are you talking about...risk?"

"Industry figures as well as your own projections indicate that demand for large double-stress metal containers such as you manufacture is very difficult to ascertain at this point in time. In short, you may possibly be gearing up for a surge in demand that is not there."

"But I also may be gearing up for an avalanche of demand that neither you nor I can foresee at this moment."

"That's true," Harvey conceded. "What all of this means is that we need to have some of your assets pledged as collateral for this loan. Now, we want to make this as painless as possible. And that's why I want you to tell me what you would like to see used as collateral."

"As Sondra probably told you, my house and grounds--we call it Merryhurst Dell--have been appraised at $1.7 million. I own that free and clear--no shred of a mortgage on it anymore. Then, my ultra-equipped roving bus-bungalow has a market value of $400,000. Our family retreat and hunting preserve in Golden County has been appraised at $780,000. Want me to go on?"

"As a banker, I'm morally opposed to forcing a client to put up his or her living quarters that may be lost in the event of default. Might there be something else?"

"My wife and I have dabbled in the stock market a little. My most impressive holding is 10,000 shares of Dudley-White-Bertelli Pharmaceuticals. A share of Dudley-White-Bertelli sells right now on the market for around $75, and the financial periodicals I've been reading say the price is still moving upward. After a moment of calculating, Harvey Felch said: "This means that your Dudley-White-Bertelli holdings are worth $750,000. That's more than sufficient to cover this loan. Great! That's what we'll use."

And so, the loan papers were drawn up and signed. Harvey Felch had ready for Filbern's use a line of credit of $500,000 at a reasonable rate of interest--the principal amount to be paid out as needed or in one lump sum immediately. Mr. and Mrs. Jason Filbern were prepared to cash in their 10,000 shares of common stock in Dudley-White-Bertelli Pharmaceuticals should they not be able to repay the $500,000 loan.

Harvey Felch felt good about his handling of his first loan. There was a good deal of uncertainty--often called risk--about the situation, but that uncertainty was covered by an overly- sufficient holding of common stock in a very viable pharmaceuticals firm. This was a loan, Harvey felt, that he would not have to worry about and that would not cause him sleepless nights. But a rude jolt was coming.

One Tuesday morning in January, as a blizzard swept across Walshton, Harvey reported to work and found on his desk a small note that read: "See me as soon as you arrive. Sondra." Harvey prepared some coffee in the bank's dayroom, poured himself a cup, added cream and sugar, then shuffled down the hall to Sondra's office.

You sent for me, Sondra?"

"Yes I did. I've been wondering how closely you keep up with the stock market."

"Well, I read The Wall Street Journal regularly and glance at the stock pages now and then, but I'm no expert."

"From now on, Harvey, you may want to become more of a stock expert if you're going to be a successful loan officer. For example, do you know what a share of Dudley-White-Bertelli common stock is selling for right now?"

"Can't say that I do."

"The answer is $41.75."

"Okay. What does that have to do with me?"

"I'm sorry I have to remind you. But it means that you now have collateral worth $417,500 backing up a loan of $500,000. May I also relate to you that financial periodicals are reporting that there is a slump in the sale of double-stress large metal containers. That $500,000 we provided for Filbern may or may not be fully paid back. Let's pray that Dudley-White-Bertelli common goes up real soon."

1. If you were asked to critique Harvey Felch's performance as a loan officer, what are some of the negative features you might emphasize?

2. Do you feel that it can always be stated that common stock is a bad form of collateral for a bank loan? Why or why not?

3. What are some sources of information and advice to which Harvey Felch could have turned to make a judgment on the viability of using this particular issue of common stock as collateral?

4. If wrong has been done here, how much responsibility for it belongs to Sondra Kelling? Explain.

ANSWERS TO TRUE-FALSE QUESTIONS

1.	F	(p. 534)	6.	T	(p. 544)
2.	T	(p. 535)	7.	F	(p. 547)
3.	T	(p. 536)	8.	T	(p. 547)
4.	F	(p. 538)	9.	F	(p. 548)
5.	T	(p. 544)	10.	F	(p. 548)

ANSWERS TO MULTIPLE-CHOICE QUESTIONS

1.	D	(p. 533)	11.	B	(p. 540)
2.	C	(p. 533)	12.	A	(p. 537)
3.	B	(p. 534)	13.	D	(p. 541)
4.	A	(p. 534)	14.	C	(p. 541)
5.	D	(p. 535)	15.	B	(p. 543)
6.	C	(p. 535)	16.	A	(p. 543)
7.	B	(p. 537)	17.	D	(p. 545)
8.	A	(p. 537)	18.	C	(p. 546)
9.	D	(p. 538)	19.	B	(p. 545)
10.	C	(p. 540)	20.	A	(p. 548)

CHAPTER TWENTY-ONE

MANAGING THE FIRM'S FINANCES

CHAPTER OVERVIEW

The overall objective of a financial manager is to increase the value of the firm and thus to increase stockholders' wealth. The cornerstone of effective financial management is the development of a financial plan. The business activity known as finance is concerned with determining a firm's long-term investments, obtaining the funds to pay for the investments, and conducting the firm's everyday financial activities. These activities include collection of funds, payment of debt, establishing trade credit, obtaining loans, controlling cash balances, and planning for the firm's future financial requirements. Errors in this latter activity can have serious consequences for a business. Some sources of long-term financing are debt financing (long-term loans and corporate bonds), equity financing (common stock and retained earnings), and "hybrid" financing via preferred stock. The relationship between risk of an investment and the return on that investment is as follows: Investors expect greater financial returns for riskier investments, but lower returns for safer investments. Some major financial considerations for the small business are establishing bank credit and trade credit, planning cash flow requirements, and knowing the availability of venture capital.

LEARNING OBJECTIVES

1.   Describe how financial managers meet businesses short and long-term needs for funds.

2.   Identify five sources of short-term financing for business.

3.   Distinguish between the various sources of long-term financing and the financial risks involved with each type.

4.   Describe how financial returns to investors are related to the risks they take.

5.   Identify the areas of financial management of particular concern to small businesses.

DISCUSSION OF THE OPENING CASE

If, in the near future, a successful entrepreneur visits your campus in order to speak to large classes about his or her tremendous accomplishments, listen carefully for the word "luck." Will you or will you not hear that word used by the entrepreneur? There is no set answer. Some entrepreneurs will use it freely in describing their business odyssey. Maybe such entrepreneurs are being humble and taking the spotlight off their own business dexterity. They will relate that no businessperson, regardless of how astute, can make the right decision at all times. Entrepreneurs of long experience will relate their many failures that have alternated with their successes. Others will protest that there is no such thing as "luck," and that entrepreneurs who stay successful do so because they have made all the right moves. We're not going to settle the issue in this commentary. But it may be interesting to note that particularly effective entrepreneurs are often able to see "bad luck" developing on the far distant forward horizon, and are able to adjust accordingly. The major such adjustments are in the financing of the firm. Ironically, when that ominous black cloud appears up ahead, the message it may send is: "What you have been doing successfully for quite some time now is exactly the wrong approach for the future. Change your ways!" Unfortunately, that is a message that is hard to receive; rigid businesspeople do not want to hear such things. There is a natural human tendency to assume that situations stay the same. In the world of business, nothing could be farther from the truth. In the saga of America West Airlines (AWA), we see at several junctures a drastic change in the airlines game. Although aggressively taking on heavy debt was the device that got AWA off and running, that same debt came back to later haunt the airline. When the Japanese route was bedeviled by jittery nerves over terrorist possibilities, such a development could not have come at a worse time for AWA. When fuel prices jumped, AWA's financial plans were jolted again. Could AWA have seen ahead what was coming? If so, could America West Airlines have done anything about storm clouds forming ahead? It's great to plan for every contingency. But if you plan for every contingency, then you will probably never have the nerve to open a business.

1. Does "luck" figure in the success of an enterprise? Why or why not?

2. Pick out some disastrous point in the America West Airlines story where you think the line could have been prepared for what happened.

3. Pick out some disastrous point in the America West Airlines story where you think "luck" was just NOT on AWA's side.

4. Pick out some high point in the America West Airlines story where you think "luck" was on the side of AWA.

ANNOTATED KEY TERMS

Finance - The business activity concerned with determining a firm's long-term investments, obtaining the funds to pay for those investments, and conducting the firm's everyday financial activities.

Financial Manager - The manager responsible for planning and controlling the acquisition and dispersal of a company's financial assets.

Cash Flow - The pattern of cash flows into and out of a company.

Financial Plan - A business plan for attaining a specific financial position.

Inventory - Materials and goods held by a company that will be sold within one year.

Raw Materials Inventory - The supplies purchased by a firm for use in its production process.

Work-in-Process Inventory - The portion of a firm's inventory consisting of goods part-way through the production process.

Finished Goods Inventory - The portion of a firm's inventory consisting of completed goods ready for sale.

Trade Credit - The granting of credit by one firm to another.

Open-Book Credit - A form of trade credit in which sellers ship merchandise on faith that payment from the buyer will be forthcoming.

Promissory Note - A form of trade credit in which a buyer signs a promise-to-pay agreement before the merchandise is shipped.

Trade Draft - A form of trade credit in which the seller draws up a statement of payment terms and attaches it to the merchandise. The buyer must sign this agreement to take possession of the merchandise.

Trade Acceptance - A trade draft that has been signed by the buyer.

Secured Loan - A loan in which the borrower is required to put up collateral.

Collateral - An asset pledged by a borrower; in the event of nonpayment of the loan, the lender has the right to seize the asset.

Pledging Accounts Receivable - Using accounts receivable as collateral for a loan.

Unsecured Loan - A loan in which the borrower is not required to put up collateral.

Line of Credit - A standing agreement between a bank and a firm in which the bank promises to lend the firm a maximum amount of funds on request. However, the firm will not necessarily have the funds to lend when they are needed.

Revolving Credit Agreement - An agreement in which a lender agrees to make some amount of funds available on demand to a firm. The lender guarantees that funds will be available when sought by the borrower.

Commercial Paper - A method of short-run financing in which large, stable companies issue unsecured notes at a face value, sell them for less than this value, then buy them back at the face value at a later date.

Factoring - Selling a firm's accounts receivable to another company.

Debt Financing - Long-term borrowing financed from sources outside the company.

Corporate Bond - A bond in which the issuing company pays the holder a certain amount of money on a certain date, with stated interest payments in the interim.

Prime Rate - The interest rate that a bank charges its most creditworthy customers.

Maturity Date - The date on which the principal of a bond is paid off.

Bond Indenture - The contract spelling out all the terms of the bond, including the principal amount, the interest rate, and the maturity date.

Bond Retirement - The way in which a bond is paid off.

Equity Financing - The use of common stock and/or retained earnings to raise money for long-term expenditures; involves putting the owners' capital to work.

Leverage - The use of borrowed money to make investments.

TRUE-FALSE QUESTIONS

1. The financial manager's overall objective is to decrease the value of the firm and thus to decrease stockholders' wealth.

2. Financial managers extend credit to all customers who request it.

3. Long-term expenditures are usually more carefully planned than are short-term expenditures.

4. Trade credit is, in effect, a long-term loan.

5. If inventory can be converted into cash easily, it is relatively more valuable as collateral.

6. With a line of credit, the firm knows the maximum amount it will be allowed to borrow.

7. Issuing commercial paper is a financing option for all firms.

8. Unlike commercial paper, bond issuers do not pay off quickly.

9. Corporate bonds are the major source of short-term financing for most corporations.

10. Investors generally expect to receive higher cash flow payments for higher uncertainty.

MULTIPLE CHOICE QUESTIONS

1. Managers responsible for planning and overseeing the financial resources of a firm are

   a. marketing managers.
   b. production managers.
   c. supervisors.
   d. financial managers.

2. A description of how a business will reach some financial position it seeks in the future that includes projections for sources and uses of funds is a

   a. corporate policy statement.
   b. corporate strategy.
   c. financial plan.
   d. budget.

3. The largest single category of short-term debt for most companies is

   a. cash.
   b. accounts payable.
   c. paid-in capital.
   d. notes payable.

4. Supplies a firm purchases to use in its production process are its

   a. raw materials inventory.
   b. work-in-process.
   c. finished goods inventory.
   d. marketable securities.

5. Land, buildings, and machinery are

   a. current assets.
   b. current liabilities.
   c. raw materials inventory.
   d. fixed assets.

6. Rules that govern the extension of credit to customers make up the firms

    a. current assets.
    b. liabilities.
    c. credit policy.
    d. collection process.

7. The granting of credit by a selling firm to a buying firm is called

    a. an accounts payable.
    b. trade credit.
    c. commercial paper.
    d. equity financing.

8. A form of trade credit in which the seller draws up a statement of payment terms and attaches it to the merchandise and the buyer must sign the agreement in order to take delivery of the merchandise is

    a. a trade draft.
    b. open-book credit.
    c. a promissory note.
    d. collateral.

9. Any asset that a lender has the right to seize in the event of non-repayment of a loan is

    a. open-book credit.
    b. a trade draft.
    c. a trade acceptance.
    d. collateral.

10. The process of using accounts receivables as collateral for a loan is called

    a. factoring.
    b. establishing a line of credit.
    c. pledging.
    d. refinancing.

11. A standing agreement between a bank and a firm in which the bank promises to lend a firm a maximum amount of funds on request is called a

    a. payment request.
    b. line of credit.
    c. compensating balance.
    d. revolving credit agreement.

12. A method of short-term fund-raising in which a firm sells unsecured notes for less than the set face value and then repurchases them at the face value within 270 days is

    a. commercial paper.
    b. a revolving credit agreement.
    c. factoring.
    d. pledging.

13. Long-term borrowing from outside the company is called

    a. equity financing.
    b. establishing a line of credit.
    c. a revolving credit agreement.
    d. debt financing.

14. The term used to describe a promise by an issuing company to pay the holder a certain amount of money on a specified date, with stated interest payments in the interim is a(n)

    a. compensating balance.
    b. a revolving credit agreement.
    c. corporate bond.
    d. common stock.

15. The interest rate the bank charges its most creditworthy customers is the

    a. bond rate.
    b. prime rate.
    c. revolving credit rate.
    d. brokers rate.

16. Raising money to meet long-term expenditures by issuing common stock or retaining earnings is called

    a. equity financing.
    b. debt financing.
    c. hybrid financing.
    d. compensation financing.

17. A middle ground between debt financing and equity financing is the use of

    a. bonds.
    b. bank borrowings.
    c. a revolving credit agreement.
    d. preferred stock.

18. The mix of debt versus equity that provides the firm's financial basis is called the

   a. asset mix of the firm.
   b. amount of bank financing.
   c. capital structure of the firm.
   d. amount of hybrid financing of the firm.

19. When borrowers increase their indebtedness to make other investments, they are said to be more highly

   a. valued.
   b. leveraged.
   c. structured.
   d. factored.

20. Bonds that are rated below investment grade are called

   a. junk bonds.
   b. legally-listed bonds.
   c. bonds in default.
   d. good quality bonds.

WRITING TO LEARN

1.   What are the functions of a financial manager? Why do businesses need funds?

2.   Discuss several sources of short-term funds for a firm. From the firm's viewpoint, is it better to have secured or unsecured sources of short-term funds?

3.   Discuss the long-term sources of funds for a firm. Why is it important for the financial manager to choose an optimal capital structure for the firm?

4. Discuss the risk/return relationship from the investors perspective. What investments are appropriate for investors seeking high (low) risk and high (low) return?

5. How does financial management differ between large and small firms? Should venture capital be used as a source of funds?

DISCUSSION OF THE CLOSING CASE

Although the emphasis in this chapter is on "Managing the Firm's Finances," we must not emphasize finance so much as to picture it as isolated from the various other facets of a business. Financial aspects can greatly impact other phases of a business. In like manner, an almost endless list of other factors within, as well as outside, the business can have financial implications. In hindsight, it is so easy to fault Sock Shops for jumping into the American market so quickly. Establishing shops in New York City must have looked like a wise financial move. Surely, no one with the firm stood up in a board meeting and said: "My dear colleagues, I know how we can lose over one million dollars in one short year. It is to open 17 shops in the New York borough of Manhattan. Let's go ahead and do it. Competition will be keen and we'll get whipped badly. Good show!" No such prediction was made, although that bleak outlook is indeed exactly what came to pass across the Atlantic. The American debacle came about because of factors that financial managers don't normally deal with. This is an extremely frustrating aspect of business for a financial manager. Sometimes he or she may find the financial domain over which he or she rules being greatly devastated by corporate decisions in which the financial manager was not invited to participate. In the case of Sock Shops, a bit of <u>marketing research</u> should have indicated that Manhattan was not a wide-open market just thirsting for Sock Shops. Well, if the firm just had to try New York, why did it have to open <u>seventeen</u> shops? In all of France, the company opened only <u>three</u> shops at first. In addition, Sock Shops management seemed to be almost trying to prevent their New York stores from turning a profit by engaging in such heavy initial financing to get the stores open. If the shops were all in high- traffic areas of Manhattan, one can easily speculate, too, as to the sky-high rents that must have been charged for this space. Under its reorganization, Sock Shops will continue to experience financial challenges through its various European outlets, but at least it will have wisely withdrawn from a market whose delicious financial fruits were only a mirage.

1. Give several reasons why the clever Sock Shop concept was not able to be a resounding success in Manhattan.

2. Let us say that Sock Shops headquarters sent you in 1987 to Manhattan to scout the potential market there for the firm's shops. What are some of the things you would have looked for in your market analysis?

3. Remembering the traditional relationship between risk and return, try to explain why Sock Shops moved ahead so enthusiastically to enter the New York market?

4. Do you think that Sock Shops will ever return to the United States? Why or why not?

AN ADDITIONAL CASE

The broad Brazos River runs through Waco, Texas, home to Baylor University. Shortly after World War II, Herbert Ryan, Jr. opened a hat store in downtown Waco--featuring hats he had made himself. The green-and-gold sign he hung over the door to his shop contained two words that today mean quality head apparel in the Southwest: Brazos Brims. The firm can equip you with a sophisticated chapeau appropriate for a downtown Dallas dandy, or put you in an over-hanging, wide-brimmed hat that the legendary cowboys of western lore made famous. In summary, it could truthfully be said, as the corporate slogan goes, that "Brazos Brims have won the respect of the West."

As these lines are being penned by a correspondent in Waco, the firm is in what King David might have called "the valley of the shadow of death" (Psalms 23:4). To properly convey the firm's present predicament, some background is necessary.

In 1982, Herbert Ryan III, son of the founder, opened a second Brazos Brims shop in Fort Worth. Simultaneously, he doubled the size of his manufacturing facility and staged a retirement party for his father. Sales in Fort Worth were so encouraging that young Herb had expanded to 27 stores in Texas, New Mexico, and Arkansas by 1991. The manufacturing facility kept pace with the retail chain. While all of this was happening, Brazos Brims had "gone public" (selling shares of their common stock on the American Stock Exchange). Although much of the nation had never heard of Brazos Brims, security analysts in New York told their clients that the firm was a "rising power in hats and a good stock buy." Up until late 1992, the firm had never become heavily engaged in long-term debt, although financial consultants kept telling young Herb and his staff that many lenders would find Brazos Brims a very attractive borrower.

Meanwhile, a cautious marketing research team from Brazos Brims was investigating new retail opportunities in Phoenix, Denver, Kansas City, Saint Louis, Omaha, Chicago, and Cleveland. After sifting through numerous findings and forecasts, the management team decided to open four stores in the greater Saint Louis area.

Why was the decision made to open four stores in one metro area rather than a single store in each of four metro areas? The marketing staff said that the costs of television advertising over Saint Louis stations would be the same for one store as for four. In a sense, you plugged four stores for the price of one. At the end of each commercial, there would be an announcer saying: "Brazos Brims available in Plaza Terrace, Higley Heights, Oak Leaf, and Cuyahoga Malls." Advertising costs (print as well as TV) would be equally prorated among the four stores.
Young Herb sent Bradley Carls, legal counsel and retail coordinator, to meet with the operators of four different shopping malls around Saint Louis. By paying a premium rent for locations in these malls, Bradley was able to extract from each a six-month escape clause. The provision allowed Brazos Brims to break a lease at the end of the first six months of operation if the hat maker felt it necessary. Bradley Carls was an ultra-conservative negotiator, but even he never dreamed that the escape hatch would have to be used. As he said to a fellow football fan: "When the Dallas Cowboys play the Kansas City Chiefs, it would be safe to have a neuro-surgeon on the sidelines--just in case...." If the worst possible scenario were to develop, pulling out of a store

would entail some major losses, as we shall see below when we note the cost of opening such a store. The pullout decision would be a case of weighing the loss of closing against the mounting losses of staying open in an unprofitable atmosphere. To open a shop in the manner required by the malls' stiff leases, Brazos Brims would certainly need some cash up front--funds that were not available in the corporate coffers at the particular moment when required. The time to wade into some long-term debt had arrived for the firm.

To redecorate, prepare, stock and equip a store in a Saint Louis mall (at least those malls dealing with Bradley Carls) would take an average figure of around $1,250,000. To provide, then, for four new retail outposts, $5 million would be needed. A Dallas bank advanced the funds with a relatively reasonable interest rate on a ten-year loan. Actually, considering the excellent financial position of Brazos Brims at this point, the bankers involved got the best of the deal. The money was to be paid back in yearly installments of around $550,000 each. It had been planned that the firm would obtain the funds for the yearly re- payment from net profits of the new stores. This meant that each store would need to clear at least $137,500 in its first year-- and every year of the nine remaining on the loan.

By some kind of miracle of timing, the six-month escape date on <u>all</u> <u>four</u> <u>stores</u> was July 14, 1993. The Waco headquarters kept close watch on sales at the four Saint Louis stores. The wide divergence in sales performances of the stores set Brazos Brims records. Consider the following figures.

The Higley Heights store's first monthly income statement indicated that if the present rate continued, the store would contribute a net income at the end of the first year of $756,000. Each succeeding month saw that figure being revised upward. The Cuyahoga store, on the other hand, if we can project from that first month, would suffer a LOSS by year's end of $114,500. Oak Leaf could possibly break even, while Plaza Terrace net income could possibly be a NEGATIVE $200,500. The mall operators all say that the second year is when profits soar to the stratosphere. But a trusted analyst in Saint Louis who knows the area well has told Waco headquarters that the Plaza Terrace and Cuyahoga stores may be open for 18 months before they register a positive monthly net income figure.

As July 14 rolled around, two major questions hung heavy in the air of the Waco headquarters. First, will we be able to make the prescribed re-payment installment to the Dallas bank at the end of our first year in Saint Louis? Second, where, if anywhere, will we exercise our six-month escape option--Plaza Terrace, Cuyahoga, Higley Heights, or Oak Leaf?

(In the interests of discussion and suspense, we shall not reveal action taken by the Waco office of Brazos Brims. If you have read of this decision in the financial press, please do not reveal its nature to your classmates. Thank you.)

1.   Do you see Brazos Brims as being able to make its first annual payment to the bank in Dallas--without acquiring funds from sources other than Saint Louis net incomes? Explain.

2. If you were advising Herbert Ryan III, which of the Saint Louis stores, if any, would you close? Why?

3. Compare the entry of Brazos Brims into Saint Louis with Sock Shops' entry into Manhattan. Which firm displayed the most wisdom?

4. What is the main item of data that would discourage you from closing any of the stores in the Saint Louis area? Explain.

ANSWERS TO TRUE-FALSE QUESTIONS

1.	F	(p. 561)	6.	T	(p. 567)
2.	F	(p. 564)	7.	F	(p. 568)
3.	T	(p. 565)	8.	T	(p. 569)
4.	F	(p. 566)	9.	F	(p. 570)
5.	T	(p. 566)	10.	T	(p. 573)

ANSWERS TO MULTIPLE-CHOICE QUESTIONS

1.	D	(p. 561)	11.	B	(p. 567)
2.	C	(p. 562)	12.	A	(p. 568)
3.	B	(p. 564)	13.	D	(p. 569)
4.	A	(p. 564)	14.	C	(p. 569)
5.	D	(p. 565)	15.	B	(p. 569)
6.	C	(p. 564)	16.	A	(p. 571)
7.	B	(p. 566)	17.	D	(p. 572)
8.	A	(p. 566)	18.	C	(p. 572)
9.	D	(p. 566)	19.	B	(p. 572)
10.	C	(p. 567)	20.	A	(p. 573)

CHAPTER TWENTY-TWO

UNDERSTANDING SECURITIES MARKETS

CHAPTER OVERVIEW

New stocks and bonds are bought and sold in primary securities markets. Investment bankers serve as financial specialists in issuing new securities. The market in which existing stocks and bonds are bought and sold is referred to as the secondary market. Par value of common stock is the arbitrary face value. Market value refers to the current price of the stock on an exchange. Book value represents stockholders' equity divided by the number of common shares. Among other differences from common stock, preferred stock has preference at dividend time. The New York Stock Exchange is the largest of all U.S. exchanges, and the second largest is the American Stock Exchange. While 4,000 stocks are listed on the organized exchanges, nearly 28,000 issues are traded "over the counter." A variety of bonds are issued by the federal government as well as by state and local governments. Corporate bonds are the largest source of long-term financing for U.S. corporations today. The retirement of bonds at maturity can involve callable bonds, sinking funds, serial bonds, and convertible bonds. Mutual funds pool investments from individuals and other firms to purchase a portfolio of stocks, bonds, and short-term securities. Futures contracts are bought and sold on commodities markets. A stock option is the right to buy or sell a stock. Current yield on a bond is the annual dollar coupon amount divided by the current market price. The most widely-used stock market index is the Dow Jones Industrial Average. Securities markets are regulated by the Securities and Exchange Commission.

LEARNING OBJECTIVES

1.   Explain the difference between the primary and secondary markets for securities.

2.   Discuss the value of common stock and preferred stock to shareholders and describe the secondary market for these securities.

3.   Distinguish among the various types of bonds available to investors in terms of their issuers, safety, and retirement.

4.   Describe the investment opportunities offered by mutual funds, commodities, and options.

5.   Discuss the process by which securities are bought and sold.

DISCUSSION OF THE OPENING CASE

Any treatment of Michael Milken and junk bonds should begin with this caution: This is not a simple issue, and those who understand its full ramifications refuse to sketch the tragedy in the exclusive hues of black and white. First of all, "junk bonds" are merely bonds that have not earned the higher ratings of the bond rating services (such as Moody's and Standard and Poor's). The ratings are supposed to tell us that a lower-rated bond has a greater element of default risk than a higher-rated bond. But since higher risk is accompanied by higher return on investment, so-called "junk bonds" pay higher interest than highly-rated securities. This latter fact makes them a wise, money-making investment. Just how "risky" are these lower-rated bonds? Official, credible records kept on the matter have indicated that only a very small percent of such bonds default. You might ask your professor to find out for you what that figure is at present. Even in cases of default, investors may receive some of their money back. It is wrong to equate a low-rated bond with conterfeit money. Then, there's the saga of Michael Milken. It is possible to see Michael Milken as a tragic character who did not receive a fair deal. Here is an excerpt on the subject from a "scholarly" paper: "Ivan Boesky was handed a three-year sentence for '$80 million in insider-trading profits.' Michael Milken received a ten-year sentence for 'causing losses Judge [Kimba] Wood estimated at $318,000.' Mathematically, the juxtaposition of these two sentences defies any code of logic. But an explanation for the Boesky sentence requires the utilization of a term frequently heard in gangster movies of America's 1930s: Boesky was, it has been alleged, willing to 'sing' to authorities about Michael Milken." (*) The Milken case is extremely complex, and anyone wishing to delve deeper therein to gain additional insights should follow a series of articles on the matter in The Wall Street Journal by L. Gordon Crovitz, starting in early 1990. A Journal staffer, Mr. Crovitz holds law degrees from both Oxford and Yale.

(*) Timmerman, Meinhardt, Bowdidge, Giboney. "The Accuser and the Accused: Whose Rights Are These Anyway?" Midwest Business Law Association, Proceedings for the Annual Meeting (Paul Frederickson, ed.), Chicago, 1992, pp. 83-90--incorporating material from Crovitz. "Prosecutors Must Beware 'Cooperation' as Perjury," The Wall Street Journal, January 23, 1991, p. A17.

1. From what you have been able to gather on the subject, did Michael Milken get what he deserved from the courts? Why or why not?

2. Would you be willing to invest in the so-called "junk bonds"? Why or why not?

3. If you considered investing in some "junk bonds," what are some questions you would ask about the firm issuing these bonds?

4. Is the low-rated bond something that surfaced first in the 1980s? Has the low-rated bond vanished from the face of the earth?

ANNOTATED KEY TERMS

Securities - Stocks and bonds that represent a secured (asset-based) claim against their issuers.

Primary Securities Markets - The market in which new stocks and bonds are bought and sold.

Investment Banker - A financial institution engaged in the purchase and sale of securities.

Secondary Securities Market - The market in which existing stocks and bonds are bought and sold.

Institutional Investor - An organization that invests for itself and its clients.

Portfolio - The mix of securities held by an investor.

Par Value - The face value of a share of stock, set by the issuing company's board of directors.

Market Value - The current price of a share of stock in the stock market.

Capital Gain - A profit earned by selling a share of stock for more than it cost.

Book Value - The value of a stock expressed as total shareholders' equity divided by the number of shares of common stock.

Blue-Chip Stock - Common stocks issued by well-established companies with sound financial histories and a stable pattern of dividend payouts to shareholders.

Cumulative Preferred Stock - Preferred stock on which dividends not paid in the past must be paid to stockholders before any dividends can be paid to common stockholders.

Stock Exchange - A voluntary organization of individuals formed to provide an institutional setting in which stock can be bought and sold. Broker - A person who receives and executes buy and sell orders in return for a commission.

Diversification - The process of spreading investable funds among a variety of investments to reduce risk.

Over-the-Counter (OTC) Market - A voluntary organization of securities dealers formed to buy and sell stock outside the formal institutional setting of the organized stock exchanges.

Government Bonds - Bonds issued by the federal government.

Municipal Bonds - Bonds issued by state and local governments.

Corporate Bonds - Bonds issued by businesses.

Secured Bonds - Bonds that are backed by pledges of assets to the bondholders.

Debentures - Unsecured bonds; bonds in which no specific property is pledged as security.

Callable Bond - A bond that may be called in and paid for by the issuer prior to maturity date.

Sinking-Fund Provision - A provision in a bond contract that requires the issuer to put a certain amount of money into a bank account each year; this money is used to redeem the bonds at maturity.

Serial Bond - A bond issue in which the issuer redeems portions of the issue at different predetermined dates.

Convertible Bond - A bond that can be paid off in (converted to) common stock at the option of the bondholder.

Mutual Fund - A company that pools investments from individuals and other firms to purchase a portfolio of stocks, bonds, and short-term securities.

No-Load Fund - A mutual fund in which investors are not charged a commission when they buy into or sell out of the fund.

Load Fund - A mutual fund in which investors are charged a commission when they buy into or sell out of the fund.

Futures Contract - An agreement to purchase a specified amount of a commodity at a given price on a set date in the future.

Commodities Market - The market in which futures contracts are bought and sold.

Margin - The percentage of the total sales price that a buyer must put up to place an order for stock or a futures contract.

Stock Option - The right to buy or sell a stock.

Call Option - The right to buy a particular stock at a certain price until a specified date.

Put Option - The right to sell a particular stock at a certain price until a specified date.

Price-Earnings Ratio - In stock exchange listings, the current price of a stock divided by the firm's current annual earnings per share.

Current Yield - A bond's annual dollar coupon amount divided by the current market price of that bond.

Bid Price - In OTC markets, the price an OTC dealer pays for a share of stock.

Asked Price - In OTC markets, the price an OTC dealer charges for a share of stock.

Market Index - A measure of the overall market value of stocks; provides a summary of price trends in a specific industry or the stock market as a whole.

Bull Market - A period of rising stock prices; a period in which investors act on a belief that stock prices will rise.

Bear Market - A period of falling stock prices; a period in which investors act on a belief that stock prices will fall.

Dow Jones Industrial Average - A market index based on the market prices for 30 of the largest industrial firms listed on the NYSE.

Standard & Poor's Composite Index - A market index based on the performance of 500 stocks; 400 industrial firms, 40 utilities, 40 financial institutions, and 20 transportation companies.

Discount Brokerage House - A brokerage firm that executes purchases and sales for a reduced commission.

Full-Service Brokerage - A brokerage firm that performs a variety of services for its clients, including but not limited to investment advice and research.

Market Order - An order to buy or sell a certain security at the prevailing market price at the time the order is placed.

Limit Order - An order authorizing a broker to purchase a stock only if the price of that stock is equal to or less than a specified amount.

Stop Order - An order authorizing a broker to sell a stock if its price falls to or below a specified level.

Round Lot - The purchase or sale of stock in units of 100.

Odd Lot - The purchase or sale of stock in units of other than 100.

Short Sale - A stock sale in which investors sell securities that they have borrowed from their brokers. These securities must be replaced at a specified date in the future.

Program Trading - The purchase or sale of a group of stocks valued at $1 million or more, often triggered by computerized trading programs that can be launched without human supervision or control.

Prospectus - A registration statement filed with the SEC before the issuance of a new security.

Insider Trading - The illegal practice of using special insiders' knowledge about a firm for profit or gain.

Blue-Sky Laws - State laws regulating the securities industry by requiring securities dealers to be licensed and registered with the state.

TRUE-FALSE QUESTIONS

1. The market in which stocks and bonds are sold is called the securities market.

2. Because private placements cannot be resold, buyers generally receive lower returns from them.

3. Personality differences affect investment decisions.

4. Common stocks are among the least risky type of securities.

5. Preferred stock is usually issued with a stated market value.

6. Most stock exchanges are nonprofit corporations.

7. Memberships on stock exchanges can be bought and sold like other assets.

8. In number of stocks listed, the London exchange exceeds the New York Stock Exchange.

9. Issuers of bonds are most likely to call in existing bonds when the prevailing interest rate is higher than the rate being paid on the bond.

10. The FCC regulates the public offering of new securities.

MULTIPLE CHOICE QUESTIONS

1. The sale and purchase of newly issued stocks and bonds by firms or governments takes place in the

   a. OTC market.
   b. overseas markets.
   c. secondary market.
   d. primary market.

2. To bring a new security to market, the issuing corporation needs to obtain approval from the

    a. FBI.
    b. FTC.
    c. SEC.
    d. NASD.

3. Which of the following is not mentioned by the authors of your textbook as an important banking service provided by investment bankers?

    a. underwriting the issue
    b. managing the companies financial resources
    c. advising the company on timing and financial terms
    d. creating the distribution network

4. Organizations whose investments for themselves and their clients are so large that they can influence prices on securities markets are known as

    a. institutional investors.
    b. brokers.
    c. investment bankers.
    d. private placements.

5. The mix of securities that investors hold is referred to as their

    a. debentures.
    b. par value determinants.
    c. tangible assets.
    d. portfolio.

6. The current price of one share of a stock in the secondary securities market is its

    a. par value.
    b. book value.
    c. market value.
    d. liquidation value.

7. The profit from selling stock for more than it cost is called

    a. par value.
    b. capital gain.
    c. margin.
    d. book value.

8. A voluntary organization of individuals formed to provide an institutional setting in which stock can be bought and sold is a(n)

    a. stock exchange.
    b. private placement.
    c. margined account.
    d. portfolio.

9. An individual licensed to buy and sell securities for customers in the secondary market is a

    a. financial analyst.
    b. investment banker.
    c. consultant.
    d. broker.

10. What percent of all shares traded on U.S. exchanges are traded at the NYSE?

    a. 10 percent
    b. 25 percent
    c. over 80 percent
    d. approximately 50 percent

11. Spreading investable funds among a variety of investments in order to reduce risk is called

    a. investment banking.
    b. diversification.
    c. brokering.
    d. futures trading.

12. For the investor in bonds, the chance that one or more promised payments will be deferred or missed altogether is referred to as

    a. default risk.
    b. inflation risk.
    c. country risk.
    d. callable risk.

13. Treasury bills are debts that mature in

    a. five to ten years.
    b. thirty years.
    c. one to ten years.
    d. a year or less.

14. State and local obligations used to finance school systems, transportation, and other social-welfare projects are called

   a. corporate bonds.
   b. treasury bills.
   c. municipal bonds.
   d. debentures.

15. Unsecured bonds are called

   a. mortgage bonds.
   b. debentures.
   c. callable bonds.
   d. municipal bonds.

16. The issuer of which of the following type of bond has the right at almost any time to pay the bond off at a price stipulated in the bond indenture?

   a. a callable bond
   b. a debenture
   c. a treasury bond
   d. a municipal bond

17. Any bond that offers bondholders the option of accepting common stock instead of cash in repayment is a(n)

   a. serial bond.
   b. treasury bond.
   c. debenture.
   d. convertible bond.

18. A mutual fund in which investors are not charged a sales commission when they buy into or sell out of the fund is a

   a. load fund.
   b. bond fund.
   c. no-load fund.
   d. convertible fund.

19. The percentage of the total sales price that a buyer must put up in order to place an order for stock or a futures contract is called

   a. interest.
   b. margin.
   c. a futures position.
   d. short selling.

20. Charles Schwab and Fidelity Brokerage Services are examples of

   a. discount brokerage houses.
   b. investment bankers.
   c. program traders.
   d. full-service brokers.

WRITING TO LEARN

1. What is the difference between the primary and secondary markets for securities? Are institutional investors an important segment in securities trading?

2. Distinguish between par value, market value, and book value. What are some differences between common and preferred stock?

3. Discuss how stocks and bonds are traded. How would you go about selecting a broker and placing an order?

4.   What is program trading? Does program trading have an impact on stock market activity and prices?

5.   What major pieces of legislation regulate securities markets? What role does the SEC have in securities regulation?

DISCUSSION OF THE CLOSING CASE

The effect of the <u>Barron's</u> article on the price of Marvel Comics stock is vivid testimony to the occasional displays of power wielded by the financial press. A <u>Barron's</u> sister Dow Jones publication, <u>The Wall Street Journal</u>, discovered this the hard way several years ago in the case of <u>Journal</u> columnist R. Foster Winans. It was alleged by the authorities that Mr. Winans was informing contacts before the fact of the nature of stock analysis columns he was writing. By getting into the market just before the Winans article appeared in the <u>Journal</u>, Winans's contacts were allegedly able to profit mightily. It is alleged that Winans, as an illustration, would tell a colleague that his column coming out Tuesday would indicate that XXWW Corporation was in spectacular financial shape and that its stock was a superlative buy. The colleague (and some of his friends) would then allegedly buy large lots of XXWW stock at the "bargain" price. When the Winans column complimentary of XXWW appeared in the <u>Journal</u> on Tuesday, the XXWW stock price would rise rapidly. The Winans colleagues, it was alleged, would then sell their easily-acquired XXWW common for premium prices. It was the <u>Journal</u> column, it was alleged, that was allowing a particular group of investors to make an unfair killing in the market! <u>The Journal</u> has since taken steps to prevent an occurrence of such maneuvers through its columns. Getting back to Marvel, being imbued with the typical American sympathy for the underdog, one's first reaction in reading this case is to be revolted by the <u>Barron's</u> ability to temporarily cripple a corporation. The fact that Marvel Comics has "gone public" is perhaps some justification for <u>Barron's</u> feeling compelled to yank the veil from Marvel. When a corporation's stock sells on the New York Stock Exchange, all investors and potential investors have a right to know the financial position of the issuing firm so that their sales or purchases of said stock will be wise and informed. Since the determination of a company's financial well-being is seldom simple and absolute, there is always the possibility that a given appraisal is vulnerable to distortion. The firm involved, in this case Marvel, must design ways to repair its image.

1.   What are some actions that Marvel Comics can take to project a more favorable image for itself than that cast by the <u>Barron's</u> article?

2.   What are your own personal reactions to a financial publication being able to have such a detrimental effect on a corporation?

3.   If the <u>Barron's</u> article in question is a case of inaccurate reporting, what legal recourse, if any, do you feel should be open to Marvel Comics? Explain.

4.   To keep yourself abreast of the Marvel situation, look up its common stock price in a recent <u>Wall Street Journal</u>.

AN ADDITIONAL CASE

Joann Fletcher is a successful broker in the Cincinnati office of one of the largest brokerage firms in the world. Upon the request of Troutman College, Ms. Fletcher has conducted several seminars and short courses on investing in securities for those persons interested in initiating participation in the stock market. The classes have been well attended and Troutman College's Division of Continuing Education schedules them several times a year.

Each time the formal lecture is concluded, Joann Fletcher always stays around to answer questions that could not be treated when the entire group was in session. And so it was, that on a lightning-punctuated rainy September night, young attorney George Cargill lingered after class to express an interest in preferred stock.

"If one kind of stock is <u>preferred</u>," George wondered, "then why in the world would anyone ever want to mess with <u>common</u> stock?"

"Well," Joann responded, realizing she was starting out on a long story, "you're right that preferred stock has some advantages. However, there are several good things going for common stock that we cannot say of preferred."

"Can you give me an example?" "Well, before I do that, let me tell you the main differences between preferred and common."

"Okay, Ms. Fletcher. Fire away."

"The term 'preferred' means that at dividend time holders of preferred stock will have preference over holders of common stock. If dividends are paid at all, dividends to preferred stock must be completed before a penny can go to holders of common stock. The same thing is true at liquidation time; whatever is coming to preferred stockholders must be taken care of before anything can be awarded the common stockholders."

George thought about that a minute, then offered a view on the subject: "Well, then it seems to me that preferred stock has all the advantages."

"Not completely," Joann tenderly disagreed. "For example, holders of preferred stock normally will not have voting privileges at stockholder meetings--regardless of how much preferred stock they hold. In addition, what seems like an advantage can often be a disadvantage. Here's what I mean. You've probably read that preferred stock is less risky than common. This characteristic manifests itself in less accentuated fluctuation on the nation's stock exchanges. Or we could say that preferred is less volatile. Now, the down side of this so- called stability is that prices of preferred issues will tend to respond less when great things are happening to a company. Preferred isn't that closely tied into the fortunes of the company. Holders of preferred stock will get that stipulated dividend coming to them--especially if it's a <u>cumulative</u> issue-- and, as a rule, there's nothing special coming to them even if the firm has a fantastic year of glowing profits. For example, let's say you have preferred stock in a pharmaceutical firm that discovers the cure for cancer. At such news, that firm's common stock prices will soar. At the same time, its preferred shares may experience a small fluctuation. Incidentally, the inside group of the corporation (founders, directors, top executives, etc.) will be holding <u>common</u> stock."

"Hold it right there! Explain 'cumulative' to me again, please."

"In the case of debt, such as a bond, a borrower (the issuing corporation) is bound by law to make interest payments regularly. There is no such guarantee of regularity with dividends on stock. No corporation has ever 'promised' that a dividend will be paid. That promise cannot be made on preferred dividends, either. Thus, in a bad year, a corporation may have to skip a preferred dividend. If the preferred issue of stock is cumulative, then the company must make up the missed dividend in the future when it is financially able to do so--even if it has missed dividends for several years. If the issue is noncumulative, then that missed dividend is forgotten forever, although a token dividend can be paid under these circumstances to holders of common stock in the same firm in that year when the preferred dividend is missed. That is why most people would prefer to have a cumulative issue."

"Why would anyone accept a preferred stock that was not cumulative?"

"You'll notice, Mr. Cargill.... may I call you George....?"

"Please do, Joann."

"....that there are some firms with several issues of preferred listed in The Wall Street Journal stock pages, but only one issue of common stock for that firm. This tells us that each issue of preferred has a different set of characteristics. For example, an issue that is convertible into a very attractive common stock and has a healthy dividend could be noncumulative. An issue with an unattractive dividend could compensate for that weakness by being cumulative. Each time a new issue of preferred comes out, the firm and its investment bankers have tried to determine what mix of charactersistics will be most attractive to buyers--along with considering what kind of obligation the firm wants to take on for itself."

In a possible attempt to bring the questioning to an end, George came up with: "Two questions, if you will. First, how is the best way to make a quick profit in the market? And second, would you be willing to explain it all to me over a cup of coffee?"

Without a moment of hesitation, Joann dealt with the double inquiry in a most professional manner. "In answer to your first question: buy common. I consider your second query to be an allusion to a splendid idea."

1.   Joann Fletcher is a capable broker. However, the authors have taken the liberty of allowing some erroneous information to fall from her lips. What is that error we have forced upon Joann? **[HINT: At one point, Joann says: "If the issue is noncumulative, then that missed dividend is forgotten forever, although a token dividend can be paid under these circumstances to holders of common stock...."]**

2.   Why do you think that members of the "inside group" hold mostly common stock of a firm?

3.   Respond to this statement: "Preferred stock is definitely a better deal than common stock."

4.   In your opinion, what is the most significant advantage that common stock has over preferred stock?

ANSWERS TO TRUE-FALSE QUESTIONS

1.	T	(p. 585)	6.	T	(p. 588)
2.	F	(p. 585)	7.	T	(p. 588)
3.	T	(p. 586)	8.	T	(p. 590)
4.	F	(p. 586)	9.	F	(p. 596)
5.	F	(p. 587)	10.	F	(p. 607)

ANSWERS TO MULTIPLE-CHOICE QUESTIONS

1.	D	(p. 585)	11.	B	(p. 590)
2.	C	(p. 585)	12.	A	(p. 592)
3.	B	(p. 585)	13.	D	(p. 592)
4.	A	(p. 585)	14.	C	(p. 593)
5.	D	(p. 585)	15.	B	(p. 595)
6.	C	(p. 586)	16.	A	(p. 595)
7.	B	(p. 586)	17.	D	(p. 596)
8.	A	(p. 588)	18.	C	(p. 597)
9.	D	(p. 588)	19.	B	(p. 599)
10.	C	(p. 589)	20.	A	(p. 603)

CHAPTER TWENTY-THREE

MANAGING RISK AND INSURANCE

CHAPTER OVERVIEW

Risk is uncertainty about future events. Speculative risks involve the possibility of gain or loss; pure risks involve only the possibility of loss. Risk management can be defined as conserving the earning power or assets of a firm by minimizing the financial effect of accidental losses. With insurance, individuals and businesses share risks by contributing to a fund out of which those who suffer losses are paid. Some techniques for dealing with risk are to avoid the risk, control the risk, retain the risk, or transfer the risk. A premium is a fee paid to an insurance company for accepting a certain risk, and the deductible is a previously agreed-on amount the insured must absorb in the event of loss. The law of large numbers is the statistical principle that the larger the number of cases involved, the more closely the actual loss rate will be to the statistically calculated loss rate. A stock insurance company sells stock to the public, while a mutual insurance company is owned by its policyholders. Liability insurance covers losses resulting from injury to persons or the damaging of property of other people or firms. General liability policies protect businesses in cases involving personal, professional, product, and premises problems. Some other types of insurance are property, marine, title, business interruption, credit, endowment, universal life, whole life, term, variable life, group life, health, and key person.

LEARNING OBJECTIVES

1.   Describe how risk affects business operations and the five steps in the risk-management process.

2.   Discuss the four techniques a business can use to deal with risk and loss.

3.   Explain the insurance industry and how it makes a profit.

4.   Distinguish among the different types of insurance purchased by businesses.

5.   Discuss the areas in which insurance companies' activities are regulated.

DISCUSSION OF THE OPENING CASE

When reading of Allstate's problems with the State of New Jersey, it is easy to take a side. On the one hand, many a motorist has experienced inferior service from an auto insurance firm.

Particularly frustrating is trying to obtain from the "other motorist's" insurer a fair settlement when that other motorist is clearly in the wrong as documented by a police report. There seems to be a deliberate attempt to avoid doing what is right! At times like these, one wishes that the state had some tight control over how insurance companies operate. Just to liven up the discussion, let's picture a state in which the "commissioner of insurance" is a fresh law school graduate who knows little of the law and even less about insurance and is, in practical terms, useless to citizens of the state. Good Heavens, where does a wronged insured motorist turn for help? In this atmosphere, we could suffer the further insult of having our auto insurance premiums going ever upward. Can't something be done? Of course. A candidate for governor can campaign on a platform of taming the insurance companies. Can't you hear the candidate now? "I'll get auto insurance premiums lowered by fifty percent, I'll make settlements occur four times as fast, and I'll increase coverage for motorists by 80 percent. In addition, even if you have an accident each week, I'll see that no insurance firm can turn you down!" Plainly, such campaigning is just as wrong as an insurance company that would cheat the public. There has to be a happy medium and there must be some cool heads that can mediate within a fair middle ground. Yes, an insurance company must be made to adhere to certain ethical standards of integrity and public service. At the same time, an insurance firm must retain the right to penalize (through high premiums or non-protection) those motorists whose driving records are abominable. Many states have still not come to grips with the drunken driver. Apparently, judges in such states find it hard to clamp down on these irresponsible citizens, and such drivers still roam the streets and highways. An insurance company is certainly justified in refusing to insure such a motorist. When the state develops a plan to cover such a person, is it fair that indirectly the insurance companies should fund such a program? The issue is far from clear.

1.   Does an insurance company have the right to refuse auto insurance to a habitual drunken driver? Why or why not?

2.   Evaluate this possible statement from an insurance executive: "If state government wants to provide auto insurance for bad risks, let THE STATE handle the costs involved, not insurance companies through a pool."

3.   If a state forces insurance firms to indirectly provide coverage for high-risk motorists, where is the insurance company most likely to get these necessary funds? Explain.

4.   What is a more fair way to handle the problem sketched in Number 3 above?

ANNOTATED KEY TERMS

Insurance - A system in which individuals and businesses share risks by contributing to a fund out of which those who suffer losses are paid.

Risk - Uncertainty about future events.

Speculative Risk - A risk that involves the possibility of gain or loss.

Pure Risk - A risk that involves only the possibility of loss or no loss.

Risk Management - Conserving the earning power or assets of a firm or an individual by minimizing the financial effect of accidental losses.

Risk Avoidance - Avoiding a risky situation by ceasing to participate in it or by not entering into the risky activity at all.

Risk Control - Techniques designed to prevent, minimize, or reduce losses.

Risk Retention - The practice of covering a firm's losses with its own funds.

Risk Transfer - The transfer of risk to another individual or firm.

Surety Bond - An arrangement among three parties-the principal, the obligee, and the surety-whereby the surety guarantees financial reimbursement to the obligee if the principal fails to fulfill its obligation.

Fidelity Bond - A type of surety bond that guarantees the principal's character, integrity, and honesty.

Premium - A fee paid to an insurance company in return for the insurance company's acceptance of a certain risk.

Insurance Policy - A formal agreement in which an insurer promises to pay a policyholder a specified amount in the event of certain losses.

Deductible - An agreed-upon amount of the loss that an insured party must absorb before reimbursement from the insurer.

Law of Large Numbers - The statistical principle that the larger the number of cases involved, the more closely the actual rate will be to the statistically calculated rate.

Stock Insurance Company - A private insurance company that sells stock to the public.

Mutual Insurance Company - A private insurance company that is owned by its policyholders.

Underwriting - The process of determining which applications for insurance should be accepted (and which should be rejected) and deciding the rates that will be charged by the insurer.

Insurance Agent - A person or business that represents an insurance company and is paid by that insurer to sell its insurance.

Insurance Broker - A freelance agent who represents insurance buyers, working on their behalf and seeking the best coverage for them.

Liability Insurance - Insurance covering losses resulting from damage to the persons or property of other people or firms.

Personal Liability - In business, a firm's responsibility for the actions of its employees.

Professional Liability - In business, the responsibility of an individual for the actions performed in a professional capacity.

Product Liability - In business, a firm's responsibility for its products.

Premises Liability - In business, a firm's responsibility for occurrences on its premises.

Workers' Compensation Coverage - Coverage provided by a firm to its employees for medical expenses, loss of wages, and rehabilitative service costs incurred as a result of job-related injuries.

No-Fault Auto Insurance - A form of auto insurance in which the parties injured in an accident are compensated by their own insurers for bodily injuries and property damage, regardless of which party is at fault.

Umbrella Insurance - Insurance that covers losses over and above those covered by a standard policy as well as losses excluded by a standard policy.

Property Insurance - Insurance covering losses resulting from physical damage to or loss of real estate or personal property.

Replacement Value Coverage - Insurance coverage that provides the insured with sufficient funds to replace any destroyed or damaged property.

Depreciated Value Coverage - Insurance coverage that provides the insured with an amount that deducts for the prior use of the property before it was damaged.

Coinsurance - The requirement made by insurance companies that policyholders insure to a certain minimum percentage of the total value of the property.

Marine Insurance - A form of transportation insurance covering both the act of transportation (by land, water, or air) and the transported goods.

Title Insurance - Insurance guaranteeing that a seller has clear legal right to sell a certain piece of property.

Business-Interruption Insurance - Insurance that covers losses incurred during times when a company is unable to conduct its business.

Contingent Business-Interruption Insurance - Insurance that covers losses incurred by a firm whose business is interrupted because it is dependent on another business that suffers damage.

Credit Insurance - Insurance that protects a firm against its customers' failure to pay their bills.

Life Insurance - Insurance that pays benefits to the survivors of a policyholder and has a cash value that can be claimed before the policyholder's death.

Beneficiary - The person to whom the benefits of a life insurance policy are paid.

Whole Life Insurance - Insurance coverage in force for the full duration of a person's life.

Term Insurance - Life insurance coverage in force for a term of one, five, ten, or twenty years.

Endowment - Insurance that pays the face value of the policy after a fixed period of time whether the policyholder is alive or dead.

Universal Life Policy - A life insurance policy that combines term life insurance with the higher yields of money market funds and similar investments.

Variable Life Insurance (VLI) - A modified form of whole life insurance that allows flexibility regarding the minimum value of the policy, the types of investments supporting the policy, and the amount and timing of the premiums.

Group Life Insurance - Insurance that is underwritten for a specific group as a whole, not for each individual.

Health Insurance - Insurance covering losses resulting from medical and hospital expenses and/or from loss of income because of injury or disease.

Health Maintenance Organization (HMO) - An organized health care system providing comprehensive medical care for which its members pay a fixed fee.

Preferred Provider Organization (PPO) - An arrangement whereby selected hospitals and/or doctors agree to provide services at reduced rates and to accept thorough review of their recommendations for medical services.

Medicare - A government-sponsored program that funds medical services for the elderly.

Medicaid - A government-sponsored program that makes health care services available to low-income individuals and families.

Self-Insurance - The practice of building up a pool of funds as a reserve to cover losses rather than taking out a commercial insurance policy.

TRUE-FALSE QUESTIONS

1. Designing and distributing a new product is an example of a pure risk.

2. The firm that practices risk avoidance may miss the opportunity to make a high profit.

3. All risk control techniques involve costs.

4. A surety expects losses.

5. Every policyholder should gain financially from insurance.

6. Business downturns are insurable risks.

7. Most insurance bought by businesses is written by public insurance companies.

8. Because a total loss of property is not highly probable, property owners have traditionally purchased less than the total value in coverage.

9. Term insurance has a cash value and is more expensive than any of the other forms of insurance.

10. Self-insurance is a form of risk retention by the self- insured company.

MULTIPLE CHOICE QUESTIONS

1. The chance that a firm will experience a fire in one of its warehouses is an example of a(n)

   a. speculative risk.
   b. manageable risk.
   c. known risk.
   d. pure risk.

2. Conserving a firm's (or an individual's) financial power or assets by minimizing the financial effect of accidental losses is defined as

   a. loss control.
   b. insurance.
   c. risk management.
   d. an insurable risk.

3.   Techniques to prevent, minimize, or reduce losses or the consequences of losses is the practice of

   a. risk avoidance.
   b. risk control.
   c. risk transfer.
   d. risk retention.

4.   The covering of a firm's unavoidable losses with its own funds is called

   a. risk retention.
   b. risk avoidance.
   c. risk transfer.
   d. risk control.

5.   Contract bonds covering bids, performance, payment and maintenance are prime examples of

   a. risk retention devices.
   b. fidelity bonds.
   c. deductible bonds.
   d. surety bonds.

6.   Which of the following types of bonds is most often used where an individual is trusted with handling money or other valuable assets?

   a. a surety bond
   b. a bail bond
   c. a fidelity bond
   d. a premium bond

7.   A formal agreement to pay the policyholder a specified amount in the event of certain losses is called a(n)

   a. surety bond.
   b. insurance policy.
   c. a premium.
   d. a performance bond.

8. The statistical principle that the larger the number of cases involved, the more closely the actual rate will be to the statistically calculated rate is called the

    a. law of large numbers.
    b. principle of insurable risk.
    c. bonded principle.
    d. statistical reserve factor.

9. The ultimate purpose of insurance is to

    a. pay claims.
    b. grant a bond.
    c. determine insurability.
    d. indemnify policyholders.

10. Which of the following is not noted by the authors of your textbook as one of the specific criteria to be insurable?

    a. predictable
    b. geographically spread
    c. privately insured
    d. verifiable

11. An insurance company that is owned by its policyholders, who share in its profits is a(n)

    a. public insurance company.
    b. mutual insurance company.
    c. stock insurance company.
    d. bonded insurance company.

12. A free-lance agent who represents insurance buyers rather than sellers is a(n)

    a. insurance broker.
    b. underwriter.
    c. claims adjuster.
    d. insurance agent.

13. Insurance covering losses resulting from damage to persons or property of other people or firms is called

    a. umbrella insurance.
    b. property insurance.
    c. no-fault insurance.
    d. liability insurance.

14. Insurance that would protect a surgeon who left a pair of scissors inside a patient after an operation would be

    a. personal liability coverage.
    b. product liability coverage.
    c. professional liability coverage.
    d. premises liability coverage.

15. A business's liability for injury to its employee(s) resulting from any activities related to their occupation is called

    a. professional liability.
    b. workers' compensation.
    c. premises liability.
    d. automobile insurance.

16. Insurance that covers losses over and above those covered by a standard policy as well as losses excluded by a standard policy is a(n)

    a. umbrella policy.
    b. property insurance policy.
    c. life insurance policy.
    d. liability insurance policy.

17. Under this plan, the parties injured in an accident are compensated by their own insurers for bodily injuries and property damage, regardless of which parties are at fault.

    a. professional liability
    b. workers' compensation
    c. allied lines
    d. no-fault auto insurance

18. The easiest way for a purchaser to verify that the seller has clear legal right to sell real property is through the purchase of

    a. business interruption insurance.
    b. credit insurance.
    c. title insurance.
    d. marine insurance.

19. Which of the following types of business insurance provides coverage if a business is interrupted because it is dependent on another business that suffers damage?

    a. marine insurance.
    b. contingent business-interruption insurance.
    c. title insurance.
    d. credit insurance.

20. An arrangement whereby selected hospitals and/or doctors agree to provide services at reduced rates and to accept thorough review of their recommendated medical services is the

    a. preferred provider organization.
    b. medicare plan.
    c. medicaid plan.
    d. marine insurance plan.

WRITING TO LEARN

1. What is risk? How can risk be managed? What is the difference between a surety bond and a fidelity bond?

2. Describe the law of large numbers. What criteria are necessary for a risk to be insurable? Distinguish between the different types of insurance companies.

3. Discuss the major categories of insurance purchased by businesses.

4.   Discuss the concept of coinsurance. What is an endowment policy?

5.   How has the insurance industry responded to consumers' changing needs? What role has insurance industry regulation played in the industry's new product development?

DISCUSSION OF THE CLOSING CASE

What do the cost of health care, the national government's debt, and the weather have in common? Some years ago, Mark Twain provided the answer: "Everybody talks about it but nobody does anything about it." Or so it seems most of the time. Every informed citizen of the United States, not to mention numerous citizens of other countries, is well aware that the United States has a debt that virtually defies definition. It would be foolish to provide a figure on the nation's debt as these lines are being written, because by the time these lines are being read by conscientious students, that figure will be grossly out of date. Despite unanimous agreement on the gravity of this situation, there still seems to be no way to grapple with the monster. Health care costs present a similar enigma, but individual firms are finding solutions. One solution that is being resorted to rather frequently in recent years--if indeed insurance costs are so enormous-- is to escape from entanglements with insurers. This is exercising the option termed "self-insurance" or "retain the risk." In this move, a company decides that it can, in a sense, insure its own employees. How in the world will they get the funds for this? Such a company would answer that question by saying: "Rather than have our employees pay high health-care premiums to an insurance company, we take in those premium payments and put them in a special contingency fund. When some of our employees go to the hospital, we use money from that fund to pay the bills." Actually, a large firm will NOT "form its own insurance company," but will engage an administrative service to handle claims and payments. Many such firms are reporting that they are much happier with this method of "self-insurance" than they were with being served by an insurance firm. However, the solution just sketched is hardly realistic for a small business. Say a firm has 50 employees. After two months of "retaining the risk" and collecting premiums from employees, one worker goes in for open-heart surgery. Instantly, the self-insurance fund is deeply in the red. The owner-operator would have to announce something like: "Until we build up our fund again after Herman's surgery, no one in the company can be ill. For example, Maisie's pregnancy will have to be covered from her own pocketbook." Clearly, health care costs for the small business are a pressing need demanding immediate attention.

1. What are some of the pitfalls of retaining the risk of health care?

2. Why is it that a large firm seems better able to engage in self-insurance? Which risk management principle is involved here?

3. Do you see a connection between our ultra-modern, eminently- equipped hospitals and the current costs of health care? Explain.

4. Would a national health care plan--such as extending Medicare to all citizens--be a workable solution? Why or why not?

AN ADDITIONAL CASE

Alph-Omega Surgical Group (AOSG) of Los Angeles is in the process of taking corporate form. This business entity will consist of seventeen of the most skilled plastic surgeons on the North

American continent. As you know, the medical specialty of plastic surgery is divided into two main groups--reconstructive surgery and cosmetic surgery. Reconstructive surgery comes into play in the aftermath of horrendous and traumatic injury. Severe head lacerations, for example, may leave a person's face a tangled mass of disorganized flesh. Extensive reconstructive work by skilled surgeons can restore that face to a semblance of normalcy, performing virtual "miracles" in the long, multi- operation process. Cosmetic surgery, by contrast, does not usually follow injury and is largely elective. Perhaps the set of cosmetic procedures best known to the general public are those that enhance the beauty and handsomeness of nationally-known figures. Chief among these is programmed facial rejuvenation (PFR), more familiarly known by the term "facelift," a procedure by which the patient's facial appearance can become more youthful.

Alph-Omega Surgical Group (AOSG) will deal exclusively in the cosmetic, with emphasis on programmed facial rejuvenation (PFR). Prior to opening its doors, so to speak, AOSG is going through a detailed risk management analysis. A properly-implemented "facelift" (PFR) can be of tremendous value to a public figure. However, the PFR procedure can be disastrous if the desired results are not achieved. In such an instance, a multi-million- dollar malpractice suit could well be filed. AOSG must be prepared for such an eventuality.

The coming of technically-sophisticated color television with its frequent appearances by movie stars and other national celebrities has brought a new problem to the cosmetic surgeon who serves the stars. This is it. Have you ever tuned in late to a TV show and seen an actor whose face looked vaguely familiar? His or her voice sounded even more familiar. But you couldn't place the face. After awhile, you said: "Hey, that's Brok Hooper, but he's had a facelift and he's not exactly the Brok Hooper I remember." Has that happened to you? If it hasn't yet, it will. And this is because a "facelift" (PFR) accomplishes the putting of youth back into the face while it often, unfortunately, slightly alters the high-profile person's indentifiable physiognomy. In an extreme case, such a public person could claim that he or she had "lost" a part of their most important asset--a face as a trademark. Imagine Brok Hooper telling his cosmetic surgeon: "I can't appear on talk shows anymore as the much-loved Brok Hooper. I don't even look like Brok Hooper. For the movies, the makeup people can fix me up for a shoot, but not for live interviews. I'm suing you for everything you're worth, Doc; you've finished my career!"

Being aware of the gravity of such suits, the seventeen members and four administrators of AOSG commissioned a risk management presentation by Claude J. Thorntin, CLU, CPCU, ARM.* Following is the essence of Mr. Thorntin's comments.

Your organization faces considerable pure risk. Now, there are several ways to cope with the problem. Let me briefly sketch them for you.

Instead of operating as individual lone wolves competing with one another, I would advocate that a team of three be assigned to each PFR. Build into your group the "team" concept--each surgeon working to cover his associates, to meticulously avoid errors that could well sink the organization. When first blueprints are drawn for a PFR, let each team member truthfully point up areas in which the most serious errors can be made. PFR experts, for example, have pointed out in their journals that administering flesh around the cheek bones is a valley of danger. In addition, every member of AOSG should attend as many continuing education seminars as possible, considering the workload here at the clinic. Call the whole cautious approach "quality control," if you wish.

Another alternative is to place in escrow some 20 percent of every fee charged by AOSG. This fund will grow quickly, and that is because you ladies and gentlemen are the premier cosmetic surgeons of our time--and your fees show it! Should there be a suit against AOSG, that fund can be your backstop. Before we get into the specifics of such a fund, we'll need some statistics and some recent history on malpractice in cosmetics to enable us to establish realistic goals, as well as requirements, for the fund's growth.

A third alternative is to seek the services of a reliable and stable insurance firm that is willing to provide malpractice insurance. You'll need broad coverage, and I'm talking about a multi-million-dollar policy. That coverage is the good news. The bad news is that such a policy could cost you exhorbitant premiums. If a major case developed against AOSG, your insurer would throw their best legal troops into the fray to protect you--and to protect their own funds. This is often the risk management move of first resort, unless the premiums become unrealistic.

Then, there is another route to travel. You can limit your practice to persons who will never qualify as "public figures." If an ordinary John or Jane Doe looks a little different after proper and appropriate cosmetic surgery, that's not the end of a career, and such an ordinary citizen will have a hard time convincing a court that looking a little different has caused a trauma. This is similar to what some other members of your medical profession have done. When they considered the severe liability that attaches itself to obstetrics and the inordinately high cost of malpractice insurance in this area, some doctors have refused to deliver babies and have turned their practice in other directions. AOSG may want to do likewise.

And, so ladies and gentlemen, you may pick one or a combination of several of these approaches to managing the risk that will be faced by Alph-Omega Surgical Group.

* = Associate in Risk Management.

1.   Go back and pick the "retain the risk" option. What are some disadvantages of such an approach?

2.   Go back and pick the "transfer the risk" option. Despite its many advantages, what is the major drawback here?

3.   Go back and pick the "avoid the risk" option. Why does this option contain the negative feature of a drop in gross revenues?

4.   What were some of the techniques and procedures suggested in the "control the risk" approach?

ANSWERS TO TRUE-FALSE QUESTIONS

1.	F	(p. 615)	6.	F	(p. 621)
2.	T	(p. 616)	7.	F	(p. 622)
3.	T	(p. 617)	8.	T	(p. 625)
4.	F	(p. 618)	9.	F	(p. 628)
5.	F	(p. 619)	10.	T	(p. 635)

ANSWERS TO MULTIPLE-CHOICE QUESTIONS

1.	D	(p. 615)	11.	B	(p. 622)
2.	C	(p. 615)	12.	A	(p. 622)
3.	B	(p. 616)	13.	D	(p. 623)
4.	A	(p. 617)	14.	C	(p. 623)
5.	D	(p. 618)	15.	B	(p. 623)
6.	C	(p. 618)	16.	A	(p. 624)
7.	B	(p. 618)	17.	D	(p. 624)
8.	A	(p. 619)	18.	C	(p. 627)
9.	D	(p. 619)	19.	B	(p. 627)
10.	C	(p. 621)	20.	A	(p. 633)

CHAPTER TWENTY-FOUR

UNDERSTANDING THE LEGAL SYSTEM AND BUSINESS LAW

CHAPTER OVERVIEW

In the United States, laws fall into three broad categories. Statutory laws are created by legislative acts and constitutions. Common law consists of court interpretations of statutory laws. Regulatory (or administrative) law is made by decrees of government agencies. Much of the responsibility for law enforcement falls to the courts. When one person sues another in court, the party who feels wronged is the plaintiff, while the party charged with the wrongdoing is the defendant. A contract is any agreement between two or more parties that is enforceable in court. A contract must meet certain standards--agreement of both parties, real consent of both parties, capacity of both parties, consideration to both parties, legality, and proper form. A tort is a civil (non-criminal) injury to people. Torts can be intentional or can result from negligence. One area of torts that is particularly worrisome to businesses is product liability. An example of tangible real property is a house. An example of tangible personal property is an automoibile. Three kinds of intangible personal property are patents, copyrights, and trademarks. The Uniform Commercial Code (UCC) has been accepted by every state except Louisiana. A warranty is a seller's promise to stand by its products or services. A business bankruptcy may be resolved through a liquidation plan, a repayment plan, or reorganization.

LEARNING OBJECTIVES

1. Identify the meaning of law and the sources of law.

2. Describe the structure of the U.S. judicial system.

3. List the six criteria of a valid contract and three types of torts.

4. Explain the legal classifications of property, the principal/agent relationship and the role of the Uniform Commercial Code in regulating the behavior of buyers and sellers.

5. Describe the conditions under which businesses and individuals use bankruptcy laws.

DISCUSSION OF THE OPENING CASE

The breast implant controversy as explained in your textbook contains at least two key aspects. First, product liability can be an ominous black cloud hanging over a manufacturer. As these lines are being written, there have been several lawsuits against breast implant manufacturers.

342

However, as these lines are being read by college and university students, there is the apalling possibility that many such suits may be in progress with untold millions of dollars awarded to plaintiffs. Such suits can put a small manufacturer of breast implants out of business completely. Note that one firm withdrew from the transplant market altogether. Often, that is a way to avoid a liability suit--if the firm withdraws soon enough. Second, there is the ethical facet of the problem. The case narrative indicates that Dow- Corning allegedly knew of the gel-leakage problem in the implants before they went on the market, and specific Dow-Corning employees allegedly chose to hide these facts. This is the kind of story that is handled by the CBS program "60 Minutes." Can't you just hear Mike Wallace asking a breast implant manufacturer: "Do you mean to look me in the eye and tell me that executives with your firm <u>knew</u> of the gel leakage from these implants, and yet you continued to market them, and refrained from warning people who had already used your implants?" One wonders if someone at an implant manufacturer might have, at some stage in the story, gone into the highest executive suite and said: "Sir, are you aware that those breast implants we are distributing are faulty? Gel in those implants will quite possibly leak into the system of a woman who is using one of our implants. What's that, Sir? You knew all along? Then, why aren't you doing something about it? No one will ever find out, you say? Sir, I beg to differ with you. The word will get out eventually, and our company will be seen in a most unfavorable light." Knowing that the general public will someday find out the truth about a faulty product such as the implant, how can a business executive still proceed to market the product? Perhaps the answer defies simplification.

1. If you were the CEO at an implant manufacturing firm, and an employee had with you the conversation just quoted, what action would you take?

2. Come to the defense of a CEO who knowingly allows a faulty product on the market, with possible life-and-death implications. Explain his or her reasoning for such action.

3. In a discussion with your teacher and classmates, arrive at a dollar figure for the amount of product liability insurance a firm such as Dow-Corning might maintain.

4. Keeping secret the faults in a product your firm is distributing--is it a legal matter or an ethical question? Explain your asnswer.

ANNOTATED KEY TERMS

<u>Laws</u> - The codified rules of behavior enforced by a society.

<u>Statutory Law</u> - Laws created by federal, state, or local legislative acts and constitutions.

<u>Tax Law</u> - Laws concerned with the government's levying and collecting of taxes on individuals and businesses.

<u>Sales Tax</u> - A tax collected by a business on the goods and services it sells.

<u>Excise Tax</u> - A tax that is levied on the products used only by certain segments of the population.

Duty - A tax levied by a country on the goods that enter or leave its borders.

Value-Added Tax - A tax calculated on the amount of value added to a product at each stage of the manufacturing or distribution process.

Common Law - Court interpretations of statutory laws that set precedents and become the basis for later interpretations of the same laws.

Stare Decisis - The practice of judicial rulings following the decisions made in earlier cases (precedents).

Regulatory (Administrative) Law - Laws made by decree of government agencies or commissions.

Appellate Court - A court of appeals on either the state or national level.

Plaintiff - The party in a lawsuit that feels wronged.

Defendant - The party in a lawsuit that is charged with wrongdoing.

Discovery Process - The process by which both parties to a lawsuit learn more about the other party's evidence and exact position on the issue.

Pretrial Motion - In a lawsuit, a petition to the judge to establish certain limits regarding testimony, evidence, and other important issues.

Contract - Any agreement between two or more parties that is enforceable in court.

Capacity - In legal terms, the mental competence that is necessary for an individual to enter into a binding contract.

Consideration - In legal terms, any item of value that is exchanged between parties to create a valid contract.

Breach of Contract - A violation of one or more of the terms of a contract by a party to that contract.

Tort - A civil (noncriminal) injury to people, their property, or their reputation for which compensation must be paid.

Slander - Spoken defamation of character.

Libel - Written defamation of character.

Intentional Tort - A tort that results from the deliberate actions of a person or firm.

Punitive Damages - Fines that must be paid by the guilty party over and above the actual loss to the defendant.

Negligence - In legal terms, a lack of reasonable care and caution.

Product Liability - A form of tort in which a company is held responsible for injuries caused by its product.

Strict Product Liability - A form of product liability in which a company is held responsible for harm caused by its product, even though no deliberate tort or negligence was involved.

Property - In legal terms, anything of value to which a person or business has sole right of ownership.

Tangible Real Property - Land and anything attached to it.

Tangible Personal Property - Any movable item that can be owned, bought, sold, or leased.

Intangible Personal Property - Property that cannot actually be seen but has written documentation.

Intellectual Property - Property created through a person's mental skills.

Patent - A form of intellectual property protection granted by the U.S. government to the inventor for 17 years.

Trademark - The exclusive legal right to use a brand name or symbol.

New Property - In legal terms, the rights of citizens to certain benefits.

Deed - A written contract that transfers ownership of real property.

Transfer of Title - The transfer of personal property.

Agent - A person who acts for, and in the name of, another party.

Principal - A company or an individual that authorizes an agent to act on its behalf.

Power of Attorney - The legal granting of power to an agent to act on the principal's behalf.

Express Authority - An agent's power to bind a principal to a certain course of action derived from a written agreement.

Implied Authority - An agent's power to bind a principal to a certain course of action derived from business customs.

Apparent Authority - An agent's power to bind a principal to a certain course of action based on the principal's silent compliance.

Uniform Commercial Code (UCC) - A body of standardized laws governing the rights of buyers and sellers in every state except Louisiana.

Warranty - A seller's promise to stand by its products or services in the event of a problem after the sale is completed.

Express Warranty - A warranty whose terms are specifically stated by the seller.

Implied Warranty - A warranty whose terms are dictated by law.

Negotiable Instrument - Any form of business paper used in place of cash.

Bankruptcy - Permission granted by the courts to individuals and businesses not to pay some of their debts.

Involuntary Bankruptcy - Bankruptcy proceedings that are initiated by the creditors of an indebted firm or individual.

Voluntary Bankruptcy - Bankruptcy proceedings that are initiated by an indebted firm or individual.

TRUE-FALSE QUESTIONS

1. The common law created by the courts is older than the Constitution.

2. Onced passed, agency regulations have the force of statutory law and are subject to review by the courts.

3. The discovery process involves petitions to the judge regarding the limits to be imposed on testimony, the appropriateness of various pieces of evidence and the like.

4. Very few of the cases that go to trial are subsequently settled before a jury verdict.

5. According to the authors of your textbook, the simplest element of a contract is agreement.

6. Contract law does not require contracts to be rational.

7. All contracts must be in writing.

8. Ten percent of tort suits involve charges of negligence.

9. Sellers are always the plaintiffs in product liability suits.

10. By law, deeds must be recorded in the local office of public records.

MULTIPLE CHOICE QUESTIONS

1. The codified rules of behavior enforced by a society are

   a. rules of behavior.
   b. court cases.
   c. court procedures.
   d. laws.

2. Court interpretations of statutory laws are called

   a. statutory law.
   b. tax law.
   c. common law.
   d. administrative law.

3. A special type of tax levied on domestic products such as alcohol, tobacco, and gasoline is called a(n)

   a. duty.
   b. excise tax.
   c. value-added tax.
   d. corporate tax.

4. Most judicial rulings follow precedents (the decisions of earlier cases), a practice called

   a. stare decisis.
   b. administrative fiat.
   c. administrative statute.
   d. district court procedure.

5. Courts that hear specific types of cases such as tax evasion, fraud, and international disputes are called

   a. district courts.
   b. appellate courts.
   c. trial courts.
   d. special courts.

6. If a party disagrees with a ruling made by the lowest-level courts, and if that party can show grounds for a retrial, the case may go before a state or federal

    a. district court.
    b. trial court.
    c. appellate court.
    d. administrative court.

7. In a lower court action, the party who feels wronged is called the

    a. appellant.
    b. plaintiff.
    c. defendant.
    d. judge.

8. The process that allows each side to learn more about the other side's evidence, information such as the names of its witnesses, and its exact position on the issue is the

    a. discovery process.
    b. pretrial motion.
    c. judicial complaint.
    d. subpoena.

9. Any agreement between two or more parties that is enforceable in court is a(n)

    a. discovery process.
    b. pretrial motion.
    c. warranty.
    d. contract.

10. An agreement is a legally binding contract only if it includes an exchange of items of value, which is called

    a. capacity.
    b. discovery.
    c. consideration.
    d. real consent.

11. Written defamation of character is called

    a. slander.
    b. libel.
    c. breach of contract.
    d. specific performance.

12. Torts that result from the deliberate actions of another person or firm are referred to as

   a. intentional torts.
   b. negligence torts.
   c. statutory torts.
   d. criminal torts.

13. Suits that hold a company responsible for injuries caused by its product are

   a. libel torts.
   b. slander torts.
   c. criminal torts.
   d. product liability torts.

14. Anything of value to which a person or business has sole right of ownership is called

   a. a tort.
   b. a statute.
   c. property.
   d. bankruptcy.

15. A house, a factory, and built-in appliances or machines within the home or factory are examples of

   a. tangible personal property.
   b. tangible real property.
   c. intangible real property.
   d. intellectual property.

16. Bank accounts, stocks and bonds, and trade secrets are examples of

   a. intangible personal property.
   b. tangible personal property.
   c. intangible real property.
   d. intellectual property.

17. Which of the following give exclusive ownership to the creator's rights for books, articles, and films?

   a. patents
   b. trademarks
   c. real property law
   d. copyrights.

18.   Trademarks are issued by the U.S. Patent and Trademark Office for

      a. 50 years after the death of the creator of the mark.
      b. 17 years at a time.
      c. 20 years at a time.
      d. 1 year at a time.

19.   Checks, bank drafts, certificates of deposit, and promissory notes that are covered in Article 3 of the UCC are called

      a. warranties.
      b. negotiable instruments.
      c. real property.
      d. public property.

20.   Companies and individuals can receive court-granted permission not to pay some or all of their debts by filing for

      a. bankruptcy.
      b. a negotiable instrument.
      c. real property liens.
      d. a discovery process.

WRITING TO LEARN

1. What is law? Is there a difference between statutory, common, and regulatory law?

2. Describe the operation of the U.S. judicial system. Discuss, in detail, the U.S. court system and what to expect when going to court.

3. What conditions are necessary for a contract to be legally enforceable? What breach of contract remedies are available to the injured party?

4. Discuss the duties and responsibilities of the principal and the agent in a business relationship.

5. What do Articles 2 and 3 of the Uniform Commercial Code concern? What is a negotiable instrument?

DISCUSSION OF THE CLOSING CASE

The narrative about the troubles of Macy's is a perfect answer to the question: "How does a firm wind up in bankruptcy?" The starting point seems to be taking on too much debt. In finance circles, the correct terminology for such action is "being too heavily leveraged." Sometimes, however, being heavily leveraged is the necessary bold step without which significant growth of the firm cannot take place. Perhaps, it's all a matter of timing. Notice how Edward S. Finkelstein appreciably increased Macy's debt by acquiring two chains on the West Coast. After such a step, a firm can survive its debt problems so long as good economic times ensue: sales revenues will be up; new acquisitions begin turning a profit early; customers flock in during the Christmas rush. But when an "economic downturn," such as the one the United States has been experiencing in the late 1980s and early 1990s, comes calling, the necessary funds for paying debts are not developing. But there is nothing wrong with expanding through debt--if the timing is right! You may recall that in Chapter Nineteen of the text, one of the cases dealt with an aggressive entrepreneur by the name of Chang Yung-fa and his Evergreen Group's fleet of container ships. When large water transportation firms were experiencing diminishing revenues, Chang went out and bought 24 ships--for $30,000,000 each. This bold step, characterized as foolish by his competitors, enabled Evergreen to grow and grow. This growth occurred because the timing was right. Had shipping clients the world over been experiencing a recession, those 24 new ships would have been a heavy millstone of debt for Chang to carry around. The increased sales revenues would not have been there to provide funds for servicing the firm's debt. Unlike Chang Yung-fa, the timing was wrong for Ed Finkelstein. There is a more specific answer to the query: "How does a firm wind up in bankruptcy?" For Macy's specifically, the answer is when your assets total to $4.9 billion and your liabilities total to $5.3 billion. This means that if Macy's had been able to sell off (liquidate) all of its assets, there would still not be enough cash available to pay all the bills that are owed. Getting as much as $4.9 billion in cash for all the firm's assets may not be possible. Hopefully, reorganization of Macy's will enable this proud institution to survive.

1. Should Macy's, considering its present problems, continue to go to all the expense of sponsoring the Thanksgiving Day parade? Why or why not?

2. Let us say that you are with Prudential Insurance and you have agreed to renegotiate Macy's debt owed to your firm. What stipulations would you make as a part of this new deal?

3. The case indicates that Ed Finkelstein "is widely recognized as an excellent merchandiser." How will this help Macy's in its current predicament?

4. Would you advise Ed Finkelstein to close all the Macy's stores and then open them up to look like Wal-Marts? Why or why not?

AN ADDITIONAL CASE

(We are indebted to Mrs. Millicent J. Thorbes, secretary to the chief executive officer of Comet Sporting Goods, Limited, a large manufacturer of equipment for the major team sports. Her service to us has been the arranging of unrestricted access to a series of internal memorandums regarding the new Comet baseball bats made of the secret compound known as WJ76--perhaps the most sophisticated wood substitute known to science. When it became known that Mrs. Thorbes had furnished us these memos, she was forced into retirement by Comet.)

DATE: June 27
TO: Mr. Ned Nelson, CEO
FROM: Jack Swan, Engineering
SUBJECT: WJ76 Bats

In reply to the question you asked me yesterday about our new bats, I regret that I must give a rather disappointing report. My crew and I have subjected these WJ76 bats to several tests and the results are attached. Here is a summary of what we discovered.

Using the Forester 7791 pressure generator, we gave stress tests to 50 of the WJ76 bats. The pressure setting was the very same that we have always used when testing bats made of genuine "tree" wood. Of the 50 bats thus tested, 13 shattered at the normal setting. To be sure that we had not inadvertently set the wrong pressure on the Forester 7791, each of my crew and I checked the setting and then ran 50 more bats through the test. This second trial, we had 16 bats that shattered.

Knowing that in a game of baseball, players do not normally subject their bats to the kind of pressure that the Forester 7791 is capable of delivering, we organized a batting practice session with the local college team. Two players suffered what they thought was a "broken bat." We did not tell them that this was a WJ76 bat. For safety's sake, each college batter we used wore a special batting helmet we had rigged up for this special batting practice. Let me stress that it is good that we took this precaution. When the second bat shattered, several large wood fragments struck the right side of the helmet at great velocity-- a totally different effect from that of a normal "broken bat" experienced in a normal game. Had the batter been a young kid in a pick-up game at some grammar school, serious injury to the child could have resulted.

My crew and I are tempted to conclude that a bat made of WJ76 is not safe enough to be marketed nationally under the Comet trademark. Knowing of the funds that this company has placed in this breakthrough, I am hesitant about insisting that you drop WJ76 bats. On the other hand, the product liability suits that could justifiably emanate from our issuing of the WJ76 bats might be a far more serious blow to the firm.

- - - - - - - - - -

DATE: July 7
TO: Mr. Jack Swan
FROM: Ned Nelson
SUBJECT: WJ76 Bats

Ned, it's at moments like this that I am glad we have you aboard. In your depressing memo on the WJ76 bats, you have offered the ideal solution. Since broken bats do occur from time to time in organized baseball, we can claim that a WJ76 shattering is nothing more than one of those phenomena always associated with the national sport. A broken bat here and there will not sully our reputation. For any major league team that buys our bats, we can replace every broken bat free of charge.

- - - - - - - - - -

DATE: October 31
TO: Mr. Ned Nelson
            CEO, Comet Sporting Goods, Limited
FROM: Del Kramer
            Continental-National-Union Insurance (CNUI)

As you know, CNUI is proud to have provided a superior quality of product liability insurance for Comet Sporting Goods for many years. As my colleagues and I pull together a new liability package for your firm, it is mandatory that I have some information. We at CNUI are concerned over the new WJ76 bats that have begun to be distributed toward the end of the baseball season. Please furnish me with safety trials on the WJ76 bats. Let this memorandum be your first official notice that unless the WJ76 report is clean enough for our company's standards, then our liability coverage for Comet will cease as of December 1. Should your safety report not reach us by November 30, then, in that event too, our liability coverage for Comet will cease effective December 1.

- - - - - - - - - -

DATE: November 1
TO: Mr. Del Kramer
FROM: Ned Nelson

My quality control people are assembling the data you have requested. In the meantime, let me assure you that the WJ76 bats are perfectly safe.

- - - - - - - - - -

DATE: December 16
TO: Mr. Ned Nelson
FROM: Myrna Watson-Clevenger
             Attorney at Law
SUBJECT: Liability Litigation; WJ76 Bats

As the enclosed documents will indicate, I am initiating legal civil action against you and Comet Sporting Goods on behalf of my client, Billy Joe Massengale, age 14. On or about November 17, at approximately 3:17 P.M., young Massengale sustained significant injuries to the right portion of his face as a result of an exploding bat made of WJ76 and manufactured by your firm. The initial suit asks compensatory and punitive damages of $11,000,000.

----

1.   What could Ned Nelson have done to avoid the product liability lawsuit brought against himself and Comet Sporting Goods, Limited?

2.   How much responsibility in this matter do you feel should be assigned to Jack Swan of Engineering?

3.   You know little of Ned Nelson. Nevertheless, using what little you have learned, comment upon the general ethical standards of Mr. Nelson.

4.   Does a free bat replacement for any Comet broken bats cover the matter sufficiently? Why or why not?

ANSWERS TO TRUE-FALSE QUESTIONS

1.	T	(p. 657)	6.	T	(p. 662)
2.	T	(p. 657)	7.	F	(p. 662)
3.	F	(p. 660)	8.	F	(p. 664)
4.	F	(p. 661)	9.	F	(p. 665)
5.	T	(p. 661)	10.	T	(p. 667)

ANSWERS TO MULTIPLE-CHOICE QUESTIONS

1.	D	(p. 655)		11.	B	(p. 664)
2.	C	(p. 657)		12.	A	(p. 664)
3.	B	(p. 655)		13.	D	(p. 665)
4.	A	(p. 657)		14.	C	(p. 665)
5.	D	(p. 659)		15.	B	(p. 665)
6.	C	(p. 659)		16.	A	(p. 665)
7.	B	(p. 660)		17.	D	(p. 666)
8.	A	(p. 660)		18.	C	(p. 666)
9.	D	(p. 661)		19.	B	(p. 670)
10.	C	(p. 662)		20.	A	(p. 671)

CHAPTER TWENTY-FIVE

UNDERSTANDING INTERNATIONAL BUSINESS

CHAPTER OVERVIEW

Absolute advantage exists when a country can produce something more cheaply than any other country. Oil from Saudi Arabia is an example. A country has a <u>comparative</u> advantage in goods that it can make more cheaply or better than other goods. The world economy revolves around three major marketplaces--North America, the Pacific Rim, and Europe. The balance of trade is the economic value of all products imported into a country compared to the total economic value of all products exported. In recent years Japan has had a trade surplus, while the U.S. has run a deficit. Balance of payments refers to the flow of money into or out of a country. An exchange rate is the rate at which the currency of one nation can be exchanged for that of another nation. Planning an international business requires that managers become thoroughly familiar with the environments in which they are conducting business. There are at least three levels of involvement in international trade. A firm may act as an importer or exporter. A firm may organize as an international business. Or a firm can operate as a multinational firm. Examples of multinational firms are Royal Dutch Shell, IBM, and Ford. Countertrading is a complex form of bartering often pursued by countries with a weak currency but a strong comparative advantage for some product. Some barriers to trade are social and cultural differences, economic differences, legal and political differences.

LEARNING OBJECTIVES

1. Describe the importance of importing and exporting and explain how absolute advantage and comparative advantage have fostered international business.

2. Discuss the factors involved in deciding to do business internationally and in selecting the appropriate levels of involvement and organizational structure.

3. Describe some way in which social, cultural, economic, legal, and political differences between nations affect international business.

4. Explain how trade agreements and international financial institutions assist world trade.

DISCUSSION OF THE OPENING CASE

The account of the worldwide expansion of Toys 'R' Us contains several of the standard elements that usually make up a story of success in globalizing. First, Charles Lazurus had the notion that there were many families outside the United States that would like what Toys 'R' Us had to offer. To refuse to harvest in such fertile fields would be to pass up a supreme opportunity. As it turned out, Europe, especially, was far more enthusiastic for the Lazurus concept than even Lazurus had allowed himself to believe. He was fortunate to find that European families buy more toys for their kids than is the case in the United States. Second, although Lazurus had perfected his approach to retailing toys, he was always open to making adaptations to accommodate local conditions and customs. This adapting seemed to be more called for in the Orient than in Europe. American firms--in industries other than toys--that had preceded Lazurus had found that they, too, had to adapt. Dan Fujita was particularly helpful to Toys 'R' Us in this matter of adapting. Third, the utilization of Fujita's skills is symbolic of the willingness of Lazurus, at some point, to turn the business over to the local nationals. And this means at high levels within the hierarchy of the foreign operation. If a firm wants to have the adaptability referred to above, then a key is to have the local nationals very much a part of decision making. Fourth, Charles Lazurus was opportunistic--taking advantage of any unique opportunity that came his way. For example, in early 1992, President George Bush paid a visit to Japan. That trip's most memorable moment, unfortunately, was the President's falling ill and collapsing--before news cameras--at a state banquet. On that same trip, President Bush was on hand for the opening of a brand-new Toys 'R' Us store. You're in the tall cotton when you can get the President of the United States to preside at a store opening for your chain. A fifth ingredient for success--locally as well as internationally--is the matter of proper timing. Note that Lazurus placed large orders for toys at a time of the year when toymakers normally experienced relative inactivity.

1.   What are some reasons why breaking into the Japanese market was more difficult than doing the same thing in Europe?

2.   How important is it for a toy retailer to stay abreast of what's popular with kids almost on a minute-by-minute basis? Has Charles Lazurus been able to do this?

3.   Although he is noted for bringing American toys to foreign countries, to what extent has Charles Lazurus brought foreign toys to the United States?

4   What chances of success would Toys 'R' Us have if it were to expand into countries of the Third World? Explain.

ANNOTATED KEY TERMS

Imports - Products made or grown abroad but sold domestically.

Exports - Products made or grown domestically but shipped and sold abroad.

Globalization - The process by which the world is becoming a single interdependent system.

Absolute Advantage - A nation's ability to produce something more cheaply than any other country can.

Comparative Advantage - A nation's ability to produce some products more cheaply or better than it can produce others.

Balance of Trade - The total economic value of all products imported into a country minus the total economic value of all products exported out of that country.

Trade Deficit - A negative balance of trade; the situation in which a country's imports exceed its exports.

Trade Surplus - A positive balance of trade; the situation in which a country's exports exceed its imports.

Balance of Payments - The flow of all monies into or out of a country.

Exchange Rate - The rate at which the currency of one nation can be exchanged for that of another nation.

Fixed Exchange Rates - An exchange-rate system in which the value of any country's currency relative to another country's currency is constant.

Floating Exchange Rates - An exchange-rate system in which the value of one country's currency relative to another's varies with market conditions.

Exporting Firm - A firm that exports a product to a single (or very small number of foreign countries.

Importing Firm - A firm that buys products in foreign markets, then imports them into its home country for resale.

International Firm - A firm with a significant portion of its business in foreign countries.

Multinational Firm - A company that designs, produces, and markets products in many nations.

Independent Agent - A foreign resident or business that agrees to represent the interest of an exporting company.

Licensing Arrangement - An arrangement in which firms choose individuals or companies in a foreign country to manufacture or market their product in that country.

Royalties - Payments made to a license granter from a licensee, usually calculated as a percentage of the licensee's sales.

Branch Office - An office set up in a foreign nation by an international or multinational firm.

Strategic Alliance - An international business arrangement in which a foreign company finds a partner in the country in which it would like to begin business. The company and its partner(s) then contribute approximately equal amounts of resources and capital into the new business.

Direct Investment - An international business arrangement in which a firm buys or establishes a tangible asset in another country.

Countertrading - A form of bartering in which a country requires that a foreign company buy products in that nation in exchange for the privilege of selling its goods there.

Quota - A restriction on the number of products of a certain type that can be imported into a country.

Embargo - A government order forbidding exportation and/or importation of a particular product or all the products of a particular country.

Subsidy - A government payment to a domestic business to help it compete with foreign firms.

Tariff - A tax on imported products.

Revenue Tariff - A tariff imposed to raise money for the government.

Protectionist Tariff - A tariff imposed to discourage imports of a particular product.

Protectionism - The practice of imposing quotas, tariffs, or subsidies to protect domestic industries from foreign competition.

Local-Content Laws - Laws that require products sold in a particular country to be at least partly made in that country.

Cartel - An association of producers whose purpose is to control supply and prices.

Dumping - Selling a product for less abroad than at home.

General Agreement on Tariffs and Trade (GATT) - An international trade agreement in which 92 countries agreed to reduce tariffs.

European Community (Common Market) - An agreement among Western European nations to eliminate trade barriers within their group but to impose quotas and high tariffs on goods imported from nonmember nations.

Free Trade Agreement - An agreement between the United States and Canada to eliminate most trade barriers between the two countries.

International Monetary Fund (IMF) - A United Nations agency that makes loans to nations that are suffering from a serious negative balance of trade.

World Bank - A United Nations agency that makes loans to less developed countries to help them improve their productive capacity.

TRUE-FALSE QUESTIONS

1. The total volume of world trade today is around $1.3 trillion each year.

2. Examples of absolute advantage are rare.

3. Relatively small trade imbalances are quite common and not very important.

4. The success of any firm depends largely on how well that firm is managed.

5. An organizational structure that works well in one country will work equally as well in other countries.

6. An importing or exporting firm entails the highest level of involvement in international operations.

7. The location of a multinational's headquarters is almost irrelevant.

8. In international business, independent agents usually specialize in one product or market.

9. Direct investment makes a firm a "corporate citizen" of a foreign country.

10. The ultimate form of quota is the embargo.

MULTIPLE CHOICE QUESTIONS

1. Products made or grown domestically but shipped and sold abroad are called

   a. world trade items.
   b. comparative advantage products.
   c. imports.
   d. exports.

2. When a country can produce something more cheaply that any other country, the country has a(n)

   a. comparative advantage.
   b. trade imbalance.
   c. absolute advantage.
   d. quota.

3. Japan, China, Thailand, Hong Kong, and Australia are countries in the marketplace and business center called the

   a. European Community.
   b. Pacific Rim.
   c. North America.
   d. Europe.

4. The situation in which a country's imports exceed its exports is called a

   a. trade deficit.
   b. trade surplus.
   c. balance of trade.
   d. exchange rate.

5. The flow of money into or out of a country is referred to as the

   a. trade deficit.
   b. trade surplus.
   c. exchange rate.
   d. balance of payments.

6. The rate at which the currency of one nation can be exchanged for that of another nation is called the

   a. balance of payments.
   b. trade deficit.
   c. exchange rate.
   d. gross national product.

7. A firm that buys products in foreign markets and then imports them into its home country for resale is a(n)

   a. exporting firm.
   b. importing firm.
   c. wholesaler.
   d. retailer.

8.   IBM, Ford, Nestle, and Royal Dutch Shell are examples of

a. multinational firms.
b. domestic firms.
c. independent agents.
d. branch offices.

9.   A foreign resident or business that agrees to represent the interest of an exporting company is a(n)

a. international firm.
b. branch office.
c. foreign interest.
d. independent agent.

10.   In return for granting exclusive rights to a product, the exporting firm typically receives a fee, plus ongoing payments called

a. agent arrangements.
b. salaries.
c. royalties.
d. administrative fees.

11.   When a firm buys or establishes a tangible asset in another country, it is engaging in

a. licensing.
b. direct investment.
c. channel control.
d. strategic alliances.

12.   A complex form of bartering often pursued by countries with a weak currency but a strong comparative advantage in some product is

a. countertrading.
b. quota establishment.
c. direct investment.
d. foreign exchange.

13.   Around what percent of all international trade involves some degree of countertrading?

a. 10 percent
b. 15 to 20 percent
c. 80 percent
d. 30 to 40 percent

14. A government payment to a domestic business to help it compete with foreign firms is a

   a. barter.
   b. tariff.
   c. subsidy.
   d. quota.

15. Which of the following requires that products sold in a particular country be at least partly made in that country?

   a. a license agreement
   b. local-content laws
   c. a franchise agreement
   d. the EC treaty

16. Associations of producers whose purpose is to control supply and prices is called a(n)

   a. cartel.
   b. franchise.
   c. trade agreement.
   d. local-content law.

17. Belgium, Denmark, France, Greece and the United Kingdom are members of the

   a. OPEC cartel.
   b. pacific rim trading group.
   c. SEATO.
   d. EC.

18. Which of the following was signed in 1989 by the U.S. and Canada to eliminate most trade barriers between those countries?

   a. the EC Agreement
   b. the IMF treaty
   c. the Free Trade Agreement
   d. the OPEC Cartel treaty

19. Which of the following organizations makes loans to nations that are having problems because of a negative balance of trade?

   a. OPEC
   b. the International Monetary Fund
   c. the World Bank
   d. the Common Market

20. Which of the following organizations funds improvements in a nation's productive capacity?

   a. the World Bank
   b. the International Monetary Fund
   c. the Common Market
   d. the U.S. Bank for Reconstruction

WRITING TO LEARN

1. What is the difference between absolute and comparative advantage? What are the three major marketplaces and business centers in the world economy today?

2. Are continually large trade deficits important to a country? What is the difference between fixed and variable exchange rates? What role does foreign competition play in determining a country's trade surplus or deficit?

3. Is there a difference between domestic and international business management? Should every company conduct business internationally?

4. Discuss the levels of involvement that a business may take in conducting business internationally. What is countertrading?

5. What are the major barriers to trade that a firm may face in its international operations? What is GATT? Do business practice laws vary from country to country?

DISCUSSION OF THE CLOSING CASE

Hal Hickman's trip to that German trade show turned out to be a most rewarding one for his Action Machinery. Here we have discovered an item that should be added to textbooks in business. Such textbooks offer a short list of ways for a company to get its feet wet in international trade. We read such things as export or import a little, get involved in a licensing arrangement or a joint venture, or set up a branch office in a foreign country--to name a few. To the list we should add: "Before you seriously consider going into international trade, attend a trade show in a major foreign country!" Right there assembled in one spot were any number of wonderful contacts for Hal Hickman and his Action Machinery. At the very least, Hickman left the trade show with a much better idea of how to begin international trade. At the very most, Hickman left the trade show with several very hot prospects who were ready to hear more about what Action Machinery could do for them. As for SeaSpace, note the reason that SeaSpace was able to get the order from the Japanese Fisheries Agency. It was because Robert Bernstein was something more than an American businessman wanting to open up new commercial opportunities. Yes, Bernstein was a trained oceanographer, and this background "provided an excellent knowledge of the Japanese Fisheries Agency's research and technological requirements." In addition, the software Bernstein offered was superior to that of two bidding Japanese firms. This tells us something. If an American firm wants to gain new markets for itself abroad, it must deliver a product whose superiority over those of competitors is unquestionable. It is unwise for an American firm to assume that consumers in foreign countries are just waiting for any American product and that a firm from the U.S. can unload on the foreign market anything that did not succeed here at home. The fact that American-made jeans and records by American artists are extremely popular in Europe cannot be generalized to all things American. In fact, in some parts of the world, some consumers may discriminate against anything made in the U.S.A.

1. Let's assume that Hal Hickman--like most Americans--spoke only English. How do you feel he would have been helped at the German trade show if he was also fluent in German, French, and Italian?

2. Reread the part about Hal Hickman at the German trade show and define in that setting the term "networking."

3. Regarding getting started in international business, evaluate this statement: "Frankly, it's really not worth all the trouble!"

4. What was the major contribution of SeaSpace software adopted by the Japanese Fisheries Agency?

AN ADDITIONAL CASE

Although founded as a customizer of software for large manufacturing concerns, Oudine Systems of Saint Paul (OSSP) has expanded to become the second largest "automater" in the United States. In the summer of 1980, Len Oudine attended several trade fairs in Europe. This sojourn left him with the distinct impression that what he had to offer would receive a relatively warm reception from certain French and German businesses.

Accordingly, some four years ago, Oudine Systems arrived in Paris. Len Oudine sent Mark Stephens to establish a small office at 15 rue Marbeau (75016). Mark took with him a sharp young programmer just out of University of Minnesota, Henley Steffard. To complete the staff, Mark was able to add a Parisian with lots of sales and computer experience--Pierre-Marie Renaud. Mark slowly added to staff. Fortunately, the people he added were sharp and productive. Before long, the Paris office of OSSP had a staff of twenty-seven and had moved to much larger quarters at 112 rue de Sevres (75015). As he added human resources, Mark Stephens added two Americans for every French citizen. Whatever his formula was, it must have been working, because the Paris office had very quickly signed several significant clients-- firms that wished to fully automate their office systems. And numerous potential customers were waiting in the wings.

Mark Stephens had his "troops" organizd into seven three-person teams. A team leader, an American, would be a skilled programmer. The French member was a hardware specialist, while the third member (American) saw to the redesign of the physical setting to be most affected by the automation. Since not every team was racing to its own deadline all the time, temporarily idle teams served as reserve forces.

Len Oudine and the home office were delighted by the progress of the Paris office. However, reading between the lines of reports from Mark Stephens clearly indicated that OPPS had not landed a major account. Oudine felt that to service small-business clients was not reason enough to maintain an office on a foreign shore.

An excerpt from a fax sent by Mark gave a clue to what was happening: "Here I was with Team #4 in the executive suite of one of the largest insurance companies in Europe, making a detailed presentation on what OSSP could do for the insurer. Our proposal was definitely better than those of a Japanese firm and two French companies. But the weaker of the French proposals won the contract."

As a matter of fact, Len Oudine received several fax messages saying just about this very same thing. He had spotted the problem and was flying to France to correct it.

With all the proper fanfare due the founder of a company who has come all the way from America, Len Oudine was ushered into Mark Stephens' office at 112 rue Sevres. After some informal bavardage, Oudine took command.

"Mark, let me tell you why I'm here. In my eyes, the problem with the Paris office is that you don't have enough French personnel. My experience has been that you will NEVER land a <u>major</u> account until one of your teams can make its entire presentation in French. And the best way to do this is to have more and more of your teams made up of energetic French young people."

"Well, uh, you know.... I've been taking French lessons...."

"But, Mark, it doesn't show. For example, tell me what this memo says."

At this, Len Oudine picked up a sheet of paper from Mark's desk. It said:

> **Je vous ecris pour confirmer le rendez-vous qu'a pris Mlle. Sylvie Latour de notre part (le lundi 1er juin a 11 heures au siege de la OPPS).**
>
> **Je vous prie d'agreer, Monsieur, l'expression de mes sentiments les meilleurs.**
>
> **Jeanne Piaf ****

"Len, I don't know what it says, but my secretary does. I'll call her...."

"That won't be necessary. What I want you to do is fill every new opening with a French national. In addition, it is company policy that all presentations to prospective clients will be made in French from here forward. Let's set some goals here. Within a year, I want twenty percent Americans in this office--no more. Two years from now, I want you to be the only American. Three years from now, I want this to be an all-French office. You've got to understand that fitting in with the French is not the only problem. Also, keeping an American over here costs OPPS far more per year than hiring a French national."

"Will I be left out in the cold?"

"Now, Mark, don't worry about your career with OPPS; I'll always have a spot for you. In fact, your experience here will be a priceless asset; I might ask you to set us up in Athens, Istanbul, Cairo, or even Singapore. In fact, since you are our first real foreign manager, we may need you someday to head up the whole OPPS-International Unit."

** = The memorandum says: "I am writing you to confirm the rendezvous that Miss Sylie Latour has set up for us for Monday, June 1st at 11:00 A.M. at the headquarters of OPPS. Sir, I hope you will accept the expression of my best regards. Jeanne Piaf."

1.   Do you agree with what Len Oudine has been telling Mark Stephens? Why or why not?

2.   In a more general sense, do you feel that Americans assigned abroad should work hard to be fluent in the language of the land where they are sent? Why or why not?

3. Show where in the narrative we see evidence that Mark Stephens realized his teams were weakened by having two Americans on each.

4. If indeed Mark Stephens follows his stint in Paris with service in Athens, Istanbul, Cairo, or Singapore (that's four new languages), should it really matter that all he handles fluently is English? Explain.

ANSWERS TO TRUE-FALSE QUESTIONS

1.	F	(p. 679)	6.	F	(p. 686)
2.	T	(p. 679)	7.	T	(p. 686)
3.	T	(p. 683)	8.	F	(p. 689)
4.	T	(p. 684)	9.	T	(p. 691)
5.	F	(p. 684)	10.	T	(p. 694)

ANSWERS TO MULTIPLE-CHOICE QUESTIONS

1.	D	(p. 679)	11.	B	(p. 691)
2.	C	(p. 679)	12.	A	(p. 692)
3.	B	(p. 680)	13.	D	(p. 693)
4.	A	(p. 682)	14.	C	(p. 695)
5.	D	(p. 682)	15.	B	(p. 696)
6.	C	(p. 682)	16.	A	(p. 696)
7.	B	(p. 685)	17.	D	(p. 697)
8.	A	(p. 686)	18.	C	(p. 697)
9.	D	(p. 689)	19.	B	(p. 697)
10.	C	(p. 690)	20.	A	(p. 698)

CHAPTER TWENTY-SIX

INCREASING PRODUCTIVITY AND QUALITY

CHAPTER OVERVIEW

Productivity is a measure of economic performance. Productivity considers both the amounts and quality of what is produced. Quality may be defined as fitness for use. The United States is still the most productive nation on earth, although it has been experiencing a slowdown in the growth rate of its productivity. To be considered are national productivity, industry productivity, and company productivity. Gross domestic product is the value of all goods and services produced in the economy. Capital productivity is total outputs divided by capital inputs. Total quality management is the total set of activities necessary to getting quality goods and services into the marketplace. Quality ownership is the idea that quality belongs to each person who creates it while performing a job. Some tools for total quality management are statistical process control, quality-cost studies, and quality circles. The latter are groups of employees who work in teams to improve their work methods with the aim of maintaining high quality standards. Benchmarking is finding and implementing the best quality practices of other companies in order to improve their own products. Quality-oriented firms are committed to a long-run perspective for continuous improvement. An aspect of quality that some firms are emphasizing is the quality of the employee's work life. Productivity and quality management concepts apply to services as well as products.

LEARNING OBJECTIVES

1. State the connection between productivity and quality.

2. Describe the decline in U.S. productivity and why some consider it a crisis.

3. Explain total and partial measures of productivity and how they are used to keep track of nation, sector, and company productivity.

4. Identify the activities involved in total quality management and describe three tools that companies can use to achieve TQM.

5. List six ways in which companies can compete by improving productivity and quality.

DISCUSSION OF THE OPENING CASE

The first "winds of change" came at Motorola in a staff meeting in 1979. Company historians, official and unofficial, point to this meeting as the instant at which Motorola changed its whole quality philosophy. As has been pointed out elsewhere in this study guide, at some firms quality control did not necessarily mean only striving for high quality. The term also covered exercising "controls" to see that striving for quality did not involve more expenses than were budgeted. In other words, "Let's keep our quality efforts under control. No customer expects a <u>perfect</u> product." From a businessperson's standpoint, that quality approach made good sense. Then, the Japanese began ringing our alarm clock. Certain Japanese firms were producing "perfect" products. If our business-as-usual firms were to compete with the Japanese, then they would have to change their ways of thinking. From a real world vantage point, what is amazing about the Motorola turnaround is that it happened at all! As the readers of this study guide move up the managerial rungs of large organizations, they will discover that change is slow and difficult to implement. In the average corporation, a meeting such as the 1979 meeting at Motorola will--at best--result in a committee of unimportant middle managers being formed to look into the quality problem. The committee will be asked to make a report every six months or so. Perfectly apropos is the famous and oft-repeated H. Ross Perot comment concerning the difference between his firm, EDS, and General Motors, which bought up EDS. Roughly paraphrased, Perot is reported to have said: "When we find a snake at EDS, we kill it. When they find a snake at GM, they form a snake committee. The committee discusses snakes for two years. Then the committee disbands, concluding that there are no snakes." It is a tribute to Robert Galvin, chairman of Motorola at the time, that he (1) realized the gravity of the situation, and (2) got on his horse and galloped off to do something about the problem. May the gentle reader work for at least one such business organization in his or her lifetime.

1.   Looking back to the case narrative, what were Robert Galvin's steps taken to change the entire complexion of his organization.

2.   What was the most important factor that forced Motorola to take quality more seriously? Explain.

3.   Do you feel that the case discussion in this study guide has sketched too negative a picture of how organizations make changes? Why or why not?

4.   If you were to become a new CEO of a stumbling organization, what steps would you take to speed up decision making on issues such as quality?

ANNOTATED KEY TERMS

<u>Productivity</u> - A measure of how much is produced relative to the resources used to produce it.

<u>Quality</u> - A product's fitness for use; how well it succeeds in offering the features that consumers want.

Level of Productivity - The dollar value of goods and services produced relative to the dollar value of the resources used to produce them.

Growth Rate - The increase in a nation's output in a given year over the previous year.

Value-Added Analysis - The process of evaluating all work activities, materials flows, and paperwork to determine the value they add for the customer.

Total Factor Productivity Ratio - A measure of productivity that takes into account all types of input resources: labor, capital, materials, energy, and purchased business services.

Partial Productivity Ratio - A measure of productivity that takes into account only certain input resources.

Materials Productivity - A partial productivity ratio calculated by dividing total output by total materials inputs.

Labor Productivity - A partial productivity ratio calculated by dividing total output by total labor inputs.

Gross Domestic Product (GDP) - The value of all goods and services produced by an economy.

Capital Productivity - A partial productivity ratio calculated by dividing total output by total capital inputs.

Total Quality Management (TQM) - The sum of all activities involved in getting quality goods and services into the marketplace.

Quality Level - The overall degree of quality in a product or service; how well the product performs or how well the service is performed.

Quality Reliability - The consistency of quality from unit to unit of a good or service.

Quality Ownership - The concept that quality belongs to each person who creates it while performing a job.

Competitive Product Analysis - The process by which a company analyzes a competitor's products or services to determine the improvements it should make in its own products.

Statistical Process Control (SPC) - Statistical analysis techniques that allow managers to analyze variations in a company's production data.

Process Variation - Variations in a firm's products that arise from changes in the inputs used in the production process.

Process Capability Study - A statistical process control method in which samples of a product are measured to determine the amount of process variation.

Specification Limits - The boundaries of acceptable quality in the production of a good or service.

Control Chart - A statistical process control method in which the results of test sampling of a product are plotted on a diagram that reveals when the process is beginning to depart from normal operating conditions.

Control Limit - The critical value on a control chart that indicates the level at which quality deviation is sufficiently unacceptable to merit investigation.

Quality/Cost Study - A method of improving quality by assessing a firm's current costs and identifying the areas with the greatest cost-saving potential.

Quality Circle (Quality Improvement Team) - A TQM technique in which groups of employees work together as a team to improve quality.

Benchmarking - The process in which a company finds and implements the best practices of other companies to improve its own products or services.

Continuous Improvement - The endless commitment to improving products and processes, step by step, in the pursuit of ever- increasing customer satisfaction.

TRUE-FALSE QUESTIONS

1.   Productivity and quality are inseparable.

2.   A productivity decline increases a nation's total wealth.

3.   The United States is the most productive nation on earth.

4.   Manufacturing is primarily responsible for recent increases in the nation's overall productivity.

5.   High productivity gives a company a competitive edge because its costs are higher.

6.   Japan's highest honor for industrial achievement is the Stempel Award for Quality.

7.   Every business experiences unit-to-unit variations in its products and services.

8.   Studies indicate that many U.S. manufacturers incur very high costs for internal failures.

9. U.S. business investment in R&D has increased in areas other than national defense.

10. Part of the decline in innovation among U.S. firms is the result of a common long-run perspective.

MULTIPLE CHOICE QUESTIONS

1. A measure of economic performance that compares how much is produced relative to the resources used to produce it is

   a. quality.
   b. dependability.
   c. the CPI.
   d. productivity.

2. A product's fitness for use by offering features that consumers want is defined as

   a. productivity.
   b. dependability.
   c. quality.
   d. price.

3. The dollar value of goods and services produced versus the dollar value of resources used to produce them is the current

   a. growth rate.
   b. level of productivity.
   c. level of quality.
   d. value-added amount.

4. The increase in productivity in a given year over the previous year is called the

   a. growth rate.
   b. level of GNP.
   c. quality measure.
   d. value-added per unit of cost.

5. The evaluation of all work activities, materials flows, and paperwork to determine the value they add for the customer is called

   a. determining the growth rate.
   b. measuring productivity.
   c. quality attainment.
   d. value-added analysis.

6. The value of all goods and services produced in the economy is referred to as

   a. capital productivity.
   b. labor productivity.
   c. gross domestic product.
   d. research and development.

7. The ratio of all of the outputs divided by the capital inputs of all firms is

   a. gross domestic product.
   b. capital productivity.
   c. labor productivity.
   d. the growth rate.

8. Any activity necessary for getting quality goods and services into the marketplace is a part of

   a. total quality management.
   b. gross domestic product.
   c. capital productivity.
   d. control charting.

9. The overall degree of quality in a product or service and how well the product performs or how well the service is performed is called the

   a. total factor productivity ratio.
   b. partial productivity ratio.
   c. gross domestic product.
   d. quality level.

10. The idea that quality belongs to each person who creates it while performing a job is found in the concept of

    a. factor productivity.
    b. gross domestic product.
    c. quality ownership.
    d. quality control.

11. The process by which a company analyzes a competitor's products or services to determine the improvements it should make in its own products is called

    a. a process capability study.
    b. competitive product analysis.
    c. quality/cost study.

d. benchmarking.

12. Statistical analysis techniques that allow managers to analyze variations in a company's production data are referred to as

a. statistical process control.
b. quality ownership.
c. specification limits.
d. benchmarking.

13. Variations in a firm's products that arise from changes in the inputs used in the production process results are

a. product changes.
b. control limits.
c. benchmarking.
d. process variations.

14. The boundaries of acceptable quality in the production of a good or service are called

a. quality circles.
b. statistical process controls.
c. specification limits.
d. product changes.

15. To detect the beginning of bad conditions, managers can check production periodically and plot the results on a

a. competitive product analysis.
b. control chart.
c. quality level.
c. PERT graph.

16. The critical value on a control chart that indicates the level at which quality deviation is sufficiently unacceptable to merit investigation is the

a. control limit.
b. productivity guide.
c. capital productivity level.
d. total factor productivity ratio.

17. A method of improving quality by assessing a firm's current costs and identifying the areas with the greatest cost- saving potential is the

a. process capability study.

379

b. competitive product analysis.

c. process variation method.

d. quality/cost study.

18. Groups of employees who work in teams to improve their quality work methods are referred to as

a. control teams.

b. matrix committees.

c. quality circles.

d. task forces.

19. The process in which a company finds and implements the best practices of other companies to improve its own products or services is called

a. competitive product analysis.

b. benchmarking.

c. a process capability study.

d. a quality circle.

20. The endless commitment to improving products and processes, step by step, in the pursuit of ever-increasing customer satisfaction is known as

a. continuous improvement.

b. competitive product analysis.

c. benchmarking.

d. a process capability study.

WRITING TO LEARN

1. Are productivity and quality related? Discuss U.S., industry, and company productivity trends and measures.

2. What is total quality management? How can a firm plan, organize, lead, and control for quality?

3. Discuss the tools that are available to management for measuring total quality management. How can a quality circle be used to improve quality?

4. What can a firm do to compete effectively on the basis of productivity and quality? Should a company adopt a short- term or long-run perspective for innovation?

5. Are small firms able to increase productivity? What roles do employee attitude and service have in the manufacturing and service sectors?

DISCUSSION OF THE CLOSING CASE

The final line of the detailing of the glass art studio of Dale Chihuly may establish for us a relationship between the cost of quality and the benefits thereof. In short, there is a fabulous payoff awaiting the Chihuly studio when one of its works of art has been commissioned and/or purchased. If indeed, the financial rewards are all in line with a $60,000 pricetag for the very smallest works, then the Chihuly studio can easily be motivated to establish and maintain the highest quality standards. The other side of this coin must be that certain projects (in whatever industry) may not be worth the trouble to set high quality levels. The traditional cost-benefit analysis is often an integral part of the decision process about quality. A part of the trade-off is follow-up service. A typical example is your automobile. Since few, if any, car manufacturers can guarantee a trouble-free auto for you [in this chapter we'd call that a high-quality-standard product], a car manufacturer compensates for lack of quality by offering abundant service. As another example, a manufacturer of manufacturing equipment (let us say a plastic-bottle blowing machine), will offer: "As we build this blowing machine for you, we cannot vouch for its quality. BUT, we'll send a crew to your factory to get it into superior operating condition, and for the first two years we'll have an 800 number you can call in case of difficulty and we'll have a serviceman at your location within 24 hours." A firm making the blowing machine may also sometimes be under terrific time pressures. A frantic customer may be saying: "Forget the quality runs at your plant. We need that machine in here by the first of the month. Even if it spits out a defect in every ten bottles, that's better than the machine not arriving on time." To take the extra time required for a high level of quality under such circumstances means, perhaps, the loss of a customer. The customer has dictated that the blowing machine will be raced to completion and a trouble-shooting crew will go along with it. There is nothing wrong with extreme pride in workmanship. It is an admirable quality. But in the real world of manufacturing, realistic considerations may necessitate some compromises and some compensations.

1. What do you think really motivates the high quality standards of the Chihuly studio?

2. If the Chihuly studio got an order for one million drinking glasses, would this alter Dale Chihuly's concept of quality? Should it alter his concept of quality?

3. Following up on the situation presented in Question 2 above, how much personal attention do you feel Dale Chihuly would be able to give to each glass being made to fulfill this particular order?

4. While responding to Question 3 above, please incorporate (if you feel appropriate) this legend about Walt Disney. It has been said that frequently Walt Disney himself would walk around the grounds at Disneyland, looking for and picking up pieces of trash that may have fallen on the ground.

AN ADDITIONAL CASE

Before we reveal the story of Elaine and Leilani, it is necessary that you know something of the unique opportunity that fell in the lap of Henri Bruder. For many years, Henri had been a middle manager at Threskinger Systems of Dayton. This firm of several thousand employees provided health insurance coverage for its workers and required that there be an extra payment from each employee who wished to have <u>family</u> coverage. Health insurance premiums were paid to Western American Cascade Certified Casualty Insurance (WACCCI) of Southern Oregon, Incorporated. It was Henri's impression that health insurance premiums went up every year for employees of Threskinger Systems of Dayton and that the efficiency of WACCCI went <u>down</u> year by year. Claims were settled very slowly and numerous mistakes were made. To Threskinger employees, it almost seemed as if WACCCI went to great lengths to purposely mess up the settling of an employee's medical claims. Threskinger management became disenchanted with WACCCI, and soon discontinued that relationship.

What especially embittered Henri Bruder was the TV commercials run in Dayton by WACCCI. One of the commercials showed a distinguished looking gentlemen who was identified as an officer of WACCCI. He said: "At Western American Cascade Certified Casualty Insurance, we put the insured first. We settle hospital and medical claims in record time--because we care about our insured." Disgusting! Record time? "Of course," Henri would say, "they take <u>longer</u> than any other firm of their kind. That's a record."

Henri got another shock. While visiting the office of a federal medical plan, to gather some information for his aging father, Henri was completely floored when the federal employee said: "We <u>answer</u> <u>questions</u> about our federal medical benefits for retired persons, but <u>the</u> <u>claims</u> <u>are</u> <u>all</u> <u>handled</u> by Western American Cascade Certified Casualty Insurance." Henri couldn't resist bellowing at the clerk:

"Good heavens! No wonder your system is so fouled up!"

"Please lower your voice, Mr. Bruder," the clerk requested.

This background explains why Henri Bruder was on a holy crusade when he was named Director of Claim Settlement for one of WACCCI's rivals, the new Brotherhood Medical Plans.

The Section Chief within Claim Settlement was Leilani Lavoisier, an extremely efficient administrator whom Henri brought over from Threskinger Systems. Leilani had the task of organizing the section dedicated to documentation. She inherited some tired workers who lacked a zeal for serving customers. As smoothly as possible, Leilani eliminated these staffers. Other spots were found for them in the organization. As Henri put it: "We wish them a happy career with Brotherhood Medical Plans--but NOT in Claim Settlement."

Leilani was able to attract Elaine Melvin to her section. Elaine had an excellent record in administrative tasks at Threskinger, and Leilani wanted her as her top sidekick in Claim Settlement. As expected, Elaine moved through claims rapidly and with authority. She processed simple claims in minutes. This was in contrast to Brotherhood's previous statement at the bottom of each claim form: "Allow 30 days for processing."

Elaine's efficiency fit in perfectly with Henri Bruder's opening declaration when taking over Claim Settlement: "That old statement we used to use about claim processing taking 30 days is ridiculous. What takes 30 days is allowing the claim forms to sit in piles on clerks' desks. Processing takes only a few minutes."

Mainly because of Leilani and Elaine being so conscientious about what went on in the documentation section of Claim Settlement, other sections picked up the spirit. In addition, workers in other sections suspected that if they didn't display the same fire in getting things done, then they might be shipped out to less challenging assignments at Brotherhood Medical Plans. The word was out that Henri Bruder was looking for reasons to trim from Claim Settlement any deadwood.

So, in a sense, the flagship section or the pride and joy within Claim Settlement was documentation. And Henri Bruder openly admitted that he was very pleased with the way Leilani Lavoisier and Elaine Melvin were doing things in that unit. Letters began pouring in to top Brotherhood executives indicating surprise at how fast claims were settled. And Henri Bruder let the executive suite know that he and his old buddies from Threskinger were making the big difference.

That is why it was so surprising to Leilani Lavoisier when Elaine Melvin came in to her late one afternoon to complain about Mr. Bruder.

"What's wrong, Elaine? You know that Mr. Bruder thinks you are doing a super job. What on earth is your complaint?"

"Well, every once in awhile, he'll come in and ask what I've done about a certain case. For example, this morning he wanted to see what I had done with Elmer Furtwangler, file number 1188774775, and claim number A-7782901. I had handled the matter two days ago and passed it on for payment. Almost always, he's checking on something I've already handled. Then this afternoon, I decided to ask him what was going on. He came looking for Adrian Martouche-Clevenger, file number 1188948685, with a claim number of B-7782221. I asked him if these people had been complaining. He said they had not. I asked why the problem, and he replied that he was just checking, and then walked away. What's going on?"

"I can assure you that there is no problem. You're a smart worker, Elaine. Figure out what he's doing. He is going around picking names at random from the entry files and inquiring as to where they stand. He's doing for our service exactly what specialized engineers do about products being produced in a manufacturing plant. See what I mean? The manufacturers have a name for it."

1.   While Elaine is thinking over the matter, will you please respond by indicating which concept stressed in this chapter is being implemented in his own special way by Henri Bruder.

2.   Could Henri Bruder have been a little more diplomatic in his dealings with Elaine? How?

3. What are some of the drastic measures that Henri and Leilani have had to resort to in order to achieve their goals? Compare these drastic actions with those resorted to by Motorola.

4. Why is it important to the efficiency of the organization that Elaine be made to understand that Mr. Bruder's actions are in no way a reflection on her work.

ANSWERS TO TRUE-FALSE QUESTIONS

1.	T	(p. 704)	6.	F	(p. 711)
2.	F	(p. 705)	7.	T	(p. 713)
3.	T	(p. 706)	8.	T	(p. 717)
4.	T	(p. 707)	9.	F	(p. 720)
5.	F	(p. 708)	10.	F	(p. 720)

ANSWERS TO MULTIPLE-CHOICE QUESTIONS

1.	D	(p. 705)	11.	B	(p. 713)
2.	C	(p. 705)	12.	A	(p. 715)
3.	B	(p. 706)	13.	D	(p. 715)
4.	A	(p. 706)	14.	C	(p. 715)
5.	D	(p. 708)	15.	B	(p. 716)
6.	C	(p. 709)	16.	A	(p. 716)
7.	B	(p. 709)	17.	D	(p. 717)
8.	A	(p. 712)	18.	C	(p. 718)
9.	D	(p. 712)	19.	B	(p. 719)
10.	C	(p. 713)	20.	A	(p. 722)